ROUTLEDGE LIBRARY EDITIONS:
HISTORY OF EDUCATION

OFFSPRING OF THE VIC

OFFSPRING OF THE VIC

A History of Morley College

By

DENIS RICHARDS

Volume 29

Routledge
Taylor & Francis Group
LONDON AND NEW YORK

First published in 1958

This edition first published in 2007 by
Routledge
2 Park Square, Milton Park, Abingdon, Oxon, OX14 4RN

Simultaneously published in the USA and Canada
by Routledge

711 Third Avenue, New York, NY 10017

Routledge is an imprint of the Taylor & Francis Group, an informa business

Transferred to Digital Printing 2007

First issued in paperback 2013

British Library Cataloguing in Publication Data
A catalogue record for this book is available from the British Library

Library of Congress Cataloging in Publication Data
A catalog record for this book has been requested

ISBN13: 978-0-415-41978-9 (Set)
ISBN13: 978-0-415-43276-4 (Volume 29 hbk)
ISBN13: 978-0-415-86065-9 (Volume 29 pbk)

Publisher's Note

The publisher has gone to great lengths to ensure the quality of this reprint but points out that some imperfections in the original copies may be apparent.

Eva Hubback
Principal, 1927–1949

[*Frontispiece*

Offspring of the Vic

A HISTORY OF MORLEY COLLE

by

DENIS RICHARDS

Principal of Morley College

With a Foreword by

SIR HAROLD NICOLSON

President of Morley College

Routledge and Kegan Paul

First published 1958
by Routledge *&* *Kegan Paul Limited*
Broadway House, Carter Lane, E.C.4.
Printed in Great Britain
yman & Sons, Ltd., London, Fakenham & Reading

In memory of
Eva Hubback
Principal of Morley College
1927–1949

Contents

CONTENTS

APPENDICES

A NOTE ON ILLUSTRATION *3b*

This photograph was taken by William Rivers round about 1906. It records a gathering at 'Chippen's Bank'. Miss Everest had asked Rivers to get together a group of her special friends among the students. She then invited them to spend three Saturdays with her during the summer: the first by themselves (as here), the second with their wives, and the third with their wives and children. This practice she maintained each summer until her health no longer permitted. The members of the group, apart from Miss Everest and Miss Cons, are (*left to right*) Messrs. Drywood, Cooper, Ash, Davidson, Richards (*centre foreground*), Eyre, Perks, Underwood and Stokes.

xii

Illustrations

xiii

Preface

IN 1949 Eva Hubback, who had just completed her twenty-second year as Principal of Morley College, found herself in the grip of an illness which rapidly proved to be mortal. Her outstanding work not only for education but also for the women's movement, family welfare and many other beneficial causes clearly demanded some permanent form of commemoration. A fund was launched, and it was finally decided that the memorial should consist of a number of separate features and projects all connected with the College whose fortunes she had directed with such imagination, sympathy and success. Among these projects was the writing of a history of the College, and this task the memorial committee invited me to perform. The narrative which follows is the result of that request. Its publication has been timed to coincide roughly with the long-deferred rebuilding of the main College block after the war-time bombing, and with the reopening ceremony which Her Majesty Queen Elizabeth the Queen Mother has graciously consented to undertake during October, 1958.

xv

In writing the history, two problems not unfamiliar to historians presented themselves with some force. The first was the fact that so much of the basic documentary material had been lost. When a German bomb smote the College in 1940 almost every unprinted paper in its possession, with the fortunate exception of the Council minutes, disappeared in the general destruction. The Vic, too, was bombed, and for that and other reasons possesses much less in the way of records than might be imagined. Moreover the various bodies with which the College had been in correspondence from its early days—the Charity Commission, the City Parochial Foundation, the Ministry of Education, and the London County Council—have all since 1939 destroyed the great bulk of their Morley College files in order to save space. The story had thus to be written very largely from printed sources—and especially from the reports, syllabuses, and magazines specified in Appendix II—and from personal recollections, of which I was fortunate enough to obtain a great many. It is worth remarking that had the project of a history been left until the official centenary of the College in 1989, as might so easily have been the case, all the benefit of personal reminiscences from students of the pre-1914 days would have been lost.

The second problem was that of scale and selection. Was one to write for 'external' or for 'internal' readers? The requirements of the two were by no means identical. To adopt the first course might produce a narrative so short and generalized as to contain little that was new to Morleyites; to follow the second might result in a wealth of detail insignificant to the outside world. In the event I have tried, though doubtless with very incomplete suc-

xvi

cess, to paint a picture with enough detail to interest College readers and not too much to deter the others.

I must express my gratitude to the very many people who have given me such unstinting help in my researches. In particular my best thanks go to the Librarians and their staffs at the British Museum, the Ministry of Education, the National Institute of Adult Education, the Lambeth Central Reference Library, the Thomas A. Gilbert Reference Library (Southwark), and the Fawcett Society; to Sir Donald Allen and his staff of the City Parochial Foundation; to Mr. R. S. Morgan of the Charity Commission; to the staff of the Public Record Office; to the Education Officer's Department of the L.C.C. and the staff of the County Hall Record Room; to Miss P. Burchell, Hon. Librarian of the Vic-Wells Association; and to Mr. C. W. Nash, Curator of the Eindhoven Collection at the Victoria and Albert Museum. Among the scores of people who were good enough to contribute to the pool of reminiscences I must particularly thank Professor Norman Bentwich for a valuable memoir of Eva Hubback; Miss L. Twiselton and Mr. J. E. Brownson for their recollections of Holst and Morley College music; Miss Mary Sheepshanks; the late Major H. F. Chettle, who sent me extensive extracts from his diaries maintained over many years; Mrs. W. Rivers and Mr. A. Day, of the Old Morleyite Association, who have helped in many ways and who arranged a special meeting of old Old Morleyites for my benefit; and another old Morleyite, Mr. W. Margrie, who sent me much valuable material. On the memories of Miss M. E. Cowles and Mr. G. Cottrell I drew, of course, very frequently; and I was remarkably fortunate, in response to an appeal in

xvii

the press for material, to receive communications from, among very many others, Mr. John Keane, a student even before the official foundation of the College, and from Mr. William Goodair, a cousin of Emma Cons. My warm thanks are also due to Mr. Harold Hutchison, who performed the office of a friend by commenting on the early chapters, encouraging me to proceed, and periodically tempting me away to the golf course.

July, 1958 D. R.

xviii

Foreword

THIS history of Morley College is valuable and interesting in that it describes an educational phenomenon from several different angles. To those who, whether as administrators, lecturers, or tutors, have given their energies and talents to the service of the College, as well as to generations of students, it will be treasured as a tribute to former founders, teachers and pupils. To those who are fascinated by the tangled, planless and almost spontaneous growth and spread of adult education in the second half of the 19th century it will provide an illuminating case-history. The sociologist will find in it a striking illustration of the increasing desire for self-improvement on the part of those who have not had the opportunity of a university training, and of their resolute urge to supplement their knowledge and to expand their tastes. The educationalist will learn with surprise that, in an institution in which the curriculum is suggested from below rather than imposed from above, the dominant demand has been, not so much for practical instruction, as for the humanities and the arts. Those who have been

xix

accustomed to dismiss the British people as philistines in their indifference to music will be startled to read how wide, deep and constant has been the demand for musical education and experiment.

To the ordinary reader the story of Morley College, which its Principal, Mr. Denis Richards, has here recounted with such skill and clarity, will represent a success-story in an unaccustomed field. It is a drama of selfless rather than personal ambition; a narrative that shows how a few resolute individuals have succeeded by faith and will-power in withstanding financial stringency, economic blizzards, lassitude and prejudice, the catastrophes of two world wars, and the dizzy transformation of social values and categories. In the course of seventy years the creators of Morley College have been able to constitute an institution which, while never departing from the principles that inspired the original pioneers, has been able to adjust itself to the needs of three successive epochs and to manifest itself as an educational centre that is not flourishing only, but essentially unique.

What are the factors that have rendered and still render Morley College distinct from other centres of adult education? I suggest that there are six such factors. In the first place I should cite an abstract quality, namely 'organic vitality'. Again and again, throughout three generations, has external competition or the action of the Queen's enemies threatened the College with dissolution or extinction. Yet no phoenix has ever risen with such bright resolution from its own ashes. The College has owed much to the vision and resolve of a succession of outstanding philanthropists, directors, and benefactors. It has been inspired by the visions of Octavia Hill, forti-

xx

fied by the driving power of Emma Cons, assisted by the benefactions of that great Liberal, Samuel Morley, and rendered efficient by the character of such powerful directors as Barbara Wootton and above all Eva Hubback. But essentially it has been the students themselves who have given to the College that vitality that has enabled it to survive calamities that would have put an end to any less vigorous body.

In the second place Morley College has always been guided by democratic principles, in the sense that the students have been encouraged to play a definite part in the administration of the College, in the choice of subjects, and in the emphasis given to those subjects. They have never felt that the College is an institution imposing a rigid curriculum on them from above: they have always known that it exists to provide them with opportunities to expand their own tastes and to minister to their own individual requirements. For generations of students the College has always been 'us' rather than 'they'.

In the third place Morley College was one of the first of such institutions to proclaim and inculcate absolute equality, not merely between the several social grades, but between the sexes. The fact that in the early years the College owed so much to the guidance and will-power of four outstanding women may explain that from the very first there existed complete equality between the sexes. This assuredly was, in the days of Queen Victoria, a novel and most beneficial principle which accounts much for the present solidarity of the student body.

In the fourth place the College has always laid emphasis upon social intercourse, and on providing entertainment,

xxi

congenial companionship, clubs, and opportunities for outside activities, to those whose working days might be monotonous and whose evenings might be dull.

A fifth factor that gives its special character to the College is its intimate connection with the arts. The fact that for the first thirty-five years of its existence it was actually housed in the basement and dressing-rooms of the Old Vic meant that students were brought into close physical contact with drama and music. The good fortune that in Gustav Holst the College obtained the guidance and inspiration of a teacher of genius encouraged the passion for music which has always been one of its most distinctive and admirable characteristics. To this day there are few non-specialized institutions that provide students with such admirable opportunities for studying and practising music and the other arts.

And finally I should attribute the success and the prestige of Morley College to the high quality of the tutors and lecturers that it has been able to obtain. From the days when Morley, Lord Mount Temple, the Duke of Westminster and Gladstone himself, gave encouragement to Emma Cons, the College has always been able to comand the services of men and women eminent in science, philosophy or the arts. A list of lecturers which includes such names as Bertrand Russell, G. E. Moore, G. M. Trevelyan, Virginia Woolf, Graham Wallas, Ralph Vaughan Williams, and Kingsley Martin is such as to establish the prestige of any educational institution. The students who attend the College well know that they will be given the best the age can provide.

The phoenix, having been hit squarely and unfairly by Hitler's bombs, now rises from its rubble with new and

xxii

shining plumes. We look forward to the opening of the new buildings this autumn by Queen Elizabeth, the Queen Mother. It will be an occasion enlivened by the presence of the alert young: and sanctified by the blessing of benevolent ghosts.

Harold Nicolson

xxiii

I

Morley, 1956

THE scene is the surviving wing of a 'blitzed' building—an evening college for adults—in the Westminster Bridge Road; the time, just after six-thirty on an autumn evening in 1956. The cheerful turmoil f the students' arrival is already over, and a scholarly hush—broken only by occasional laughter from the class-rooms, the clatter of crockery in the canteen, and the relentless efforts of the choir sopranos to come to grips with a modern work in the Holst Room—pervades the corridors.

The Principal's main visitors of the evening, a group of Nigerians and Pakistanis studying the English educational system under the auspices of the British Council, approach the building. After emerging from Lambeth North, an underground station unknown to their English friends, they have waited no more than five minutes before a brief gap in the traffic has enabled them to cross the road. They have now gained the entrance steps, between a board marked MORLEY COLLEGE and a much larger board marked MISKINS—a board which the College regards with great affection, for it denotes that after sixteen years contractors are at last at work on the rebuilding. The visitors mount the sixteen-year-old 'temporary' steps, admire the view of the bombed site from an equally temporary concrete platform, and push their way through a pair of still more temporary doors. They find themselves in a small hardboard box, ten feet by ten feet by ten feet—an unquestionably temporary entrance lobby. The notices on the sides of this box, drawing attention to such forthcoming events as a showing of Jean Cocteau's *Orphée,* a concert of twelve-tone music, and a Swimming Club Dance with refreshments of sea-food, assure the visitors that they are indeed in Morley College.

Directed by Tom the doorkeeper or Cliff the caretaker—as genial a pair of giants as ever manhandled a college grand piano—the visitors ascend the short staircase to the upper floor. In the corridor before them they observe on one side a memorial table to the late Principal, Eva Hubback, bearing its customary tribute of flowers; on the other, the varied hues of dust-jackets proclaiming the latest additions to the Library. Ahead, their gaze is attracted by a large painting, the work of Colin Gill, depicting the naked Aphrodite rising from the waves—a phenomenon too common, apparently, to attract the attention of a group of dancing sailors who share the same canvas. From the level of this corridor a further short stairway, flanked by a gay and graceful brass railing, carries the visitors to the Library. They enter through the simple but substantial limed oak doors; and a brief glance at the fine proportions and harmonious decoration of the room, its brilliant Van Gogh reproductions set off by plain walls and clean-lined oak furniture, confirms them in an impression they have already received in the corridor outside. If the appearance of the surviving wing is any indication, the spirit of the College, they feel, is one of gaiety, colour, and subdued excitement. Their interest quickens, and they look more closely at the scene before them.

The visitors' second glance at the Library reveals other things. Above all it reveals the fact that the Library is, at the moment, somewhat more than a Library. Telescoped on account of the bombing into this one room are also the administrative offices, the Principal's room, the Common Room, and much of the general storage. Not that there is any separate identity about them now. The administrative offices, the visitors observe, are two large desks and a small one, occupying one end of the room, together with a miscellaneous assortment of typewriters, duplicators, filing cabinets, and lost property. At one of the large desks, through a cloud of cigarette smoke, the visitors descry the impeccably neat figure of the Principal's assistant, now in her twenty-fifth year of service with the College; at the other, more clearly, they see the scarcely less neat figure of the Secretary, in his thirtieth year of service.

At the far end of the room, in an alcove by the bookstall, stands yet another desk. It bears on it, in addition to blotter, telephone, reading-lamp, books, letters, gramophone records, tea-cups and *objets d'art,* a small notice with the optimistic inscription—PRINCIPAL—PRIVATE! Towards this desk the Nigerians and Pakistanis turn their steps. The Principal, who is simultaneously

3

signing correspondence, listening to a voluble talker at the other end of the telephone, and wondering where he can find a deputy for a suddenly indisposed tutor due to take a class in an hour's time, smiles a greeting and motions them to sit down. Within a few minutes he is hearing about their mission and telling them something of the College they have come to see.

It is, he explains, a College of unusual history and character. A night school for adults, and one of the first to be founded for both sexes on terms of perfect equality, it was born in the 1880s. In its own premises in the Westminster Bridge Road since 1924, it was so heavily bombed in 1940 that only a quarter of the fabric survived. Nevertheless, classes have continued as before, with the help of overflow premises outside the College, and each year nearly 3,000 men and women enrol as students. Some of them take one, but others two, three or even four classes a week. A few devoted souls are to be found in the place six nights a week—or, when a Sunday concert makes it possible, seven.

The visitors are interested, even a little impressed. After all, 3,000 students is a fairly impressive total—almost as many as at Cambridge University, for instance, before the war. But who are these students—what was their previous education, where do they live and work, what qualifications do they hope to acquire at the College? The Principal explains that some are university graduates, while others left school at anything down to thirteen years of age; that some are youngsters of seventeen, others veterans in their seventies; that they come not only from London, but from eight other counties; and that by occupation they range from civil servants to

4

carpenters, salesmen to shorthand-typists, teachers to taxi-drivers. In fact there is practically only one thing which can be said about them all. None of them comes to Morley for the sake of qualifications.

The eyes of the visitors widen a little. Then what do they come for? They come, the Principal explains, for a hundred different reasons—but mainly for the love of learning. They can acquire no degrees, no certificates. In technical jargon, the classes are 'non-vocational'. The students come, not for qualifications, but for fun.

The visitors approve. The idea is novel to them, but not unacceptable. And what do the students study? The Principal deals round a handful of prospectuses, and invites the visitors to glance inside. Their eyes travel through the formidable list of 120 or more classes. English Literature, the Art of Writing, a Theatre School, Public Speaking, Philosophy, Psychology, Religion, Economics, History, Law, Biology, Astronomy, Medicine, Ornithology, Modelling, Painting, Wood-carving, Book-binding—like the parade of kings before Macbeth, the list stretches on and on. It includes, the visitors note, a large number of foreign languages—the Western ones and Russian—and a generous array of physical activities such as fencing, ballet and folk-dancing. And it also includes—how it includes!—music. History of music, appreciation of music, theory of music, composition of music, choirs, orchestras, wind and string ensembles, recorder classes—the visitors cease reading, and turn slowly to the Principal for enlightenment. He explains that the College has a great musical tradition. Moreover the twentieth century, he informs them, is England's second great age of music, her true musical renaissance.

No wonder then that among Morley's 3,000 students more than 600 now study music. A little more surprising, perhaps, that even in the fastnesses of the Workers' Educational Association, where working men were wont to concentrate on the study of economics and history and political science and all the things that would unlock the doors of power and privilege, very large numbers of students nowadays enrol for music.

A little baffled by this extreme devotion to a study bearing so little relation to colonialism, atomic energy or the balance of payments, the visitors turn to more practical matters. How much do the students pay? The Principal explains that the students, if they live or work in London, for the most part pay a pound for their first course, and six shillings for each subsequent course. If they take three classes, their 108 evenings of instruction during the session cost them a little over thirty shillings. An evening's tuition, to use the current economic standard, for the price of two cigarettes. Nominal fees of this kind, the Principal hastens to add, are a tradition in British adult education. They cover, in fact, only a quarter of the College's annual expenditure, the remaining three-quarters coming from the rates and taxes.

And how, the visitors inquire, is the College governed? What is its official 'status'? It is, the Principal tells them, a semi-independent body. It is independent in that it has its own governing council, its own buildings and great latitude in developing its own traditions; but in as much as three-quarters of its income comes as a grant from the London County Council, its programme of classes, its fees, and its rates of tutorial remuneration have to be such as that body will approve. In official parlance, it is an

6

'aided institute'—and in view of its kind of classes, an 'aided literary institute'. But the Principal emphasizes that neither he nor anyone else connected with the College thinks of it as one of a type: they think of it as the unique thing it is—Morley College.

For the word 'College', he goes on, is in this case no mere piece of window-dressing. It expresses a deep reality. Morley has its own building—drastically reduced by the bombing, but still its own. It has its own sports ground. It has a great range of social activity—activity catered for in twenty or more clubs, all run by the students, and ranging from football, hockey and tennis to German, art, and folk-dancing. It has a vigorous and most public-spirited Old Morleyite Association; and an equally vigorous and public-spirited body of well-wishers known as the Friends of Morley College. Once upon a time, before the bomb, every student was brought into contact with this social activity by the mere fact that to reach his class he had to pass through the large Common Room; and one day, before too long, this admirable idea of the College founders will again find expression in the new building. But the clubs and the social amenities, the Principal stresses, are only half the story; for the feeling of being a College, of being much more than a collection of evening classes, of being in fact a band of brothers and sisters and even closer relations—the matrimony rate is high!—is also powerfully fostered by the College's very democratic constitution.

'Democratic': the Nigerians and Pakistanis nod approvingly. This is more their meat than music. They incline their heads attentively and absorb the details. Each class, the Principal explains, elects a secretary, who

7

among other things represents its wishes to the Principal. Each club elects a secretary. Periodically, the class secretaries meet together to confer with the Principal; and so do the club secretaries. And each year the class secretaries and the club secretaries choose some of their number to serve on the Student Executive Committee—a body to which other members are also elected by direct popular vote throughout the College. This Student Executive Committee, the Principal adds, supervises the clubs and the whole range of College social activity, runs such annual events as the Christmas Party, the Ball, and the Garden Party, and moreover elects two of its members to serve on the governing College Council. 'So that as Principal,' the Principal concludes, 'I am responsible to a Council which includes two of my own students. Could democracy go further?'

Smilingly, the visitors ask if the system works, and are assured that it does—very well. Moreover, the Principal explains, it gives the students a real stake in the College; large numbers of them come to feel that it is on their efforts, as well as on those of the administrative officers and tutors, that the College depends for its continued well-being and progress. 'The social side and the student democratic organisation,' the Principal concludes, 'are the mortar which binds together the educational bricks of the classes.'

The metaphor is not very original, but he has talked too long for his taste, and is a little tired. So are the visitors. He suggests a brief glance at some of the classes. The visitors rise quickly to their feet, and in a minute or two the procession leaves the Library.

* * *

It is, the Principal explains as they pass down the brass-railed staircase, not exactly an easy matter to obtain a bird's-eye view of the College within an hour or so. A group of half a dozen visitors may wander into a practical class without undue disturbance, but not into a lecture class. So he proposes that they look briefly together at a few practical classes, and then—if they wish—separately and for a longer period at a lecture class. The visitors see the point. Putting thoughts of their waiting hotel dinner resolutely behind them, they decide to see the evening out at Morley College.

By this time the sound of the choir is becoming still more insistent, and the Principal leads the little group into the Holst Room. As the visitors sidle towards a seat they quietly register their approval of the *décor*: the rose-pink walls, the ebony chairs, the pale-blue ceiling spangled with silver stars. The Principal whispers that the room was equipped by public subscription in memory of Gustav Holst, one of the College's most famous directors of music, and that the stars on the ceiling are a reference to his best-known composition, *The Planets*. He adds that although the room holds only 150, it is the largest left to the College; intended only for music, it has perforce been used since 1940 for public lectures, plays, dances, gymnastics and other pursuits to an extent which would have made many a famous composer—but not Holst—turn in his grave.

The visitors smile, but are naturally more interested in the choir. The sopranos have now succeeded in getting their difficult bit right, and a stream of coherent, if unfamiliar, sound emerges from the whole ensemble of some seventy voices. After frequent halts they are singing

9

their modern work 'straight through', and at the end the choir-master—and present director of music—nods his approval. 'Not at all bad,' he proclaims: 'Not bad at all.' The choir relaxes, gratified to hear that the piece is 'coming on'. After all, their tutor should know: he wrote it.

The moment is opportune to move: the visitors steal out and proceed along the lower corridor. Outside the end room they pause. The Principal explains that since the bombing this has become the 'art-room'. On three nights a week it serves for modelling and pottery, on two for drawing and painting. Tonight is an oil-painting night. The visitors edge gently into the room and find themselves at once amid a welter of stools, easels and students. One or two of the students are trying to realize on canvas some private day-dream, but most are busy depicting a female model, an ancient bedame apparently selected for 'character'. Understandably reluctant to gaze too long at their subject, they alternate brief glances at the lady with slow, considered strokes of the brush. It is apparent that they are all deeply absorbed. So too is their tutor, a well-known artist still on the right side of thirty-five, who is is sitting on the stool of one of the younger students and showing her how the thing might be done. It seems a pity to disturb them; so after glancing quietly over the shoulders of a few of the painters, and tripping not so quietly over the legs of one or two of the easels, the visitors discreetly retire.

On this particular evening the remaining seven classrooms in the Morley building are occupied by classes of the lecture or discussion type. So the Principal leads the visitors outside the building and some 500 yards down the St. George's Road. They halt at the secondary modern school in West Square, a large and barrack-like building originally dating from the 19th century but recently refurbished inside by the L.C.C. in attractive style. Here the College is allowed to accommodate its overflow: an overflow which consists in the main of such classes as are too large, too noisy or too active to fit conveniently into the parent building. As the visitors cross the playground to one of the innumerable entrance-doors, an extraordinary noise assails their ears. Some familiarity with the time-table, coupled with careful aural analysis such as is achieved by the ornithologist who can resolve the local dawn-chorus into five sparrows, three blackbirds and a couple of chaffinches, enables the Principal to announce that the sound emanates from one string orchestra, a group of recorders, a violin, a clarinet, two pianos, and a set of bagpipes, all playing different pieces. Undaunted, the visitors enter the building and direct their steps towards the main noise on the ground floor. It turns out to be a highly rhythmic melody of Jerome Kern's, firmly but attractively rendered on a school piano.

Mystified, the visitors gaze through the glass doors whence these syncopated strains emerge, and are surprised to see a large concourse—some fifty or so—of ladies engaged in physical exercise. With graceful sweeping motions of the arms, carefully co-ordinated with turning movements of the upper torso, they bend and stretch to the music. Their faces express a pleasure which is only occasionally belied by the creaking or clicking of joints. Here, the visitors quickly conclude, are Morley's devotees of physical poise and culture. They are a little disappointed to learn from the Principal, however, that the class is inspired less by the principles of yoga than the desire to keep, regain or acquire for the first time a slender figure.

Moving to a similar hall on the floor above, the visitors next discover the *raison d'etre* of the bagpipes. In several sets, light-hearted addicts of various ages are dancing an eightsome reel. The lassies, most of whom wear tartan skirts, heavily outnumber the lads, few of whom wear the kilt; but this is a gala evening—hence the bagpipes—and joy is unconfined. Making no attempt to explain to the visitors the *mystique,* and still less the movements, of Scottish dancing, the Principal leaves them a while to enjoy the exhilaration of the scene, and then leads them to the floor above.

It is Chopin now that strikes most clearly upon their ear: the immortal melodies that make up *Les Sylphides.* And here the visitors discover with something of a shock that beneath the cool front of the most unexotic Englishwoman may lurk the demon of romance, impelling her to spend arduous evenings mastering *jetés* and *foutettés* in order that one day her body may move, obedient to her command, in the controlled ecstasy of the ballet. Some, so to speak, are already more than half-way there; for others the road will still be hard and long. But all are intent on the goal; and in this, if not as yet in every movement, the visitors rightly discern a kind of beauty.

Slightly awed, the visitors now move on again, past rooms from which emerge the screechings of a violin or the wailing of a clarinet. 'Individual musical tuition,' the Principal explains. A different and concerted sound, indefinable except in its own terms, floats along the corridor. 'Recorders,' the Principal adds. He leads his visitors into a room where some sixteen students of widely diverse ages are grappling with the first stages. Already they have mastered Exercises A and B; and Exercise C is almost theirs. In equal proportion their expressions betray determination, self-consciousness, amusement and pride. Some are learning so that they can later instruct others, some because above all things they adore the recorder, some because they have never managed to master any other instrument. In any case, the task remains the same. In methodical and business-like fashion, yet enjoying every note of it—'grim but gay'—the elementary recorder class proceeds.

The visitors' schedule is a tight one, and after two minutes of Exercise C the Principal hurries them out and up the St. George's Road to the College building. They have just time for coffee and biscuits before they plunge into their lectures. It is seven-thirty now, and most of the classes are enjoying their break. The canteen, into which the visitors pass, presents an animated scene. A long and aged wooden hut, it was brought up from the College sports ground after the war and re-erected for use as a temporary buffet until full restaurant facilities could be restored in a new building. It is still, very palpably, a long and aged wooden hut. But it is nevertheless a very gay one, with light walls, brightly coloured pictures, and a profusion of flowers and greenery. It is gay, too, with something even more exhilarating—the chatter and banter of some scores of students as they refresh themselves against the final hour of their class and the journey home.

By-passing the queue at the counter, the Principal obtains refreshments for his visitors and repairs with them to one of the tables. While they sample yet one more version of how the English make coffee, the Principal dilates a little on the function of the canteen and points out two groups where refreshment is apparently being combined with a business meeting. The faces are familiar to him. 'That,' he says, 'is the Committee of the Film Society planning its next show. And over there is the Committee of the Rambling Club—a club which has arranged a walk for Morley students every week-end in term for more than twenty-five years.'

Over coffee the visitors discuss which classes they will join for the next hour. Two, with an interest in natural history, decide for 'Wild Life of the Countryside', two more for 'Science in the Home'. Another pair settle for 'Psychology', a three-year 'Tutorial' class run, like several others in the College, under the auspices of the Extra-Mural Department of London University. The last pair, after wavering between 'Current Events' and 'Everyday Law', finally decide to sample a foreign language class—'Advanced Spanish'. The crowd in the canteen is thinning now. The Principal quickly leads the visitors to the classes of their choice, inserts them with a word of introduction to the tutor, and returns, more than a little thankfully, to his desk in the Library.

An hour quickly passes. During this, the Library presents an atmosphere of comparative quiet, broken only by the periodic ringing of the telephone and the resulting conversations. The Principal deals with correspondence and discusses future arrangements with his assistant. The Librarian weeds out battered or out-of-date volumes from the shelves. The Secretary toils silently over his accounts.

The Library clock shows 8.30 p.m., and soon the situation becomes distinctly more *mouvementé*. In ones and twos the students enter from their classes till a dozen or

14

so are ranging the shelves, another half-dozen sitting at the tables, and small queues forming in front of the Secretary, the Principal's assistant, and the Librarian. Two students together tackle the Principal about an object of interest to their class, while a third hovers watchfully a few yards away, ready to move in as soon as the others have finished. A few more minutes, and the activity is increased by the return of the foreign visitors.

This time their conversation with the Principal is very brief. They are hungry, and there is just a chance that their hotel dinner may still be 'on'. But they are also lively and appreciative. The visitors to the 'Wild Life' class mention the superb colour slides, and the Principal remarks that the photographs have all been taken by the tutor. The 'Science in the Home' visitors are astonished at the elaborate electrical and other equipment which the tutor has gathered together and installed. The pair who have sampled 'Psychology' are impressed by the technique of discussion by the students in small groups, and are still smiling at one of the tutor's anecdotes. And the visitors to 'Advanced Spanish' speak with admiration, indeed almost incredulity, of the liveliness and fluency of the students, and of the variety of ways in which the tutor draws them into active participation. It suddenly occurs to the Principal that all these four tutors, though as a group no more than middle-aged, have been connected with Morley for more than a quarter of a century. He points out that behind their success lies not only experience but a long and deep affection for the College.

Gratefully, then, the visitors take their leave. They have seen a good deal in a very short time; and they leave the Principal in no doubt that they enjoyed what they saw.

He assures them that there are whole ranges of activity of which they have had no glimpse, from plays and concerts and public lectures to the Saturday night dances in the Holst Room and all the manifold diversions of the sports ground. They reply that they have seen enough to appreciate both the nature and the spirit of Morley College. They look forward wistfully, but not very optimistically, to the day when Morley Colleges will flourish in Nigeria and Pakistan. And they impress on the Principal that if ever he passes through Lagos, or Karachi, he must on no account fail to look them up. So saying, they are gone, but not before their warmth of smile and handshake has convinced him that they mean what they say.

The students, too, are leaving now, and as nine-thirty approaches only an odd two or three are left in the Library. In the canteen the lights are going out, and from the Holst Room emerge the enthusiasts of the Ballroom Dancing Club, who have fitted in an hour of practice after the end of the choir meeting. Already Cliff the caretaker is making his rounds, hoping that he can see the last straggler off the premises before ten o'clock. The early hours brought about by World War II have persisted, and by 10 p.m. Morley is duly bedded down for the night, lights out and the burglar alarm set.

The 10 p.m. close is not the only difference from the pre-war days. Still less is it the only difference from those more distant days of the 1880s, when a large part of the neighbourhood was hungry, and another large part drunk, and a middle-aged woman named Emma Cons was bringing the College to birth in the dressing-rooms of the Old Vic.

16

II

Ancestry

THE social conditions of the late 1870s were so unlike those of today that we can now recall them only by study and a considerable effort of the imagination. This is scarcely surprising when even matters which at that time roused the nation to furies of controversy have receded into an apparently forgotten and far-distant past. The Public Worship Act against 'ritualism' in the Church, the 'Big Bulgaria' crisis, the disasters at Kabul and Isandhlwana, the realization that Income-Tax (at 2*d.* in the pound) could not, after all, be abolished—these now seem little less remote than the struggle of Roundhead against Cavalier. Yet many of us have parents still alive who were born in the 1870s, and few of us can be unacquainted with healthy veterans whose memories, if tested, would take them back at least to 1880.

It is an instructive exercise to ask such elderly folk

17

what they consider to be the outstanding differences between the years of their youth and the present day. Their replies almost invariably concentrate on three points. The greatest changes they have seen during their lifetime are the tremendous developments of scientific invention, the increased threat of world war, and the immense lessening of the gulf between rich and poor. This last point may be put from different angles. Some may emphasize the lower standards of the better-off, particularly in domestic accommodation and staff; far more will stress the almost incredible improvement in the wages, hours of labour, diet, clothes and housing of the 'working man'. If pressed, many will select this as the most striking of all the changes they have seen.

To recall the life of the poorer classes in London towards the close of the 1870s, we need not look beyond the districts of Southwark and Lambeth, with which Morley College has always been associated.[1] Even today these two boroughs contain many desperately mean streets which the greater prosperity of the ordinary wage-earner seems somehow to have passed by. In the 1870s conditions in much of Southwark and Lambeth were grim indeed. Southwark, a traditional refuge since the early Middle Ages of criminals, actors and other unorthodox characters not acceptable within the City of London, had not greatly changed since some of its worst quarters had featured in the pages of Charles Dickens. It had provided striking material for Henry Mayhew's *London Labour and the London Poor* in the fifties and sixties, and in the nineties it was still to appear, in Charles Booth's monumental

[1] Morley College has always been within Lambeth; but its first home, the Old Vic, is only a few yards from the Southwark boundary, and its present home a few feet.

18

survey, *Life and Labour of the People in London*, as among the very worst-off areas. Indeed, one of its parishes figures in that work as the very poorest district of all. Booth's yardstick in his initial survey was 'overcrowding', defined as the occupation of accommodation by an average of two or more persons to a moderate-sized room. By this test not merely was St. Saviour's, Southwark, the poorest parish, but the whole of the Central South London area, with 47 per cent of families living in conditions of overcrowding, was the poorest of all the twelve regions under which he surveyed the metropolis.[1]

Lambeth, nowadays a very large borough stretching from the Thames as far south as the boundaries of Croydon, in the 1870s contained less poverty than Southwark, just as it does today. The heart of it was the old historic parish of Lambeth covering the northern or Thames side parts of the modern borough. Apart from the district round Lambeth Palace, the boat-building yards along the river and the sites of a few old-established industries such as pottery and glass-making, Lambeth had remained very undeveloped until the mid-18th century, largely because of its extensive marshland. The construction of Westminster Bridge in 1750 opened up new possibilities for the future, but the highways which followed, notably Westminster Bridge Road and Kennington Road, were for long flanked by the merest fringe of houses.[2]

[1] By the close of his survey in 1901 Booth had developed these comparisons by area and regrouped them under fifty census registration subdistricts. In order of worst social conditions, judged by crowding, poverty and high birth- and death-rates, St. Saviour's and Waterloo came first and Lambeth eighth.

[2] In the undeveloped marshland, and on the site of the present Waterloo Station, the naturalist William Curtis ran a botanical garden during the

(*continued overleaf*)

19

It was not in fact until after 1817, when Waterloo Bridge was completed, that streets and houses began to cover most of Lambeth marsh. Some of these, as surviving buildings show, were unpretentiously elegant in the admirable style of their period; but they had barely been in existence twenty years when through their midst came the devouring juggernaut of the London and South-Western Railway. In 1848 an extension was built from Nine Elms, where that line had previously ended, to a new terminus at Waterloo. The construction of this great station and the lines leading to it left an indelible mark on the neighbourhood and at once lowered its character. Jerry-built shops and terraces suddenly sprang up on the unoccupied ground; and from the older houses the more substantial citizens quickly departed to pleasanter and healthier districts, leaving only those who could not afford to travel to their work. Amid the grime and the smoke, the spoilt streets and dingy railway arches, only the poorer families remained. And these were by no means all 'respectable' poor. In particular, one group of streets south of the station between the Waterloo and the Westminster Bridge Roads quickly became a veritable Alsatia, almost entirely given up to thugs, drabs and the dregs of the criminal classes. It was to enjoy an almost

1780s. He finally closed it for causes which, since they for long afterwards afflicted this part of Lambeth, and in some (but fortunately not all) respects still do, may be worth quoting: 'I had an enemy to contend with which neither time, nor ingenuity, nor industry could vanquish, and that was the smoke of London, which, except when the wind blew from the South, constantly enveloped my plants. In addition to this grand obstacle, I had to contend with many smaller ones—such as the obscurity of the situation, the badness of the roads leading to it, and the effluvia of the surrounding ditches, at times highly offensive.'

(*Flora Londiniensis*)

unprecedented reputation as a centre of low-life debauchery until finally obliterated by further railway building during the 1870s and 1880s.[1]

By the close of the 1870s, then, North Lambeth and Southwark were areas marked by great poverty and by more than their fair share of rough characters. Through them ran some of the fine wide thoroughfares which distinguish South London; but even these were rapidly losing their better-off inhabitants. From the river to the Elephant and Castle, whether by way of Westminster Bridge Road or Waterloo Road, Blackfriars Road or the Borough High Street, though there were hundreds of small shops there was not one store of size and importance. And immediately behind these main roads lay the mazes of mean streets in which the all too numerous poor waged, with varying energy and success, their ceaseless battle for existence.

The dozen years of full employment since 1945, coming on top of all the municipal schemes of clearance and rebuilding during the 1930s, have made most of the younger generation of today almost unacquainted with the reality behind the word 'slum'. But no one who remembers certain areas in London, Manchester or scores of other towns during the early 1930s, when work and cash were hard to come by, will have much difficulty in conjuring up a picture of housing conditions among the urban poor at the end of the 1870s, when municipal schemes had barely begun. As Charles Booth's survey showed a few years later, almost a third of the population of London was living in poverty, two or more to a room. In houses

[1] It was known as the 'Granby Street' area, and has been vividly described in Michael Sadleir's novel *Forlorn Sunset*.

supplied with water—the supply was usually on for only ten or fifteen minutes a day—these folk washed at the kitchen sink (if they could get to it), or from basins in other rooms, or from a tap outside in warm weather. But very large numbers of houses still had no water laid on, and depended on a common tap (or a common water-butt periodically refilled) and a common closet in a courtyard. In such conditions those who tried to maintain decent standards—the majority—had a desperately hard task, while a large minority soon gave up trying.

Within the 30 or more per cent of the London population living on or below the poverty line—and not to be confused with the 50 per cent above that line enjoying 'solid working-class comfort'—Booth found four main classes of family or person. Of the lowest group he wrote that they 'could not be associated in any regular way with industrial or family life. . . . The common lodging house caters for their necessities and the public house for their superfluities. Their ultimate standard of life is almost savage, both in its simplicity and in its excesses'. Of the next group above, the very poor, whose earnings were not only small but irregular, the prevailing characteristic was incompetence, 'often aggravated by indulgence in alcohol'. Their staple diet was bread, tea and potatoes, supplemented when money was to hand with margarine, jam, bacon, fried fish and the cheaper parts of beef and mutton. They wore cast-off and disreputable clothing, and the group could 'almost be distinguished by its deplorable boots'. Their homes were miserable and unsavoury, containing only furniture not worth pawning—'things not only broken and shabby but foul'. In their rooms, used alike for living, sleeping, cooking and washing, remains of food were always about, together with 'an unwashed cup or two and a cracked plate'; while the window, 'broken, patched and dirty', indicated perhaps more than anything else the absence of any housewifely pride. Little less significant of the group, which Booth reckoned at some 300,000 souls in London, was the 'foul and acrid smell which is the almost invariable characteristic of the homes . . . and of which the very streets reek where their houses are found'.

Beyond these two lowest groups, but still within the one-third living in poverty, Booth distinguished two further groups of much higher standards. One had fairly well-paid, but irregular and uncertain work; the other, work where the wages were not high, but at least came in regularly week by week. These groups enjoyed a more varied diet, wore clothing which was often new if cheap, paid much more attention to their children, who were 'at once the plague and pride of their parents' lives', and kept their homes on an altogether higher plane than the two lowest groups. All told, however poor or overcrowded, they showed the virtue of self-respect, and their existence was enjoyable but subject to a distinctive curse—'the narrow margin between such a life and destitution, the lack of any protection against "the slings and arrows of outrageous fortune"'.

Such, in sum, were the varying lives and homes in 1890—and the position was not very different ten years earlier—of nearly one-third of the population of London, and nearly one-half of the population of Southwark and North Lambeth. Of the other half in those two districts—the half above the poverty line—by far the great majority were the working class in regular and reasonably-paid employ,

23

accustomed to buying new and hard-wearing clothes and enjoying every day a dinner of meat and vegetables and a pudding. The upper ranges of this group, the foremen and highly paid artisans 'at the summit of working-class life', lived very comfortably, and often saved money or insured their lives for a considerable sum. Beyond them stretched the middle classes and above, with their servants and their different way of life. Not more than 10 per cent of the inhabitants of Southwark and North Lambeth in 1880 would have claimed to belong to these more fortunate classes.[1]

Of all the evils which beset the one-third of the inhabitants of London and the one-half of the inhabitants of Southwark and North Lambeth who by Booth's reckoning were living in poverty, in 1880 three stood foremost. The first, as already stated, was the lack of any adequate protection against bad luck in the form of illness, injury or dismissal through declining trade. The second was the widespread practice of drinking too much or too often in the all too abundant taverns: over-indulgence in drink by a lower-class breadwinner, even when it did not lead to quarrels and brutality, drastically lowered his whole family's standard of life by the inroads it made into his small earnings. The third was the overcrowded and generally deplorable housing accommodation in which so many were forced to spend their lives. In such conditions it was impossible to avoid contact with the diseased, the gross and the base, and many a fundamen-

[1] Booth's rough estimate in 1890 was that two-thirds of the London population belonged to the working class (with one-third on or below the poverty line) and one-third to the middle class and above. In a Gallup poll taken in 1952 49 per cent of the sample (not confined to London) claimed to belong to the middle class, and 46 per cent to the working class.

tally decent mother soon gave up the unequal struggle against disorder and filth.

By the late 1870s a generation of agitation by various pioneers had made the force of these three evils sufficiently recognized for measures against them to have reached the statute book. The relics of *laissez-faire* philosophy as yet prevented much direct 'cushioning' of working-class existence beyond the harsh and unsatisfactory Poor Law, but at least in the beginnings of elementary education the poor were being helped to help themselves. The evils of over-drinking were sufficiently serious to have brought into being not only powerful temperance (or rather abstinence) movements, but also the Licensing Act of 1872—a measure nevertheless so unpopular that Gladstone considered it cost him the ensuing General Election.[1] To the evils of bad and overcrowded accommodation, too, public opinion was at last awakening. In 1875 Richard Cross, the enlightened Home Secretary in Disraeli's second ministry, put through Parliament the Artisans Dwellings Act, which empowered local authorities to purchase land and buildings for clearance or improvement, and to undertake new building schemes 'with special regard to the accommodation of the working classes'. It was only a permissive measure, of which few municipalities at once availed themselves; but in Birmingham at least it enabled the radical mayor, Joseph Chamberlain, to make good his famous boast: 'By God's help the town shall not know itself.'

Among those who had helped to awaken public opinion to the evils of overcrowded and insanitary accommodation, and to inspire the passing of the Artisans Dwellings

[1] 'We have been borne down in a torrent of cheap gin and beer.'

Act, was one who has been described as 'the second greatest woman of the nineteenth century'. She was by no means, of course, the first campaigner in this field: as far back as the 1830s and 1840s, Dr. Southwood Smith, Edwin Chadwick, Lord Shaftesbury and others had attacked such aspects of bad accommodation as deficient drainage and water supply, and had even secured the passage of the first Public Health Act of 1848. This set up a General Board of Health, empowered under certain conditions to create local boards—over which it then had practically no control. The compromise proved difficult to work. Moreover Shaftesbury and the ultra-efficient Chadwick, who were members of the Board, were more conspicuous for zeal than tact. They even proposed to take under the Board's control the whole water supply and burial system of London. Not surprisingly, from the outraged municipalities and J.P.s and improvement commissioners and from all the vested interests of property, storms of protest arose as suggestions for sanitary improvements began to issue from London, and in 1854 the force of this opposition swept away the Board. 'We prefer,' wrote *The Times* in welcoming the demise, 'to take our chance of cholera and the rest, than to be bullied into health.'

The further cholera epidemic of 1865–6, however, caused the merits of undiluted freedom to be examined somewhat more critically. At the same time the benefactions of George Peabody, the Baroness Burdett-Coutts and Sir Sydney Waterlow were directing attention to social problems of which many worthy citizens had remained entirely unaware. The changed climate of public opinion before long resulted in a Royal Commission on the sanitary laws in the late sixties, the creation in 1871 of a supervisory Local Government Board (precursor of the Ministry of Health) at the centre and a more uniform system of sanitary authorities at the circumference, and the passing of a fresh Public Health Act in 1875. By this time the 'Clean Party' which (according to Palmerston twenty years earlier) existed in every town had manifestly triumphed over the 'Dirty Party'. By 1875 it was administratively possible, if the central authority decided, to see that better standards of sanitation, both in regard to public water supply, sewerage and the like, and to private domestic accommodation, were observed throughout the country. It was also possible, as we have seen, for local authorities to engage in slum clearance and the building of municipal housing estates. Towards these desirable reforms a decided, and perhaps decisive, impetus had been imparted since 1864 by the work of Octavia Hill.

It has been given to very few people, even in the 19th century, to accomplish quite so much for their fellow-citizens as did this remarkable woman. A pioneer in the development of housing associations, she was also one of the main forces in bringing to a halt the continued enclosure of common land in or near the cities. To her efforts, as much as to anyone's, Londoners owe the fact that they can wander on Primrose Hill and a sizeable Hampstead Heath. This preservation of open spaces for the town dweller against all the urgent claims of builders and railway companies was but a part of the same vision that inspired her to fight for the preservation of old footpaths and places of great natural beauty in the countryside, and that finally, with the potent aid of Canon Rawnsley and Sir Robert Hunter, brought into being that

27

imaginative and ever-fruitful conception, the National Trust. Fundamentally all she strove for and accomplished, whether in housing or Poor Law reform or the retention of open spaces or even the foundation of the Army Cadet Corps, stemmed from the same root—the belief that health and fresh air and beauty and a fair chance in decent surroundings should not be the prerogative of favoured classes, but the birthright of all. Given the decent surroundings, and encouraged in appropriate ways to maintain them, all but a very small minority of the poor would respect them and profit from them, so that in time their standards of citizenship would become higher and their lives fuller and more acceptable to themselves, their fellow-men and God. This was the creed of Octavia Hill. It was one which had inspired many social reformers in the past, and one which will never cease to inspire others in the future.

* * *

The eighth daughter of a radical corn-merchant and banker, and the granddaughter on her mother's side of Dr. Southwood Smith, who had fought for years to establish the connection between fever epidemics and bad sanitary conditions, Octavia Hill had reforming instincts in her blood. Her father's prosperity having been abruptly shattered during the bank failures of the 1840s, she was brought up in straightened circumstances, happily enlarged by the generosity of Southwood Smith, who re-established the family at Finchley, then a country village. At the age of thirteen she moved into London with her mother, who had become manager of the Ladies' Co-operative Guild, a handicraft enterprise sponsored by the newly formed Christian Socialist group. Already

28

possessed of considerable artistic talent, she soon began to specialize in the Guild's main activity—paintings on glass for table-tops and other decorative furniture—and before long was also managing an associated section devoted to the making of toy furniture. This was staffed not by ladies but by Ragged School working girls, whom she at once treated as individuals and as friends. Her contacts with these girls and their homes, her growing knowledge of the poorer parts of Marylebone so close to the Guild Centre off Fitzroy Square, her reading of *Oliver Twist,* Charles Kingsley's *Yeast* and *Alton Locke,* and Mayhew's *London Labour and the London Poor* (as it appeared during the fifties), all confirmed her inherited instincts of reform. So too did her increasing acquaintance with her mother's Christian Socialist friends, headed by the two clergymen, Frederick Denison Maurice and Charles Kingsley. In fact it is not too much to say that by the age of fourteen she was already looking forward to a life of social service.

It was very shortly after this that Octavia Hill first met John Ruskin, a man whose physical and mental maladjustments have recently been so thoroughly explored as almost to obscure his real and generous devotion to social reform. Soon after the beginning of their acquaintance the Ladies' Guild collapsed, and Octavia Hill, seeking for other artistic work, found in Ruskin a ready friend and patron. For ten years or more he gave her free instruction in drawing and regular employment copying Turner and the old masters. She still needed, however, other remunerative work. At the age of eighteen, in 1856, she accordingly accepted an offer by F. D. Maurice to become the part-time secretary, at ten shillings a week, to some women's classes run in conjunction with the recently founded Working Men's College. In this we may discover one more of the many threads which, if followed, lead up to the foundation of Morley College.

The Working Men's College, that remarkable pioneer venture in adult education, was founded by F. D. Maurice and his fellow Christian Socialists in 1854. The Christian Socialist movement itself had been born six years earlier after the final collapse of Chartism: deeply Christian in inspiration and half-Chartist in sympathy, it employed the word Socialism not in the doctrinaire sense of state ownership but in the wide and general sense of co-operation. 'The watchword of the Socialist,' wrote Maurice, 'is co-operation, and the watchword of the anti-Socialist is competition. Anyone who recognizes the principle of co-operation as a stronger and truer principle than that of competition, has a right to the honour or the disgrace of being called a Socialist.' But the Christian Socialists' first attempts to organize self-governing bodies of workers—tailors, builders, bakers and others—for co-operative production on Owenite lines all came to grief, like the Ladies' Guild; and Maurice, Kingsley, Thomas Hughes and the other middle-class leaders became convinced that another form of co-operation was necessary before groups of working men became fit for co-operative production. This was co-operation in education—a venture over which Maurice and his friends, as professional men, were particularly well fitted to preside. Already for some time they had been running, in a Hall of Association constructed by the builders' co-operative, evening classes in the Bible, Grammar, History, and many other subjects, together with periodic lectures and debates. Spurred by the fact that in 1853 Maurice was expelled from his professorship in theology at King's College, London, for his unfashionable opposition to the conception of eternal punishment, and was available for other educational work, the Christian Socialist leaders now expanded and developed these evening classes into a permanent corporate body. So came into being what was virtually a new conception in adult education, and one the potency of which is by no means yet exhausted or even fully realized. The novelty lay not in specific instruction for working men—the Mechanics' Institutes founded by Dr. Birkbeck and others from the 1820s onwards were already providing this—but in instruction for working men with an emphasis on continuous courses in the liberal studies, given in a true College possessing its own distinctive corporate life and constitution.[1]

It was not long before the Working Men's College had its female counterpart, the Working Women's College—which has unfortunately not survived.[2] For this, as for the classes from which it grew, Octavia Hill acted not only as paid part-time secretary but also as an unpaid teacher. Meanwhile in the Working Men's College her new friend and patron John Ruskin was giving art lessons and introducing as a fellow voluntary teacher the leader of the Pre-Raphaelites, D. G. Rossetti, to be followed later by Ford

[1] In this ideal the promoters of the Working Men's College were inspired by the example of the People's College of Sheffield, founded in 1842.

[2] It split up in 1874 over the question of mixed classes. The majority group, retaining the original building in Queen Square, became the College for Men and Women, which was wound up in 1901. The smaller group formed the College for Working Women, later renamed the Frances Martin College; this for long occupied premises in Fitzroy Street and, on a reduced basis, still exists (now within the Working Men's College).

31

Madox Brown and Burne-Jones. All these, like Kingsley, Hughes and Lord Shaftesbury, Octavia Hill came to know through her original family contacts with Maurice. As she passed into her twenties her circle of acquaintance was steadily widening and her daily life, with its painting and secretarial work and teaching, growing even busier. Yet at the same time, she was becoming increasingly possessed by a desire which, when it became translated into action, soon left her no time for any of these. In 1864 in a conversation with Ruskin—who had recently inherited his father's fortune—she confessed her ambition to do 'something to provide better homes for the poor'. He at once encouraged her to work out the details of a scheme she already had in mind. More, he promised financial backing if the project appeared practical and likely to be self-supporting.

Octavia Hill's scheme, when it came down to details, was to buy the leases of three slum houses in Marylebone, in a vile courtyard characteristically misnamed Paradise Place, and to recondition both the property and as many as possible of the inhabitants. To this, within a year, was to be added a similar project with five cottages and a small piece of waste ground in Freshwater Place—another glorious misnomer. The task was no light one, as Octavia Hill's own description of the second group of properties makes clear. Roofs were leaking, plaster dropping from the walls, wallpaper hanging down in strips, drains blocked up, banisters missing—having been burned as firewood by the tenants—grates falling forward into the rooms. Windows were everywhere broken and pasted over with paper or rags: out of the 192 panes in the five cottages, only 8 were intact. Vermin abounded; and from the solitary dustbin, standing in front of the houses, boys were in the habit of dragging 'unseemly objects' and spreading them over the court. There was no proper water supply: 'One large but dirty waterbutt received the water laid on for the houses; it leaked, and, for such as did not fill their jugs when the water came in, or had no jugs to fill, there was no water.' Yet nearly every room in the five cottages, as in the houses in Paradise Place, was the home, not merely of an individual, but of a family—a family in some cases as many as six or seven in number.

With Ruskin's money the leases were secured and he became the legal owner. He had suggested a return of 5 per cent on his capital, instead of the usual 15 or more obtained from such property, and this figure governed the rents. To Octavia Hill fell the responsibility of management. As soon as she had got rid of the resident landlords or 'middlemen' she installed better water and sanitary arrangements and had the stairs, passages and yards cleaned and redecorated. She also set out at once to establish personal relationship with the tenants, visiting them herself to collect the rent, and enlisting their confidence by various kindnesses, particularly to their children. She gave them firmly to understand that the prompt payment of rent was an essential—no one was allowed to owe for a second week—but that if the rents were paid, and if wilful damage ceased and the rooms were cleaned up and kept clean, some portion of the rents would become available as a surplus for improvements suggested by the tenants. Thanks to her strong and warm personality, her admirable business sense, and her gift for inspiring willing helpers, the project began to work. A few incorrigibles had to be evicted: the great majority settled down to co-operate in

33

the task of transformation. Within eighteen months or so the properties were clean, in good repair, and supplied with water; Paradise Place was beautified by flowers in window-boxes; the derelict ground in Freshwater Place was transformed—against strenuous opposition from the rougher elements—into a garden and children's playground. Moreover a new self-respect had come into the lives of the inhabitants, who were encouraged where possible to occupy two rooms rather than one. Yet the rent exacted was considerably less than that taken before, and Ruskin had received back part of the borrowed capital, as well as his 5 per cent.

To restore these properties and to maintain them in good order was for Octavia Hill only the beginning of the battle. Fundamentally her concern was not with bricks and mortar but with souls and bodies. Her tenants must not be denied the healing qualities of a daily glimpse of beauty—hence the window-boxes and the garden—and they must not be driven, for lack of comfort at home, to spend their spare time in the ubiquitous public house. As soon as she took over the houses in Paradise Place she accordingly determined that their inhabitants should have at least a hall where they could meet for social and educational activities and hold parties for their children. In the Place itself there was no room of suitable size, just as there was no space for the garden she also longed to provide. But not far away, behind her own home in Nottingham Place, were some stables which might serve for a hall if cleaned out and redecorated, with two rooms above them which could be made into an additional tenement. The decision was quickly made. With the help of one of her oldest friends, a young woman whom she had known as an

34

art student in Gower Street, and as a pupil of her mother's and a fellow-painter in the Ladies' Guild—she set to work. Together they cleaned up the premises, whitewashed the walls, painted the woodwork, reglazed the windows. Within a short time Octavia Hill's tenants had an admirable meeting-place for conversation, classes, and children's parties.

The young lady who shared in this task of transformation had already been helping in Paradise Place itself. She was in fact the first and foremost of Octavia Hill's colleagues in the work of housing reform. As such she was expected to possess—and soon possessed—not only unflagging energy and devotion and the ability to handle folk tactfully, but also considerable competence in bookkeeping, household maintenance and repair, sanitary science, and the law relating to landlord and tenant. From 1864 onwards, braving the roughs and the drunks and the dirt, she collected rents, aided the tenants in their various troubles, helped in all the steadily expanding projects as the experiments of Paradise Place and Freshwater Place were repeated in the still more dreadful Barrett's Court—a place where the tenants even used one of the empty rooms as a dustbin, and where the filth was so firmly encrusted on the stairs that it could be removed only with a shovel. The young lady shared, too, in Octavia Hill's ever-growing circle of acquaintances as the work in Marylebone became more widely known and brought its authors growing public recognition. By 1875, when Octavia Hill was a figure with a national reputation, consulted by the Home Secretary on the provisions to be included in the Artisans Dwelling Act, her fellow-artist and friend, now in her later thirties, had behind her more

35

than ten years' experience of every problem which could confront a housing manager and a worker among the poor. She had, too, methods of her own—she heartily disliked Octavia's practice of evicting the 'incorrigibles' —and she was already applying them with success in her own field of operations round Drury Lane, then among the worst of London's slums.

It was at this juncture that she was asked to take over the management of a block of 'model' dwellings which had failed either to pay its way or to create model tenants. The block was situated in Lambeth, and so she decided to transfer her main activities, and herself, south of the river. It proved a momentous move for a district which, as we have seen, was one of the poorest and most sordid in London. For the lady was Emma Cons, who before long was not only to make the model dwellings live up to their name but also to transform the Old Vic and create Morley College.

36

III

The Royal Victoria Coffee Hall

THE convictions which inspired the founder of Morley College will by now be sufficiently clear. As the colleague of Octavia Hill, Emma Cons believed that the poor no less than the rich should have a fair chance to reach their full stature as human beings. Towards this, better accommodation was a start; but the poor must also be given the educational facilities which would help them to a higher life. They must have too, places of recreation to which they could escape from their overcrowded homes —but places where they were not faced with the constant temptation to consume alcohol. It was the combination of these diverse but closely related beliefs that led to the great experiment of the Old Vic.

Born in 1838, Emma Cons was one of a family of eight —three boys and five girls, the latter all possessing Christian names beginning with E. Her grandfather,

37

Elias Konss, had come to England from Germany only in 1770; but her father, Frederick Cons, who was apprenticed to the piano manufacturing firm of Broadwood's, became thoroughly anglicized and married the daughter of a cotton spinner from Stockport. Of their children other than Emma two at least played a part in this story. One was Ellen, who became one of Emma's greatest supports both in domestic life and at the Old Vic. The other was Elizabeth, the youngest, who carried on the family musical tradition by becoming a singer and by marrying another singer, Newton Baylis. From this union was born in 1874 Emma Cons's redoubtable niece and eventual successor at the Old Vic—Lilian Baylis.

After studying painting as a fellow-student of Octavia Hill, and before becoming a professional housing manager, Emma Cons had for some time earned her living as an artist. In association with two other girls, she had set up as an engraver of watch-cases—only to be beaten out of business by the bitter hostility of male engravers who resented the intrusion of women into their craft. She had then suffered the same hostility all over again as a designer of stained-glass windows for Messrs. Powell's, the famous firm in Whitefriars; but her courage, her persistence, and her talents, together with the support of the management, had enabled her to win through and establish herself as the head of a small department. In this position she had undertaken several important commissions, including an extensive restoration of stained-glass windows at Merton College, Oxford. By profession, then, she had been an artist before she became a property manager, and this, allied to her parentage, perhaps helps to account for her deep conviction that the poor should

38

not be without the uplifting influence of the arts. In 1874 we find her persuading Elizabeth and Newton Baylis to present an operetta to the tenants of Barrett's Court—whom she had already encouraged to form a brass band. Round about this time, too, another of her social undertakings, a girls' hostel and married women's crèche in Drury Lane, brought her increasing contacts with the theatrical world. Before long all these interests were to play their part in suggesting to her a new and unprecedented venture in the realm of social reform.

Like almost everyone else seriously concerned with working-class conditions in Victorian England, Emma Cons was a passionate believer in the cause of temperance. It was, wrote Lilian Baylis later, 'the one subject on which this exceptionally broad-minded woman was intolerant'. From her earliest days with Octavia Hill she had seen at the closest quarters the terrible prevalence of drunkenness in working-class life—a prevalence which, because it has so completely disappeared nowadays, we are apt to forget continued with little diminution up to the days of the First World War. Education, widespread recreational facilities, and dearer and weaker drink have since combined to make the sight of a drunken man in the streets a rarity; but the spectacle was all too common to the older generation still amongst us, and commoner still to Emma Cons, who in the course of managing her tenants had to wrestle daily with the effects of strong drink. She saw within her own dwellings not merely the needless poverty and the slow deterioriation of mind and body brought about by over-indulgence, but also the active brutality—the quarrels, the fights, the blows that fell on wives and children. And especially she became aware that

39

the bruises and the black eyes were at their worst after Saturday night, when the men had enjoyed their main evening of leisure at the public house or the music-hall.

It was her close experience of all this which made Emma Cons one of the leaders of the 'coffee tavern' movement during the later 1870s. The plan was to set up cafés for the working class at which alcoholic drinks would not be served—for such places hardly existed. Support was forthcoming from many philanthropists and temperance reformers, and the movement spread rapidly. To the three companies formed to promote this work prior to 1877, were added in the next three years no less than fifty-three more. A 'Coffee Public House Association' was formed under the presidency of the Duke of Westminster, with Emma Cons on the executive committee, and in London three companies set up establishments. To the first of these companies—the Coffee Tavern Company, her own particular creation with Thomas Hughes—Emma Cons acted as honorary secretary: the chairman was Lord Mount Temple, like the Duke of Westminster an ardent worker in good causes.[1]

By the end of the 1870s a dozen or more coffee taverns

[1] The Duke of Westminster and Lord Mount Temple remained firm supporters of Emma Cons's ventures until the end of their lives. The Duke, a Liberal who split with Gladstone over Home Rule, had a reputation in many fields. Sportsman, racehorse-breeder and patron of art, he was also a model landlord, a great promoter of agricultural and technical education, and an unfailing leader in charitable causes. In the latter part of his life he made Grosvenor House 'a centre of far-reaching philanthropic effort' (*D.N.B.*). Lord Mount Temple, the first and last of the title, lives in history as William Francis Cowper Temple, the proposer of the famous Cowper-Temple amendment to Forster's Education Bill. By this clause, which the government accepted, purely denominational religious teaching was forbidden in the new rate-built schools. The son of the fifth Earl Cowper, he adopted the surname Cowper-Temple after he had inherited the estates of Henry Temple Lord Palmerston (who had become his stepfather). In the 1860s as Commissioner of Works he was responsible for

40

were open in London where men and women, from 5 a.m. to midnight, could get a cup of coffee for a penny, a cup of tea or cocoa for a halfpenny, and a plate of hot beef for sixpence. Most of them had recreation rooms and some also offered cheap beds for men.[1] In fact the need they met, for cheap meals or a cheap cup of tea or coffee in modest but completely respectable circumstances, was so great that commercial companies soon followed the trail blazed by the philanthropists. The result was that during the 1880s Messrs. Lockharts, 'Pearce and Plenty', and others began to make the coffee tavern superfluous. The companies responsible for them accordingly faded away, the last to survive in London being the Coffee Tavern Company, which was wound up in 1892. It had enjoyed a vigorous and useful life of sixteen years.

Meanwhile Emma Cons, who was soon to be living in a cottage in Surrey Lodge, an attractive quadrangle of working-class cottages, tenements and shops built to her own design at the junction of the Lambeth and the Kennington Roads, had become more than ever convinced of the need not merely for temperance cafés, but for temperance entertainment. She had accordingly set out to link the coffee tavern movement with a still more ambitious venture. Once more support was forthcoming, and in

[1] When General Gardiner was taken round the new sleeping accommodation in the Walmer Castle Coffee Tavern, in Seymour Place, he was heard to remark to a friend: 'We should some of us have been very glad of as good a bedroom as this at the University!'

---

he Thames Embankment. He also came to the fore in the Commons Preservation movement, and in 1871 was one of the leading figures in the successful struggle to save Epping Forest. His last decade of life, in the 1880s, was given over to philanthropic effort. The Criminal Law Amendment Act of 1887, passed after W. T. Stead's revelation of the traffic in young girls, owed much to his support.

1879 a meeting was held at the Walmer Castle Coffee Tavern. It was presided over by the indefatigable Lord Mount Temple, and its purpose was to consider Emma Cons's proposal 'to provide for the working and lower middle classes recreation such as the music-hall affords, without the existing attendant moral and social disadvantages'. These disadvantages were too well known to require stating on paper. They were unclean jokes, heavy drinking, and the large number of prostitutes soliciting in the bars and promenades.

In her preliminary circular Emma Cons mentioned 'what seemed to be the best way of achieving the desired end'—namely 'by opening music-halls in various parts of London—at which a purified entertainment shall be given and no intoxicating drinks be sold'. 'It is not proposed,' the circular went on, 'to provide for a higher class of audience than that which at present frequents music-halls, but only to offer that class an entertainment which shall amuse without degrading them, and to which men may take their wives and children without shaming or harming them.' In this spirit, after speeches by Lord Mount Temple and other gentlemen—Emma Cons being a woman was not expected to address a public meeting—a resolution was duly taken to form the Coffee Music Halls Company Ltd., with the programme of providing 'several large music halls in various parts of London, at which a purified entertainment shall be given and no intoxicant drinks be sold.[1]

In point of fact, no such music-halls were ever pro-

[1] Among the first directors of the company were Carl Rosa and F. D. Mocatta. Its shareholders soon included the Marchioness of Lothian, Lady Brabazon, the Countess Ducie, the Duchess of Richmond, Mrs. E. Montefiore, Mrs. Gladstone and Dr. James Martineau.

vided by the Company, except one—the Old Vic. The exception is very large and owes its existence to a number of factors. One was that the theatre had for long been surviving only on the most precarious basis, and was standing empty available for lease or purchase. Another was the fact that it was close to Surrey Lodge and other dwellings in Lambeth. A third was the interest of John Hollingshead, the lively and well-disposed manager of the Gaiety Theatre, who was the first to suggest the acquisition of the Old Vic, and who was willing to act as its manager under the new dispensation. This last offer, however, was not accepted by the Company. 'Eventually I found,' says Hollingshead in his autobiography, 'that my connection with the Gaiety Theatre was not considered a good and safe qualification for me to take a leading part in carrying out my idea. Being a philosopher, I left it in the capable hands of Miss Cons, and have watched its rise and well-deserved progress with that interest which an abandoned parent takes in the career of a prosperous and proper child.'

At all events, after a further meeting of 'influential persons' in February, 1880, had been held in the Jerusalem Chamber of Westminster Abbey under the chairmanship of Dean Stanley, sufficient support was forthcoming for the Coffee Music Halls Company to take an eighteen-year lease of the Victoria Theatre. As honorary secretary to the company, and organizing genius of the whole venture, Emma Cons's charter was clear—to stop the drinks and the soliciting, and to 'improve and elevate' the character of the entertainment. The transformation involved would be considerable, as a glance at the previous history of the theatre will make clear.

* * *

43

The place of entertainment which Emma Cons took over in 1880 had first opened its doors sixty-two years earlier as the Royal Coburg Theatre. It owed its origin to the building of Waterloo Bridge and the anger of two lessees of the Surrey Theatre at being refused a renewal of their lease except on grossly extortionate terms. The name capitalized the patronage of Prince Leopold of Saxe-Coburg, the husband of the Prince Regent's only child, the Princess Charlotte—the heiress presumptive to the throne. Of the actual building, it is sufficient to say that it was a fairly large theatre, with a stage about the size of that of the present Her Majesty's, and a huge gallery. In the construction considerable difficulty was encountered from the swampy nature of the soil—for though the New Cut ran along the front and the Waterloo Bridge Road down one side, the neighbourhood was still very undeveloped. To overcome the swamp, the architect used in the foundation large numbers of stones from a famous building then being demolished—the old Savoy Palace in the Strand; and to overcome the various dangers from the undeveloped neighbourhood (and its frequenters), the Waterloo Bridge Company provided special patrols on the bridge and along the main road.

In the state of the law as it then stood, only two theatres in London, the privileged houses of the Theatre Royal, Drury Lane and the Theatre Royal, Covent Garden, were entitled to present every type of theatrical entertainment including the 'legitimate' drama. If one of the so-called minor theatres, like the Coburg, wished to present Shakespeare, it could legally do so only by concocting some altered version and then interrupting this by repeated outbursts of song and dance. Anything more faithful to

44

the original, as the Coburg soon found, could easily call down an attack at law from one of the two patent theatres. This restriction, which persisted until the doctrines of free trade and *laissez-faire* eventually triumphed in the Theatres Regulation Act of 1843, hamstrung the Coburg during the vital years when its reputation was being formed. Before programmes which consisted of melodramatic spectacles and harlequinades, varied by scenes and sketches incorporating aquatic effects and pony races, the initial *éclat* of the royal patronage soon wore off. It soon wore off too, before the inconvenient and poorly lit journey, and the dubious character of the local clientèle. As early as 1820 Hazlitt—admittedly a notorious exaggerator—had extremely harsh things to say not merely of the entertainment but of the audience. 'You felt yourself,' he wrote, 'in a bridewell, or a brothel, amongst . . . pickpockets, prostitutes and mountebanks, instead of being in the precincts of Mount Parnassus or in the company of the Muses. The object was not to admire or to excel, but to vilify and degrade everything. The audience did not hiss the actors (that would have implied a serious disapprobation and something like a disappointed wish to be pleased), but they laughed at, hooted at, nicknamed, pelted them with oranges and witticisms, to show their unruly contempt for them and their art. . . .'

Although during the 1820s and 1830s the theatre enjoyed (besides much rubbish) several meritorious performances and a few moments of distinction, the prevailing tone of the audience remained low. This was repeatedly commented upon by the critics. *The Times,* for instance, in its review in 1824 of *George III, The Father of His People: a new grand historical and dramatic memoir,* heavily remarks that 'a very profound dustman and two chimney-sweepers in the gallery seemed to enjoy the whole performance with that quiet delight which might be expected from persons of their taste and breeding'. And it was the Coburg audience which in 1831 inspired the best-remembered curtain speech in theatrical history, when Edmund Kean, after suffering noise and inattentiveness during his playing of Othello, together with a good deal of partiality towards a local Iago, first delayed in facing a call at the end, and then, when the house insisted, hurled at them the immortal words: 'I have played in every civilized country where English is the language of the people; but I never acted to an audience of such unmitigated brutes as you are.' [1]

It was in 1833 that the Coburg, passing into fresh hands, acquired its later and more famous name. Princess Charlotte was dead, her husband King of the Belgians; and in honour of a new heiress presumptive the theatre was renamed the Royal Victoria. Soon after the reopening the young princess herself visited the theatre, together with her mother the Duchess of Kent, to see a musical version of *Guy Mannering*. For some years the new management strove not unsuccessfully to redeem the reputation of the house; Phelps played on occasion, Sheridan Knowles frequently, and Macready once (on Knowles's benefit night—though he felt it 'rather a descent to play at the Victoria'). On one memorable evening Paganini gave a farewell charity concert. During this period disorders became rare, and when a boy in the gallery hissed during a performance of Miss Mitford's *Charles I,* the police were called in.

[1] There are other and more extended versions of this famous speech.

46

Long before the end of the 1830s, however, the new proprietors were bankrupt and the Victoria was again on the down-grade. By 1840 yet another critic (G. F. Tomkins, in his *Brief View of the English Drama*) was referring to the theatre's many vicissitudes, and to the fact that it had never pursued 'any course sufficiently steady to raise a character or secure a continuous and respectable audience'. 'Situated in one of the worst neighbourhoods,' Tomkins continued, 'its audiences are of the lowest kind, and if the English Emperor or Empress should visit it, it would be necessary to imitate the Roman potentate, by drenching the audience with rose-water to neutralize certain vile odours arising from gin and tobacco and bad ventilation. . . .'

In the 1840s, under the management of D. W. Osbaldiston, the fortunes of the theatre continued to be chequered. An attempt was made to take advantage of the liberating act of 1843, and Osbaldiston presented somewhat more authentic versions of Shakespeare, together with such new plays as a dramatic version of *Jane Eyre*. The staple fare of the house, however, soon became melodrama of the crudest and simplest kind. Sometimes these plays were fashioned from the misdeeds of well-known criminals, such as Jack Sheppard or Dick Turpin; at other times they were of the type of '*Poor Susan: or the Fate of the Village Maid*', or else vamped up from the more violent scenes in well-known novels.

Of the last kind, a memorable account has been left in John Hollingshead's description of *Oliver Twist:* 'The gallery of the Victoria was a large amphitheatre, probably containing about 1,500 perspiring creatures: most of the men in shirt sleeves, and most of the women bare-headed,

47

with coloured handkerchiefs round their shoulders, called "bandanna wipes" in the slang of the district, and probably stolen from the pockets of old gentlemen who were given to snuff-taking. This "chickaleary" audience was always thirsty—and not ashamed. It tied handkerchiefs together—of which it always seemed to have plenty—until they formed a rope, which was used to haul up large stone bottles of beer from the pit, and occasionally hats that had been dropped below. . . . It was this body . . . who were maliciously tortured by Mr. E. F. Savile and half a dozen other representatives of Dickens's criminal animal.

The murder of Nancy was the greatest scene. Nancy was always dragged round the stage by her hair, and after this effort Sikes always looked up defiantly at the gallery, as he was doubtless told to do in the marked prompt copy. He was always answered by one loud and fearful curse, yelled by the whole mass like a Handel Festival chorus. The curse was answered by Sikes dragging Nancy twice round the stage and then, like Ajax, defying the lightning. The simultaneous yell then became louder and more blasphemous. Finally when Sikes, working up to a well-rehearsed climax, smeared Nancy with red-ochre, and taking her by the hair (a most powerful wig) seemed to dash her brains out on the stage, no explosion of dynamite invented by the modern anarchist, no language ever dreamt of in Bedlam could equal the outburst. A thousand enraged voices, which sounded like ten thousand, with the roar of a dozen escaped menageries, filled the theatre and deafened the audience, and when the smiling ruffian came forward and bowed, their voices, in thorough plain English expressed a fierce, determi-

48

nation to tear his sanguinary entrails from his sanguinary body.'[1]

The building of Waterloo Station and the other railway development near by during the 1840s only served to produce a still lower grade of audience than that for which the Royal Victoria was already notorious. Round about this time, too, there are many references to the flagrancy of the immoral traffic within the theatre saloon and in the neighbouring streets and houses. The best known of these is the often quoted passage from Kingsley's novel *Alton Locke,* published in 1850. The hero, Alton Locke, a young man of high principles working in a tailoring sweat shop, recounts how he and a friend 'were passing by the door of the Victoria Theatre—it was just half-price time—and the beggary and rascality of London were pouring in to their low amusement from the neighbouring gin-palaces and thieves' cellars. A herd of ragged boys, vomiting forth slang, filth and blasphemy, pushed past us, compelling us to take care of our pockets.' . . . Alton Lock's companion, an enthusiastic Chartist, promptly drew the moral: 'Look there! look at the amusement, the training, the civilization which the Government permits to the children of the people! These licensed pits of darkness, traps of temptation, profligacy and ruin, triumphantly yawning night after night! and then tell me that the people who see their children kidnapped into Hell are represented by a government which licenses such things! Give us the Charter, and we'll send workmen into Parliament that shall find out whether something better can't be put in the way of the ten thousand boys and girls in London who live by theft and

[1] John Hollingshead: *My Lifetime.*

49

prostitution than the tender mercies of the Victoria—a pretty name! They say the Queen's a good woman, and I don't doubt it; I often wonder if she knows what her precious namesake here is like.'

It would be superfluous to describe any further the prevailing tone of the Victoria. During the 1860s the place continued to be given up to low-grade melodrama; and in the 1870s—by which time it had acquired the popular nickname of the 'Old Vic'—the only substantial difference was that the managements found it harder and harder to avoid loss. Hence the theatre eventually fell empty, and so the Coffee Music Halls Company were able to secure their lease. Right up to the last, the atmosphere had remained one of rowdyism, drunkenness, and soliciting. In the later words of Caroline Martineau, another of Octavia Hill's rent-collectors and the devoted friend and colleague of Emma Cons: 'the police . . . got extra pay for coming, and yet it was an unpopular job for they were afraid of getting their heads broken. There was seldom a Saturday without seven or eight police court cases, sometimes thirty or forty, and often on Boxing Night the gallery had to be cleared.'

Such was the theatre for which Emma Cons assumed responsibility in 1880, and such its normal audience.

* * *

After the expenditure of some £3,000 on alterations and redecorations, the Victoria reopened its doors on Boxing Day, 1880, as the Royal Victoria Coffee Hall. Prostitutes and strong drink had been strictly banished from the saloon, which had become a pleasantly fitted-out coffee tavern open both day and evening. The programme presented on the opening night consisted of standard

50

WATERLOO BRIDGE ROAD. 15 Minutes from Strand

Saturday, May 17th, and Monday, May 19th. At 8. 84	Miss PERCY, Character Vocalist. Tiny TENOR, Tyrolean Vocalist Leo STORMONT, Baritone Mr. Tom TINSLEY, Young JOHN BULL, Character Comedian. The Levina Brothers, Musical Funniosities Wonderful Hicken Family, Equilibrists Expensive Engagement of FRANCOIS DE BLANCHE, The great Parisian Humourist and exposer of Conjuring Tricks. SIGNOR MONZAWOOD, Juggler. FRED. EVANS'S Grand Pantomimical FARCICAL SCREAMER, entitled PUSSY'S HOLIDAY, OR THE DEMON CATS Characters by Arthur Bolton, Willie West, F. Evans, jun., Fred. Evans Mechanical Effects, Tricks, etc., invented by Fred. Evans, Music by A. Lee, Esq.
Tuesday, May 20th. Gallery, 1d. Pit 2d. Balcony, 6d. Stalls, 1s.	At 8 o'clock.—Selections by the Band. 8-30—PENNY SCIENCE LECTURE. Prof. H. G. SEELEY, F.R.S. on "A WORKING MAN'S DINNER." With Dissolving Views. Chairman, Samuel MORLEY, Esq., M.P. To conclude with VARIETY ENTERTAINMENT.
Wednesday, May 21st. At 8.	ENTERTAINMENT for the benefit of Bro. Chas. Osborn, P.C.N., by the BEEHIVE Lodge, O.G.O.T.A.S.P. See Special Bills.
Thursday, May 22nd. At 8.	Grand Ballad Concert! Under the direction of Madame FRANCES BROOKE. Vocalists—Madame Frances Brooke, Miss Jeannie Rosse, Miss Eva Lynn, Miss Edith Daniel, Mr. John Cross, Mr. Lynde, Mr. Frederic Wood, Mr. A. G. Pritchard, Miss Jane Levien, and Mr. L'Estrange.
Friday, 23rd. At 8. Prices same as Tuesday.	GRAND TEMPERANCE NIGHT! Chairman, B. WHITWORTH, ESQ., M.P. John M. R. Todd, Esq., Kilburn, & Two Navvies. Working Men's Choir of the Holy Trinity Branch, C.E.T.S., will give Temperance Choruses, Recitations and Short Addresses, after which Variety Entertainment—Leo Stormont, Signor Monzawood, Bros. Levina, Francois de Blanche, The Hicken Family, Fred. Evans's Screaming Ballet, PUSSY'S HOLIDAY.

PRICES—Gallery 3d. Pit 6d. Balcony 9d. Pit Stalls 1s. Balcony Stalls 1s. Orchestra Stalls 2s. Reserved Stalls 3s. Boxes 6s. 10s. 6d. and 21s. Her Majesty's Soldiers and Sailors in uniform admitted at Half-price to all parts. Bill Orders not admitted on Saturday or Wednesday. Conductor, Mr. F. EPLETT. Acting Manager, Mr. T. MILNES. Hon. Sec., Miss CONS

Bowers Bros., Printers, 89, Blackfriars Road, S.E.

2a Vic Handbill, 1884

2b The Vic and its Coffee Tavern, 1880

variety acts with a careful eye given to the extent of the innuendo. Emma Cons and her friends helped to serve the tea and sandwiches, and a large crowd enjoyed the convivial but abstemious evening. Lilian Baylis has recorded how her mother was one of the amateur waitresses, and how when asked by a patron 'for a couple of thick 'uns' she failed to grasp the allusion and handed him two of the thickest mugs.

In the course of the ensuing weeks Emma Cons found that it was one thing to fill a music-hall on a Saturday night, and quite another thing to fill it during the week. The ordinary music-hall could compensate for an indifferent mid-week attendance by the profits from the bars. The Royal Victoria Coffee Hall could not, and in consequence soon found itself unable to afford an attractive bill every night. Fortunately there was an honourable alternative. Emma Cons was in any case keen to vary the fare which the hall would put before the public. She knew that there were many among the poor who could rise to higher levels of entertainment than music-hall variety; and for these she was soon providing ballad concerts on Thursdays, and a temperance meeting followed by a talk 'with dissolving views'—a lantern lecture—on Fridays. On Wednesdays variety was diluted with something less expensive—a public practice by the newly formed Royal Victoria Choir. The other nights remained devoted, as before, entirely to variety, harlequinades and the like. On Saturday afternoons there was a variety show for children, and on Sundays the hall was let for religious services.

All these activities were well supported; but because of the small price of admission—as little as 1*d.* for the gallery on the choir and temperance evenings—none of them

51

paid their way except the Saturday night variety and the Thursday ballad concerts. The latter did so only because Madame Sainton-Dolby and other eminent musicians gave their services free; but at least there was no doubt of their popular appeal. 'The hard-working enthusiastic dwellers in the New Cut,' wrote the *Illustrated London News* on April 2nd, 1881, 'crowd the place to suffocation to hear Sir Julius Benedict play, and Miss de Fonblanque sing. The better the music, the more it is appreciated; and the rough working men are as courteous and enthusiastic as the fashionable folk in St. James's Hall.' The *Pall Mall Gazette,* a few days earlier, put the matter a little more laconically: 'The experiment is certainly one of the most interesting and admirable that has been made in the direction of giving to the workers of London some of the humanizing pleasures hitherto reserved for the idlers.'

Over all these entertainments it was intended that Emma Cons should keep a supervisory eye, while the actual work of theatrical management was discharged by a professional manager. Clearly it would not be easy for the normal manager to fit into such a venture; and the first one, though recommended by Carl Rosa, soon proved unsuitable. After eight months' working, the disheartening picture then emerged of a loss of £2,800. There were no funds, and not likely to be any, by which a continuing loss of this order could be accepted. The prices of seats were already as high as it was thought the audience could or would afford. When the dog-days of August, 1881, arrived, the performances were accordingly suspended. Within less than a year the whole venture had reached the point of crisis.

In this situation the majority of the directors of the Coffee Music Halls Company, after examining the possibilities, were for realistically acknowledging defeat and winding up the project at the Victoria. The unexpired part of their tenure could then be disposed of for its market figure; while the concerts, which were an unquestioned success, could be carried on at a different place. Something would thus be saved from the wreck. Such counsels of prudence, however, did not suit Emma Cons. She pointed out that if the hall were sub-let to any ordinary management it would at once revert to all the bad old practices; that to cease activities would discourage others from trying any similar scheme; and that the shareholders were much less interested in the financial aspects of their investment than in the philanthropic. In sum, to admit defeat at this juncture would be productive of evil and positively immoral.

These arguments in committee she reinforced by a powerful appeal in her official report on the eight months' working. 'Of the *moral* success of our work at the Vic,' she wrote, 'I can scarcely find words strong enough to give a true idea to anyone, except those working in the neighbourhood. Some idea may be gathered by talking to the neighbouring clergy, who when we began were all against having another Music-hall in their district, as the others did so much harm to their people. None of them would come to our hall; in fact many of them spoke against us, and advised their people not to come to it. But now they have nearly all joined our Temperance Committee: have spoken at our meetings: and concur in saying that a wonderful work is being done. I should like you to see their letters to me: they say that the streets are

53

quite different since we came, both for drunkenness and immorality. The Police say the same, from the Chief Superintendent downwards, noting a wonderful decrease in drunkenness and immorality. The general charges of the neighbourhood have decreased on an average from forty to four; while taking the charges arising directly out of the Vic, there has not been one in our time, whilst before they say "There was never a night without one or two, and at holiday time there were as many as thirty, forty and even fifty charges at one time". Not one policeman only, but without exception every policeman and person to whom I have spoken in the neighbourhood, joins in the same theme of thankfulness and rejoicing. If I were rich I should think no money so well spent: as it is, I can only give my life and that I give freely!'

Even such a statement by itself could not have prevailed against the majority opinion. But Emma Cons had several devoted friends more affluent than herself. From one of them, who wished to remain anonymous at the time (but who in fact was Mrs. Richard Martineau, the mother of Caroline) she secured a promise of £1,000 if the work should continue. From others came lesser but equally acceptable offers. In short, disappointed in the majority of the directors, Emma Cons found others who would be willing either to help in the scheme or to lend it financial support. Among the directors or principal shareholders themselves, her main encouragement came from Constance Marchioness of Lothian and from Lord Mount Temple, who most generously gave a personal guarantee to meet any deficit incurred in the ensuing nine months.

Faced with this, the majority of the directors were quite agreeable to letting the scheme proceed under different

54

auspices. A new committee came into being to continue the Victoria project on the same lines as during the first eight months and this committee hired the hall from the Coffee Music Halls Company. At its first meeting it also took a formal resolution 'never to run into debt'. By the autumn of 1881 the first great crisis had been overcome; the experiment of purified variety in teetotal surroundings —and diversified by temperance meetings, lectures and ballad concerts—could continue.

In October, 1881, the Victoria therefore reopened its doors. For the new season Emma Cons had found a new manager—one who was himself destined to add (in other places) some important pages to theatrical history. William Poel was a man of genius who was already proclaiming that the right way to present Shakespeare was on the platform stage and in the costume of Shakespeare's own period, and with concern not for the pleasures of declamation or spectacle but for the meaning of the text. But at the Royal Victoria Coffee Hall Poel remained only a little over two years. He seems to have done admirable work during his first season—when he raised the tone of entertainments, reduced expenses and drew large audiences—but to have been less sucessful in 1883, when financial worries again became pressing. To judge from his later utterances, he felt that the committee was 'aiming too high', with too much emphasis on education and not enough on entertainment. At all events he departed at the end of 1883 to become stage manager for Frank Benson. And when he left he was not replaced. From then on Emma Cons not merely exercised general responsibility over the whole project but also carried out the detailed work of theatrical management—all, of course, while

55

continuing a host of other activities including the management of the South London Dwellings Company.

During the earlier and more successful part of Poel's management the hall enjoyed some notable moments—though in connection with the musical rather than the theatrical side of the entertainments. On February 9th, 1882, for instance, the Prince and Princess of Wales—who ever afterwards remained good friends of the venture—were present at an Irish ballad concert. According to the *Daily News* the following morning, they seemed to be 'much amused at the free and easy style of the pit and gallery', who 'though vastly different to the "gods" of fifteen years beforehand,' were still 'true to some of the traditions of the place'. 'Ever and anon the flash of the stricken lucifer and the kindling pipe shone through the gloom, for the Prince with his usual kindliness had expressed a desire that none of the customs of the concert should be altered on his account. In the front row some young fellows took off their coats, and paid Madame Liebhart the compliment of listening to her "Harp that once through Tara's halls" in their shirt sleeves. As their fervour warmed they loosened their collars and finally rose to the sublimity of tucked-up shirt sleeves, and so, with their naked arms gracefully disposed on the ledge they enjoyed the remainder of the concert.'

Several times during the rest of this season the Thursday concerts successfully appealed to a much higher level of musical taste. The week after the Prince's visit there was an evening devoted entirely to Mozart, and the following Thursday saw a performance of the supreme masterpiece of Handel. 'The *Messiah*,' reported the *Echo*, 'drew an immense audience, and the grand old oratorio

56

was followed with the deepest attention by all present. The great bulk of the audience were the hardworking people of the class commonly called by some "the lower orders". Mechanics, factory men and women and even costers in humble habiliments, were plentiful in pit and gallery, who listened without a murmur of restlessness to the 57 numbers of the Messiah, exclusive of choruses. And not only did they listen patiently, but they rapturously applauded each soloist and redemanded "Unto us a child is born" and would have encored nearly every solo and chorus had they been permitted. Leaning over all round the gallery, the threepenny spectators, a great number with knotted handkerchiefs round their necks, and nearly all with the humble "clay" in their mouths, harkened earnestly to the marvellous orchestration and the world-famed vocal music with which Handel's masterpiece abounds. . . . Such an event deserves to be noted, especially by those (and they are many) who think that audiences in poorer neighbourhoods can never be got to relish anything beyond music-hall trash and plays of the Sweeny Todd class.'

By the end of Poel's first season, in the summer of 1882, substantial progress had thus been achieved. The variety artistes were proving more responsive to the *ethos* of the venture—'we have continually less and less trouble in controlling words and gestures', reported Emma Cons—and the financial loss had been less than in any corresponding period since the hall opened. It was therefore all the more disappointing when in the next season, from the autumn of 1882 to the summer of 1883, audiences began to fall off. The programmes were running much as in the previous season, with variety on Mondays, Tuesdays, and

57

Saturdays, choir (and band) on Wednesdays, concerts on Thursdays, temperance meetings and lectures (always followed by an entertainment) on Fridays, and the hall let for mission work on Sundays; yet support was perceptibly declining. The main reason for this was probably a growing trade depression, though Emma Cons herself ascribed it to the competition of new music halls in the neighbourhood. In addition there was the permanent factor, little less true today than in 1883, 'the prevalent impression that the Surrey side of the water is almost inaccessible to the majority of Londoners, whereas this is far from being the case'.

The fact that the audiences were so poor for the variety performance on Mondays and Tuesdays helped to inspire Emma Cons's next step. Impressed with the success of the lantern lectures which usually followed the temperance meeting on Fridays, she had already in the summer of 1882 written to *Nature* appealing to scientists to come and address her audience. Caroline Martineau has recorded the result. The appeal 'was responded to by several scientific men, notably by Mr. William Lant Carpenter, who, in the following autumn, was the first to face a New Cut audience with a lecture on a scientific subject, "The Telephone', or "How to talk to a man a hundred miles away". It needed some pluck to do this. When he stopped speaking for a minute to arrange the apparatus for the next experiment, a voice from the gallery bade him "go home and learn his lesson". But this was only chaff, not meant as rudeness, and a little good-humoured chaff in reply soon turned the tide. He was followed by his father, Dr. W. B. Carpenter, Dr Dallinger, Norman Lockyer, and others of the foremost

58

scientific men of the day. And thus a fresh section of working people was added to the supporters of the Hall, those with scientific tastes. They came from long distances, since really good, well-illustrated lectures, at prices within their means, were at that time very rare in London.'

This generous response on the part of so many distinguished men encouraged Emma Cons to put lectures on a much more systematic footing. A committee of scientists was formed to assist in their running, and in place of being a pleasant adjunct to the temperance meetings on Friday, they began to occupy a night of their own —on Tuesday. Music before and after formed a subsidiary attraction; and this form of Tuesday evening became the practice from the autumn of 1883 onwards. But as the hall continued to lose money, and the deficiency was met only by subscriptions and appeals, several members of the committee came to believe—like William Poel—that Miss Cons was giving too much attention to the education of the working man, and too little to the original object of the venture—his entertainment. This, several of them thought, must inevitably take the form of music-hall variety, with perhaps occasionally a ballad concert: nor could they see the sense, financial or otherwise, of taking over a theatre and then devoting four evenings out of six to non-theatrical activities. The matter came to a head towards the close of 1883 when by the margin of a single vote the committee decided to stop not only the Tuesday lectures but also the Friday temperance meetings.

This new resolution ignored the fact that a policy of five or six nights of variety had already been tried earlier

59

on without success. The lectures and temperance meetings were duly stopped; but still the loss of money continued. Faced with this evidence that variety on a Tuesday was no more profitable than a lecture on the wonders of electricity, some of the committee came round to the minority view, with the result that the lectures and meetings were restarted. It remained painfully clear, however, both that the hall was suffering from divided counsels, and that its Guarantee Fund was fast melting away. Within a few months, it seemed, the whole venture must come to an end.

In this situation Emma Cons, who had never wavered in her belief in the lectures and meetings, again produced one of her master cards. As before, she found out side the ranks of the committee someone of similar views to her own who was willing to put up money. In this case it was a gentleman who offered £1,000 towards the purchase of the remainder of the lease from the Coffee Music Halls Company—a proposal which would save a considerable sum in annual rent. There was, however, a condition. If his offer were accepted he claimed the right—can it be that Emma Cons put the stipulation into his head?—to choose a working committee in harmony with his own ideas. These, needless to say, ran strongly in favour of continuing and indeed developing the lectures and temperance meetings.

The name of this benevolent *deus ex machina* was Samuel Morley.

* * *

An outstanding and universally respected figure in the worlds of commerce, nonconformity, philanthropy and politics, Samuel Morley was the head of the great Mid-

60

land hosiery firm of I. & R. Morley. As such he was one of the true Victorian kings of commerce. Skilful in finance and immensely enterprising, in association with his brother he had developed an already considerable family firm until it was the greatest business of its kind in the world, and he himself a millionaire. Yet everything had been done with unimpeachable integrity and with an almost unprecedented consideration for the interests of the workpeople. Though a disciplinarian of the old school, as exact with others as he was with himself, he had ceaselessly striven to establish the best possible conditions in the ever-growing number of his factories: no one in the 1880s could boast workplaces that were cleaner, better lit or better ventilated, and no one could boast work-people who for their tasks were better paid. For the firm's hand-knitters dispossessed by the advent of new machinery he had bought annuities and so started the first big pension scheme in industry. He was rewarded by the devotion of his employees, and by virtue of this and the immense volume of its business, his firm stood with rock-like solidity through all the commercial vicissitudes of the 19th century—a fact which drew from the great historian Taine the well-known tribute: 'Nothing can shake the House of Morley.'

From his earliest manhood Morley had had many interests outside the world of commerce. A sincerely religious man, very tolerant of differences in creed but with an overwhelming concern for moral rectitude, he was impelled by his powerful sense of duty to fight what seemed to him obvious evils. His sympathies were from the start strongly radical, and from the 1850s onwards he had campaigned strenuously for a number of reforms which in the fullness of time were eventually achieved. The reform of banking and the currency, the opening of the Civil Service to public competition, the abolition of the purchase of commissions, the extension of the franchise, the introduction of the secret ballot, the admission of dissenters to Oxford and Cambridge, the development of a national system of elementary education—all these owed much to Morley's advocacy. In Parliament as Liberal M.P. for Bristol from 1868 onwards he had given invaluable support to Gladstone in the great reforming programme of the latter's first ministry. It was a support all the more valued by the Prime Minister because it came from one whose power of speech, while not much exercised in the Commons, could reach out to a working- or a middle-class audience in tones and words that came direct from the heart.

But though a national figure in industry, politics, and education (where for many years he was chairman of the London School Board), Morley was even better known in the world of philanthropy. His benefactions had been almost countless—a fact picturesquely expressed by the clergyman at a meeting who remarked that 'it would be more easy to say to what good things Mr. Morley does not subscribe than to what he does'. Mid-Victorian money-making was not quite on the same scale as that of the early 20th century, and individually none of these gifts was of a size to compare with those of Lord Nuffield. Morley gave in tens, in hundreds, and in thousands of pounds; but not in tens of thousands or beyond. Nevertheless he consistently gave away some £20,000 to £30,000 a year, and cumulatively his benefactions probably exceeded those of any of his contemporaries. Moreover each gift, large or small, was deeply considered; and the larger ones, in response to appeals, were often accompanied by some condition designed to put the recipient on his mettle or to bring in further contributions. Thus the £1,000 towards the purchase of the lease from the Coffee Music Halls Company was offered on condition that the rest of the money was raised from other sources. Furthermore, a gift from Morley meant in very many cases not only money but his readiness to help personally even in the humblest of ways. 'There is that dear man Samuel Morley,' Lord Shaftesbury once remarked to Edwin Hodder, 'content to be anything or nothing, so that good is being done.'

Of Morley's innermost qualities, two facts will perhaps give sufficient indication. In 1885 he was offered a peerage by Gladstone in the warmest terms: 'I do not know,' wrote the Liberal leader, 'that I have ever had a more genuine pleasure in conveying a proposal of this nature than now, when I make it to one who had earned so many irrefragable titles to the honourable regard of his countrymen.' Nevertheless the offer was refused: Morley had always been opposed to a hereditary chamber not responsible to the electorate, and he was not prepared to compromise his principles. The second fact is perhaps even more indicative of his remarkable quality. In 1886, after W. T. Stead had earned a prison sentence by purchasing a thirteen-year-old girl from her mother in order to show up the existence of a widespread traffic in young girls for immoral purposes, an official inquiry became necessary to pierce the clouds of controversy and establish the truth of Stead's assertions. Only public men of the loftiest place and reputation could, in those days, have

63

attempted to discharge such a task without being overwhelmed by public disagreement and disapproval. The members of the committee therefore consisted of the Archbishop of Canterbury, Cardinal Manning, the Bishop of London, and Sir Robert Reid (an eminent lawyer). The chairman was Samuel Morley.

An episode of another kind says perhaps even more for Morley's character. Early in his career he had become deeply disturbed by the drunkenness then so prevalent in working-class life. 'What is to be done about the drink evil?' he wrote in 1857, 'it is the monster grievance of the present day. It seems to me something like infatuation to be building and supporting at great cost reformatories and other institutions, while this huge cancer remains unremoved.' In this spirit he had lent strong support to temperance societies, and had taken to addressing meetings in that cause. At one of these a working man boldly interrupted: 'Do you go without yourself? I dare say, if the truth's known, you take your glass or two of wine after dinner and think no harm of it. Now sir, do you go without yourself?' Morley in fact did not; he drank a modest glass of wine at dinner. 'This rather shut me up for an instant,' recorded Morley in relating the incident, 'but when I looked around at those poor fellows whom I had been asking to give up what they regarded—no matter how erroneously—as their only luxury, I had my answer ready pretty quickly. "No," I said, "but I will go without from this hour".' He lived for nearly thirty years afterwards, but never again, except once in illness under doctor's orders, did this millionaire, with every luxury at his command had he wished, permit an alcoholic drink to pass his lips.

64

So far as the Royal Victoria Coffee Hall was concerned, Morley had not at first been a supporter of the project. He had been approached in the beginning but had stood aloof as he did not approve of music-halls—an attitude which need not strike us as unduly narrow-minded when we remember that neither their entertainment nor their associations were such as to appeal to any respectable and substantial Victorian. Within a very short time, however, he had become aware of the remarkable transformation which the Cons régime was working in the theatre, and in 1882, at a meeting in the Mansion House, he stood forth as a convinced supporter of the scheme. The support was expressed in his usual practical form, and with his usual homely eloquence. He told the meeting the story of a Quaker, who, in addressing a similar gathering, had said: 'My friends, there is a vast amount of feeling being spoken about, but I should like to know how much your feelings amount to?' Morley had then added: 'I should like to ask the same question of this meeting. I feel £100 a year for five years, and I hope many others will feel the same.'

It was to a supporter of this calibre that Emma Cons addressed her appeal at the close of 1883. When he had returned from the Continent and personally investigated matters, Morley responded with the offer recorded above—of £1,000 towards the purchase of the lease, on condition of being allowed to choose a working committee in harmony with his own ideas. In the circumstances the existing committee, nearly all of whom admired him greatly, could hardly do other than accept.

65

IV

Lectures—Classes—College

THOUGH his support proved decisive, Samuel Morley was not in fact the first to come to Emma Cons's aid in the crisis of 1883–4. Another of her anonymous female friends (her lifelong friend Ethel Everest, daughter of George Everest, after whom the mountain was named) had already promised £1,000 towards the purchase of the lease. It was this which, reported to Morley by Emma Cons, encouraged him to add his own conditional offer. With £2,000 now promised towards the objective, a subscription list was opened, and within a short time the required total of £4,000 was raised. Among the contributors were no less than nine members of the Martineau family. The lease, with about fourteen years still to run, was then taken over from the Coffee Music Halls Company, so saving about £700 a year in rent.

This success was announced in June, 1884, at a meeting

66

in Grosvenor House presided over by the Duke of Westminster. The meeting also went on to subscribe the better part of a further £1,000 needed to cover running costs. Various resolutions in support of the work or the principles behind it were moved or seconded by, among others, Earl Brownlow, Cardinal Manning, Lord Mount Temple, Sir Thomas Brassey and Samuel Morley; and Mr. William Lant Carpenter (who had been the first to brave the Vic audience with a scientific exposition) explained the origins and development of the penny lectures. At one point, after Lord Mount Temple had stressed the importance of music as a civilizing influence to which the 'lower classes' were particularly responsive, Sir Julius Benedict (by this time—like Arthur Sullivan—a member of the Council) said, 'I should like to see an orchestra of working men playing in the Victoria Hall.' Interruptions from well-bred women at meetings were unusual in those days, but at this Emma Cons could not resist calling out, 'There is one!' 'Very well,' replied Sir Julius, 'have ten or twenty.'[1]

Soon after this meeting the five trustees—Emma Cons (acting Trustee), the Duke of Westminster, Sir Thomas Brassey, Samuel Morley and Charles Morley (one of Samuel's sons)—who had taken over the lease appointed a new working committee to manage the Victoria project. Of this the chairman was Samuel Morley and the honorary secretary Emma Cons. In addition there was a largely honorary Council liberally stocked with the more benevolent aristocracy, together with a President (The Duke of Westminster) and a Patroness (H.R.H. Princess

[1] Had he lived until the present day, he might almost have seen this come true in the Victoria Hall's offshoot. Morley College now has thirteen working groups of instrumentalists or singers.

67

Christian). The name of the 'Royal Victoria Coffee Hall' was dropped, and the official style became 'The Royal Victoria Hall (and Coffee Tavern)'. Round about the same time—i.e. in mid-1884—the Coffee Music Halls Company went into voluntary liquidation and its assets were transferred by vote of the shareholders to the new trustees.

The crisis over, Emma Cons applied herself with renewed vigour both to the management of the theatre and the development of the lectures. In the latter she received constant encouragement from her new chairman. During the 1884–5 session the subjects ranged from 'Our Bones, What They Are and How They Are Made' to 'Yankee Humour', but were predominantly on scientific themes; and the lecturers included such eminent men of the time as Dr. Andrew Wilson, Mr. J. M. Thompson, Dr. J. A. Fleming and Mr. Edwin Hodder. Gradually the fame of the lectures spread, and soon each Tuesday was finding some seven or eight hundred men and women—but mainly men—listening to discourses on 'Light and Colour', 'Air and Ventilation', 'Ancient British Glaciers', and similar subjects. Certainly the price was no deterrent. Patrons able to support the work financially were encouraged to take boxes at ten shillings—or even stalls at a shilling or sixpence—but the main body of the house was open to the public at the almost insignificant price of threepence for the balcony, twopence for the pit, and one penny for the large gallery. From this the series soon came to be widely known as the Penny Science Lectures, or sometimes the Penny Popular Science Lectures.

The listeners to these lectures did not as yet exhibit the finer points of audience etiquette. They were an audience,

68

reported Emma Cons at the end of the 1884–5 season, 'of a kind to put a lecturer on his mettle. Whilst as a whole they nearly always show appreciation of a really good lecture, meaning by this one which is good in manner and matter, it cannot yet be claimed that they recognize what is solidly good if delivered with a weak voice or in a hesitating manner. Perhaps few audiences do, but this particular one is specially severe on defects of manner. Most of the lecturers have expressed surprise and satisfaction at the interest shown by the silent attention of the audience, and the evident intelligence of the applause coming at the right points—and it is certain they do not applaud out of regard for the lecturer's feelings; nor will a man, who finds it difficult to hear or understand him, refrain from conversation in order that others may hear. With them silence and applause, each in its place, are honest signs of genuine pleasure'.

It was at one of these lectures that another link was forged in the long chain of events which led to the foundation of Morley College. The date was 1884; the subject Electricity; and the lecturer William Lant Carpenter. Since his first lecture some two years earlier Carpenter had been of the greatest help in suggesting other subjects and speakers, and had himself spoken more than once. At the close of his talk two or three of his audience, young men from the pit, approached Emma Cons and asked if they might discuss a point with the lecturer. They were already known to her as inveterate questioners, and she probed their intention a little further. They replied that the lectures were wonderful things, but that being only weekly, and on different subjects by different speakers, they left a host of important points unanswered. In short,

69

the young men felt the need not only for individual talks of this kind, but also for more systematic instruction. Could Miss Cons not supply this by starting regular scientific classes in the evenings?

From what they set off by their importunity, these young men deserve an honoured place in the Morley College story, and it is therefore fitting to record their names. According to the tradition within the College, one was J. G. Sparkhall, a clerk who later greatly distinguished himself in the College classes. Another was Percy Eyre, also a clerk, who later acted as the first assistant secretary and died in 1937 after more than fifty years' continuous student membership of the College and the classes which preceded it.[1]

What reply Emma Cons made to this request is not recorded. She must, however, have been impressed; and obviously what they asked would lie very near her heart. At any rate during 1885 she is found conferring with Morley on the matter, and then negotiating through Dr. J. A. Fleming with the Science and Art Department at South Kensington—a government body originally formed in the Board of Trade but later transferred to the Committee of Council on Education (the forerunner of the present Ministry of Education). The result was that she received authority to run evening classes in science under the scheme then current of 'payment by results': if the students achieved a certain standard in an examination they earned a small sum in grant for the educational establishment at which they were studying. Under these regulations, in the autumn of 1885, Emma Cons started

[1] But according to John Keane, a student of the pre-College classes who is still alive in 1958, the names of the young men concerned were Bond, McMahon, and Gristwood.

70

her first officially approved evening classes in the Old Vic. Even before this, however, she had been running—or stimulating others to run—some classes in connection with a Working Men's Club which she had founded within the theatre during 1884. 'Some space behind the stage,' she reported in June 1885, 'has been fitted up as club-rooms. In these a club of 120 working men meet every night. One room is given up to bagatelle, billiards and other games, with smoking. Above it is a reading room where the non-smokers have a room to themselves, and where classes for book-keeping, elocution, etc. are held. A third room, in the basement, is used chiefly for practising athletic exercises. . . .'

By 1885 then, there was appearing in the Victoria Hall that fusion of the educational and the social which four years later was to take fuller shape in Morley College. Clearly the achievement thus far at the 'Vic', already immense, was more than matched by Emma Cons's unfailing flow of ideas for the future. In one way the possibilities thus seemed limitless; but from another aspect, that of continued financial loss, the struggle to survive remained as hard as ever. Yet in appealing for support in her report of June, 1885, Emma Cons stressed not so much the ever-present need for money as the need for active personal help. In doing so she struck a note which was basic to her life's work, and one which certainly set the key for the subsequent development of Morley College. 'More might be done,' she wrote, 'if the motive power of personal help could be obtained. The Hall might be made a valuable means of linking together classes whose wide separation all agree in considering a crying evil. The mere fact of filling a box at a ballad concert

71

or a lecture has its value in showing that there is some community of taste between those who have education and means of recreation and those who have less; and people think much more of a performance if the "gentry" are there and applaud. "It's all right—there's *our* Lady Cavendish again" said a bricklayer in the gallery who recognized the occupant of one of the boxes. But if this is true of the Hall, still more might the Club become common ground on which different classes might meet. Many a man, as busy as he is, might spare one hour a week for teaching a class or presiding over gymnastics. If he only played games with the club members the hour would not be wasted. He would find a freshness which is sometimes wanting in the social intercourse of conventional society, in coming into contact with minds essentially like his own, but differently shaped by the different circumstances and experiences to which they have been subjected.

'It has been well said that the old Roman fable of the gulf in the Forum applies to the gulf between the classes in our modern life. What is needed to fill it up is not gold, nor armour, nor any material thing, but the best life of the nation. In places where that is forthcoming the gulf closes. Will not some of those who read this Report lend a hand in this work?'

* * *

The scientific classes began in October, 1885, in a very small way. Only four men presented themselves on the first evening. Numbers, however, quickly improved, and the two teachers obtained through the Working Men's College—Mr. Leo H. Owen and Mr. Frank Castle—were able to settle down with effective groups for the study of mechanical drawing, plane and solid geometry, and electricity and magnetism. The only accommodation available was in some small unused dressing-rooms behind the stage—wooden-walled rooms reached by a wooden staircase. The fee payable for the session's tuition was two shillings and sixpence.

After the slow start, interest soon quickened, and when the number of students stood at 46, 31 of them were entered for the government examinations. Before the end of the 1885–6 session the student roll had grown to about 60, and two further classes—in physiology and practical chemistry—had been formed. To cope with these increased numbers two rooms—and later four—were knocked into one. As their ceilings remained of different heights the appearance was odd, but to this the students were impervious. At about the same time another spare dressing-room or two was set aside for social pursuits.

Of these early classes little written record remains. Caroline Martineau, however, recalling them eight or nine years later in 1894, offers us a vivid little glimpse of the atmosphere. 'Those of us,' she wrote, 'who can remember those old days have very pleasant associations with the "saloon" where gatherings of students were held, too crowded, perhaps, for perfect comfort, but full of enthusiasm. One of the men volunteered to give away prospectuses in the streets "as if they were tracts". Another told of the interest excited among his mates by his account of the Electricity Class. He worked for the Telephone Company, where the men were "handling things they did not understand, and they wanted to understand them". We remember, too, how eagerly Mr.

73

Owen's students came together on extra nights to make their own apparatus, while the love of science which Dr. Drew infused into his Physiology Class will not leave them as long as they live.'

The successful initiation of these classes in 1885–6 gave Emma Cons immense satisfaction. In her characteristic forward-looking way, however, she regarded them as only a beginning. 'This part of the work,' she wrote in her Report of May 31st, 1886, 'is as yet in its infancy, but without in any way interfering with the regular entertainment of the hall it has in it the power of indefinite growth if increased room and teaching power are provided. . . . There are still disused rooms at the back of the stage which could be adapted for class purposes. . . .' She went on to discuss the possibility of running classes in the summer, or at least of forming a field club for botanical and geological excursions and another group for visiting museums.

In her enthusiasm for all these new educational possibilities, however, Emma Cons never lost sight of the fact that they were likely to appeal only to the more intelligent sections of the working class, and that her concern was with the poorer classes as a whole. Just as in her housing work she had insisted on retaining even her most 'impossible' tenants and trying to improve them, so at the Royal Victoria Hall she spread her differing wares before all comers. 'During the past year,' her report for 1885–6 concluded, 'the Victoria Hall has been worked on its former principles, striving on different evenings and in different ways to meet the wants, not of one clique, but of the working class generally. In these days of strongly marked distinctions, it is pleasant to pass from the rough

74

lads in the gallery, who appreciate nothing but a variety entertainment, to the eager intelligence of the students in the science class-rooms, and to think that the Hall is frequented and regarded with loyalty by every grade of working men—from the very pick of the skilled artisans to those on the edge of the so-called "dangerous classes", into which they might easily pass, if inflamed by drink or misled by vicious persons.'

But though the 'rough lads' were still being drawn to the gallery of the Old Vic, their standards of taste and behaviour were being steadfastly raised. This struck a lively reporter from the *Daily News* very forcibly when he attended in October, 1885, a Ballad Concert at which the special feature was a 'Grand Welcome Home' to General Roberts and his troops from Bechuanaland. 'The gallery,' ran the newspaper's account the following morning, '. . . the really historic gallery of the "Vic", by far the largest in London, was packed to its uttermost tier. It was the gallery audience of the good, or rather the bad, old days, but how changed! Memory still preserves the picture of what that gallery was—the terror of stage villains under its swiftly retributive shower of orange peel and ginger-beer bottles, the almost equal terror of the police. It was a show for the West End dandies, who used occasionally to go down and take a box, much as their fathers went to see the wild beasts in Exeter Change. On Boxing Night its eccentricities rose to the licence of the Saturnalia, and no mortal man attempted to control them. . . . There was a complete transformation on the night of the grand military concert, and it surpassed all the transformations of even Victorian pantomime. All coal-heaving London was still there, but it was hushed

75

to the decorum of a religious service as it listened to selections from *Lucia, Miserere Domine*, *Souvenirs of Haydn* and *O Ciel, quanti Gioel*. *O Ciel*, indeed! Think of the possible result of such an attempt twenty years ago. How many policemen would have been hurled into the pit before the end of the first line? Yet the motley audience not only listened but enjoyed. The smoking was like the free list, entirely suspended; and the eager faces, with often the sparkling eyes as the only visible feature, were thrust forward to take in every note, like a row of quaint gargoyles hanging over the pit. Their attention was rapt and earnest, and this evidently as much in compliment to the artists as in delight with the music. The silence was perfect until an intolerable pain of suppressed enthusiasm caused one gentleman to emit an unearthly whistle. It was a solitary offence, and it was no more to be laid to the charge of his good manners than the occasional yell of a converted Indian called forth by some reminiscence of the bad old life. . . . Altogether the audience behaved with discretion, temper and taste. In one word, the gallery of the "Vic" was reclaimed to civilization, and it is as great an achievement in its way as the pacification of Bechuanaland.'

* * *

During 1886 the Old Vic also witnessed many other notable moments, as when Sims Reeves sang at the ballad concerts and the first selections from opera were presented illustrated by tableaux. But the hall also suffered two heavy blows deeply felt by Emma Cons. The first was when it was fined 2*s*. 6*d* for having presented a 'stage play' the previous Christmas—though in point of fact the entertainment had been largely spectacle, and only one character had a speaking part. The amount of the fine was trivial, but the consequences were not. By the fine the law gave clear warning that so long as the Victoria held only a music-hall licence—for which the safety requirements were less stringent, and which allowed the audience to smoke and consume refreshments—it could not extend its activities into the field of the legitimate drama. A temporary dramatic licence at this time was unobtainable; a permanent one would involve expensive structural improvements and the abandonment of the music-hall entertainment and atmosphere which the Vic audience cherished. Such was the situation in which the hall management found itself. For many years after this, until the administration of the regulations changed, the hall accordingly had to fit its more serious productions into the category of variety. The only way in which this could be done was to present straight plays or operas in excerpts, usually broken by appropriate spectacle. With such a state of affairs Emma Cons remained deeply discontented, and to the end of her life no public office was a more constant target for her shafts than that of the Lord Chamberlain.

The second blow which Emma Cons and her projects suffered in 1886 was more personal and still more deeply felt. During the summer Samuel Morley became ill and in September he died. Though his active personal interest in the Victoria Hall, as opposed to financial contributions, had dated only from 1884, he had quickly assumed next to Emma Cons the leading role in the whole venture. As chairman of the executive committee, his wisdom and his influence had been of immeasurable benefit, quite apart from his generous gifts and subscriptions. His death when the success of the project still hung in the balance was a cruel grief to its originator, herself only just recovering from a severe illness.

What sort of a chairman and colleague Morley had been may be glimpsed from a letter Emma Cons wrote to Edwin Hodder when the latter undertook Morley's biography. 'He constantly expressed his determination to do his share in our "happy partnership", as he always termed our work together. And indeed it was a happy partnership for us, as his clear head and warm sympathetic heart were always a tower of strength to us against the worries and petty troubles which fritter away one's powers. His speeches aroused public attention, so that money and helpers came to our aid, and I was thankful not to have to claim his oft-repeated promises, "Now don't you worry about money. I will not let this important work flag for want of that. It is not fit that you workers should be troubled on that score!" He took such interest in every detail that in spite of his many engagements, he continually made little appointments to see me and consult about matters rather than trust to letter discussions. Then he would run into the hall for an hour, and see what lecture or entertainment was going on, and his rare keen enjoyment was quite refreshing to us who are tired out with such things. On other nights he would come to take the chair at the Science lectures, and encourage the men to a higher life. On Nov. 24th, 1884, he came to open our then newly formed Working Men's Club, and gave a splendid inspiriting address to the men. His cheery hearty way, and his grand broad tolerance of differences of creed or of politics, endeared him to all, and the men admired him so much that, whenever he came to meet them, they all (over one hundred) crammed into their small room to hear him. . . .

Samuel Morley was in no sense the founder of the Victoria Hall or of the College which bears his name. Though she would have been the first to insist that these institutions were the creation of many hands, the honour of foundation rests firmly on the brow of Emma Cons, who contributed the ideas, the determination, and nine-tenths of the work. But Morley's support at a critical juncture had saved the Vic enterprise when it was in danger of foundering, and in his last two years of life his personal exertions assured it of continued existence and development. There is something deeply admirable and not a little moving in this spectacle of a great public figure in his seventy-sixth and seventy-seventh years, with health perceptibly on the decline, mustering the time and the energy amid all his manifold responsibilities to visit the Vic on repeated occasions for the sake of helping with advice or spending an hour with the working men. A great man of business and a great philanthropist, Morley exerts his claim on the gratitude of the causes he served not only for the money that he gave but also for the exceptional depth and warmth of his personal interest. A millionaire who sat by invitation on the advisory committee of the Agricultural Labourers' Union; a Liberal who contributed to the election funds of the first Labour candidates; an immensely busy man who still had time for the smaller, thoughtful acts like sending up holly from his estate in Kent to decorate the Vic at Christmas; these are some of the tiny details of Morley's activity that impress almost as much as the great. His devotion to the Vic was throughout part of a wider devotion inspired by the belief that to love God is to love Man. He did much, and was much, but all that he sought to be was fully expressed in the brief words chosen for his epitaph: 'A servant of Jesus Christ.'

* * *

The cloud of Morley's death was still heavy over the activities at the Victoria when there was held at the theatre a meeting with momentous consequences. Following the success of Quintin Hogg's venture in Regent Street, a movement to found Polytechnics had gathered force. The government, too, was becoming increasingly aware that in many aspects of education, and particularly technical education, we were being far outstripped by Germany. In December, 1887, a conference on Technical Education, attended by representatives from the Department of Science and Art, was accordingly convened at the Royal Victoria Hall—a suitable venue not only because of its size but also because of the scientific classes which for the past two years had been running there. During the course of this meeting a statement was made, almost incidentally it appeared to those present, which was to open up immense new possibilities. A representative of the Charity Commission announced that there was now a fund under the control of the Commissioners consisting of moneys from various out-of-date charitable bequests originally administered by the City of London parishes, and that from this fund the Commissioners were prepared to endow institutions for popular education and recreation.

To this, as Caroline Martineau has recorded, 'Some of those present listened incredulously'. Nevertheless what the speaker said was true: the fund had been created by the City of London Parochial Charities Act of 1883. The statement was of course immediately followed up by all the interested parties present, with the result that several new polytechnics eventually came into being. So far as the educational activities of the Royal Victoria Hall were concerned, Emma Cons made the formal request for support to the Commission on April 18th, 1888, and this was backed up the following day by a deputation. It was introduced by Sir George Baden Powell, M.P., and comprised a dozen working men connected with the various activities of the hall, including R. W. Bowers, a printer who was secretary of the Working Men's Club, James McMahon and John Keane, two of the students of the classes, and West, the doorkeeper. They bore with them a petition signed by 200 others, and all gave up a day's work for the purpose. Following study of Emma Cons's proposals, which had included the conversion of further space behind the stage into class- and club-rooms, the official who received the deputation asked its members if they would welcome not merely a continuation of their existing club and classes, but the formation of something on the lines of the institution in Great Ormond Street (The Working Men's College). To this suggestion they gave a favourable response.

These approaches from those connected with the hall soon produced from the Commissioners an offer on extremely exacting conditions. The Commissioners would assume the trusteeship of the venture and fix upon it an endowment from the consolidated parochial charities—£1,000 a year was the sum determined upon—if the existing trustees could hand over the theatre free from any restriction of lease. To take advantage of this offer the trustees had thus to purchase the freehold. This the owner was willing to sell at a price of £17,000 if the money were put down within four months.

Undaunted by this formidable proposition, Emma Cons and her supporters at once set to work. The idea had already occurred to them, and had been broached to the Commissioners in the request for support, that to put the activities at the Victoria Hall on a firm footing in this way would be a singularly appropriate memorial to Samuel Morley. Thus far nothing had been done to commemorate him in London, though Bristol had already raised a statue in his honour. On April 25th, 1888, at a meeting at Grosvenor House, the Duke of Westminster and Lady Frederick Cavendish, one of the staunchest of the Vic's supporters, accordingly outlined the scheme. If the trustees could find the £17,000 to buy the freehold, the Charity Commission would take over the Hall, and permanence could be given to its various activities: the Victoria Hall in fact would become a People's Palace for South London. As such it would be a lasting memorial to one aspect of the work of Samuel Morley, and an appeal should be addressed to the public in this sense. How far the hall had already gained a hold on the affections of the poorer folk of South London could be seen from the fact that during the past season £1,800 had been taken, largely in pennies and twopences.

To this A. J. Mundella, Liberal Cabinet Minister, philanthropist, and another stalwart of the movement, added the weighty point that the scheme offered a great opportunity to extend scientific and technical instruction in South London. A subscription list was then opened with gifts of £1,000 each from the Duke and Lord Brassey, and with generous contributions from Samuel Morley's

82

family and executors.[1] Nevertheless the bulk of the money, if it was to be forthcoming, had to be extracted from the ordinary public, and in May the Duke of Westminster and Lady Frederick Cavendish launched the general appeal in the press.

From her cottage in Surrey Lodge Emma Cons, tirelessly assisted by Ellen Cons and Caroline Martineau, handled the whole work of the public appeal. The holiday season was approaching and after the first subscriptions money was slow in coming in. By mid-June, with less than half the desired total subscribed, the Duke of Westminster judged it necessary to write again to *The Times*. He pointed out that people were perhaps baffled by the number of schemes afoot to start new polytechnics, but as far as he knew, only two—the Regent Street Polytechnic and the classes in the Victoria Hall—already existed. He appealed for support for the latter, and announced that £9,000 was still required to purchase the freehold. The chance held good only till August 15th, for if the money were not forthcoming by then the owner would sell the freehold to another bidder—a publican who had offered £5,000 more. 'Thus,' concluded the Duke, 'if the Vic is not a people's palace it will eventually be a gin palace.'

A final period of acute anxiety then followed, but within a few days of the closing date the total was triumphantly reached. It was a matter of some little pride to the ladies of Surrey Lodge that though the bulk of

[1] Earl Brassey, or Sir Thomas Brassey as he had been earlier, was one of the staunchest supporters of the Vic venture. The son of the famous Victorian railway contractor, he was First Lord of the Admiralty in Gladstone's second ministry. He was passionately interested in two very distinct subjects—industrial welfare and maritime affairs—and is best remembered as the founder of Brassey's *Naval Annual*.

the money had come in to them in small sums, all the accounts tallied, except for a missing shilling—which was finally tracked down and found to be a contribution paid in penny stamps.

With £17,500 safely in hand the trustees straightway purchased the freehold of the theatre and the Royal Victoria Hall was at last assured of a reasonably secure if modest future. At an early meeting after this the governing body of the hall then formally decided to constitute the educational classes as a separate entity from the theatrical activities, and to organize them under the name of the Morley Memorial College. This, it was finally decided, should be not only for working men, but also for working women. During 1889 the rooms already occupied by the classes, together with some others, were accordingly separated off from the rest of the hall. Of the premises as they finally emerged, perhaps Caroline Martineau's description will give sufficient indication: 'The recreation rooms run *under* the stage, where in old days there was a wilderness of traps and theatrical apparatus. Above the ceiling is a layer of fire-proof material on which is laid down the floor of the stage. *Above* the stage is another fire-proof layer forming the floor of the library, a beautiful room which runs the whole width of our premises, from Waterloo Road to Webber Street, and is lighted by a lantern roof. At the *back* of the stage is a solid party wall, entirely dividing the College from the Hall. Thus the College runs above, below, and behind the stage, but is cut off by fire-proof walls and floors from all direct communication with it, a matter of great importance, not only in case of fire, but in order to shut out the sound of the entertainments from the classes.' To all of

84

this, access was gained through an arched entrance at the far end of the hall—where now stands the Old Vic stage-door.

So at length came the memorable evening, on September 29th, 1889, when the new College formally opened its doors for the first time. The reconstruction was far from complete, but the time for the autumn session had arrived and the building was thrown open rather than disappoint the students. 'No one then present is likely to forget that day,' wrote Caroline Martineau five years later. 'The alterations were not completed—many of the room windows were unglazed, and floors and staircases unfinished; but the enthusiasm of the students was not to be chilled by draughts, nor damped by wet walls. Those who were present marvelled at the way they flocked in those first few nights. None were admitted under 17, except a few who had previously attended the classes in the Hall, and these former students were also exempted from the payment of the shilling entrance fee. It was amusing to see the pride with which the youngest of the boys announced that they were "*Old* Vic Students", and wrote letters after their names to signify as much—O.V.S.M.M.C. (Old Vic Student, Morley Memorial College). "We'll make that as good a Degree as any of them," said one.'

Morley College is not concerned with Degrees, and never has been. The young man's boast, however, must be understood not in the letter but in the spirit. To what extent it was justified the rest of this history must bear witness.

V

The Educational Setting

THOSE who, for whatever purpose, have been called upon to describe the British system of education will be well aware of the virtual impossibility of the task. Nevertheless a brief glance at what existed in 1889 may perhaps help to establish how far the founders of Morley College were breaking new ground, and how far they were proceeding along paths already well marked and recognized.

By 1889 a national system of elementary education had been in existence for nearly twenty years. For anything from ninepence a week to nothing, either in the schools founded by the religious societies or in the new non-denominational establishments built by the School Boards, boys and girls were receiving compulsory education. Except in a few 'higher grade' and continuation schools or classes operated by the Boards with doubtful legality,

86

the work revolved firmly round the 'three R's' and the various 'standards' of attainment in these. Narrow as were the limits of this instruction, and strict as was the discipline with which it was imparted, great educational advances were already being made. The flood tide of urban ignorance and savagery resulting from the over-rapid growth of towns in the 18th and 19th centuries had at last been arrested. In the gleaming new edifices erected by the School Boards, all glazed brown brick without and glazed white tile within, even the poorest and roughest districts now possessed bastions for the defence and advance of civilization.

Between this comparatively newly organized system of elementary education and the older unsystematized institutions dispensing higher education there was as yet scarcely any link. From the 1830s, under the stimulus of Victorian and Christian idealism, the old public boarding schools had been reformed, and many new ones founded. The educational impetus had also extended to the ancient grammar and other endowed schools, which from the 1870s began to be greatly enlarged and revivified. From the 1850s, too, counterparts to these institutions had been established for girls. There were also, of course, large numbers of proprietary or private schools, boarding and day, of all degrees of excellence and none. But there was as yet no state system of secondary education, no municipal secondary school. The Board and denominational schools on the one side, the public, endowed, and private schools on the other, were worlds apart. A fair number of boys, and a much lesser number of girls, spent their earliest school years under Church or State auspices, and then passed on to an endowed school, either by scholarship

87

or otherwise. But the great majority—nine-tenths of the school population—had no acquaintance with any educational establishment which retained most of its pupils after the age of thirteen years.

If the 'secondary' school was a closed book to by far the greater part of the nation, the university was naturally still more so. By the end of the 1850s, Oxford and Cambridge had been awakened from their long lethargy, but the only other institutions in England where an education of university standard could be obtained were the fairly recently established University and King's Colleges in London, the University of Durham, and Owens College in Manchester. Nevertheless the idea of university expansion was in the air, and was soon to take the form of the 'extension' of university teaching to the industrial towns, usually by special courses of lectures. During the 1870s and 1880s, this movement largely inspired the creation of colleges working at university level in Sheffield and Nottingham, and greatly strengthened another at Leeds. In the same period local enterprise also established half a dozen other colleges, all destined in the fullness of time to become 'redbrick' universities.

Since the formal education of the overwhelming majority of the population thus ended round about the age of twelve or thirteen and was extremely restricted in content, and since there were still many among the older generations whose schooldays had been even briefer or completely non-existent, great importance was attached by the more enterprising and intelligent of the poorer classes to the possibility of 'self-improvement' in night schools. From one motive and another, night schools of various kinds had sprung up from the 18th century on-

88

wards; and by 1884, when classes first began in the Royal Victoria Hall, evening instruction was a long accepted feature of the English educational scene—though the choice of subjects was naturally restricted in comparison with the vast array available today.

The evening schools in existence during the early 1880s had in the main originated from three different motives. There was the simplest kind, to be found even in small villages, which concentrated on the three R's. The motivating force behind these had originally been religious: unless they could read and write the poor would remain ignorant of true moral principles, unable to study the Bible and a danger to society. In this spirit Hannah More had instructed the miners of Somerset at the beginning of the century, hoping by her efforts not merely to bring them to the Scriptures but also to inculcate a wise submission to the inequalities prescribed by Providence. Most of these schools, or rather classes, were by 1880 concentrating on straightforward instruction, without political undertones, for the benefit of those who were still unable to read, write or figure. From 1851 onwards state grants had been available for such work, and from 1870 the School Boards had been actively promoting such classes within their areas, though mainly for the younger adults in their teens.

Apart from this elementary type of evening school there was the more advanced kind which had long been associated with the Mechanics' Institutes, and the various Lyceums, Athenaeums, and the rest. Stemming from the initial efforts of Dr. Birkbeck and others in Glasgow, the Mechanics' Institute movement had spread rapidly during the first three-quarters of the century, in its growth

89

extending far beyond its original sphere—the study by mechanics of scientific principles and their practical application. Valuable for their social activities and libraries as well as for their classes and lectures, the Mechanics' and other institutes had since the 1850s been natural centres for the organization of advanced classes of the kind for which the Science and Art Department at South Kensington was empowered to make grants. In the 1880s, though many institutes had fallen by the wayside or become little more than clubs, on the whole they still played an important, if proportionately diminishing, part in English education. Indeed the largest of them, surviving all competition from the growing activities of the local education authorities, within the next few years were to embrace a new and assured future as Colleges of Technology.

In yet another category were those evening schools which had Chartist, co-operative or trade union origins, and where the inspiration was predominantly socio-political, rather than religious or scientific. Such classes existed in large numbers, often in the humblest premises. They aimed for the most part to enlarge the mental horizon of the working man and to offer him that acquaintance with the liberal, humanistic studies which would both enrich his personality and enable him to play a more influential part in politics. Few of these classes had in fact developed, or were to develop, into enduring educational institutions; but one such venture which had—the Working Men's College in London—was, as we have already seen, directly linked through Octavia Hill and Ruskin with the main founder of Morley College. Collegiate in organization, ethical and democratic in spirit, equipped for social activities as well as study, and

90

with its educational emphasis on continuous classes in the humanities, it had many features which profoundly appealed to Emma Cons and her associates.

During the 1870s one other institution was founded which was soon to touch off new developments in the realm of evening study. This is not the place to recount the extraordinary story of the establishment, from philanthropic motives and from 'ragged school' origins, of Quintin Hogg's Institute and its growth into the great Regent Street Polytechnic opened in 1882. It is perhaps sufficient to recall that under its founder its collegiate atmosphere, the consciousness among its students of being a band of brothers, and its devotion to liberal as well as technical studies, were all very marked, and far stronger than we would now normally associate with so large and multifarious an institution as a polytechnic. So far as Morley College is concerned, it does not appear that Emma Cons and her friends were in any way indebted to Quintin Hogg for their ideas. The outstanding success of the Regent Street establishment, however, coinciding as it did with a growing appreciation of the need for technical education, led directly to a demand for more polytechnics. This in turn first helped the scientific classes in the Victoria Hall to attract a government grant in 1885, and then greatly facilitated the task of securing from the Charity Commission the foundation endowment of Morley College.[1]

[1] At the end of the 1880s, through the combined action of the Royal Commission on Technical Education, the London Trades Council, the Charity Commission and G. T. Goschen as Chancellor of the Exchequer (who made available for technical education money raised to compensate publicans in certain circumstances—the so-called 'whisky money'), schemes were drawn up for polytechnics on the Regent Street model in various parts of London. Hence followed the Woolwich, Chelsea, Battersea, Northern, Borough and Northampton Polytechnics, all created in the

(continued overleaf)

91

One other development must also be emphasized if the 'night school' picture in the early 1880s is to be at all clear. During the 1870s, on the initiative of James Stuart, a fellow of Trinity College, Cambridge, and with the support of forward-looking dons like Benjamin Jowett, the universities began to organize lecture centres beyond their own walls. Stuart's idea of such work was that the lectures should form part of a continuous course at university level, each lecture being preceded or followed by a class in which the lecturer could discuss the subject informally with his students—from whom written work would be required. By 1878 Oxford and London had followed the lead given by Cambridge five years earlier, and courses of university extension lectures of this kind for working people were a regular feature in many towns.

If we now set against this background the objects enshrined in the foundation scheme of Morley College—a scheme drawn up in 1888 by Emma Cons and others in consultation with officials of the Charity Commission, and propounded by Order in Council in 1891, two years after the College had formally begun its activities—we shall be in a position to see how far the establishment of the College was in any sense an innovation in the broad pattern of British adult education. The official scheme defined the objects of the College in the following terms:

1. To promote by means of classes, lectures and otherwise, the advanced study by men and women belonging to the working classes, of subjects of knowledge not directly connected with or applied to any handicraft, trade or business.

1890s—as also was the Goldsmith's Institute. The educational work in the Old Vic started before this movement, on the first waves of which the proposed Morley College secured its endowment.

2. As subordinate or ancillary thereto, to assist in acquiring the requisite elementary instruction those whose age prevents them from making use of the ordinary elementary instruction.
3. To promote social intercourse among those follow-lowing the above-mentioned pursuits.

The achievement of these objects, and the ultimate control of the College, was entrusted to a governing body, known as the Council, which was eventually to consist of thirteen members. Three of these were to be appointed for six-year periods by the trustees of the City Parochial Foundation, the body created by Parliament on the initiative of the Charity Commission to administer the consolidated City parochial charity funds for their newly approved purposes—of which an annual grant of £650 to the Royal Victoria Hall and £350 to Morley College was now one. Two more members of the College Council were to be appointed for six-year periods by the Royal Victoria Hall; and two, to serve on an annual basis, were to represent the unpaid teachers. The remaining six were to be co-opted members. 'At least three' of the members were to be women—a provision inserted on the request of Emma Cons and Caroline Martineau—and it was stipulated that 'so far as practicable, two of the co-optative members shall always be present or past students of the College'.[1] In addition to this governing council the

[1] The Charity Commission's original draft had provided for elected student representatives on the Council, probably on the analogy of the Working Men's College. Emma Cons and Caroline Martineau objected to this—in effect as giving untried students too much power in a venture which others had created. The student clause was therefore dropped and it was left to the seven foundation members of the Council—Miss Cons, Lady Frederick Cavendish, Miss M. C. Martineau, Sir John Lubbock, Charles Morley, Edwin Drew, and Leonard Noble—to control the type of student representative by co-option.

College was also to have a Consultative Committee consisting of the teachers and six elected students, who would help to make the work of the College known among working men and women, make proposals to the Council about matters both educational and social, and in general 'co-operate with the Council in all matters tending to promote the welfare of the College'.

The salient facts about the new institution all appear in this foundation document. Morley was to be a true College, complete with independent endowment and premises. It was not to be governed democratically, but was to have sufficient democratic machinery to allow the views and feelings of the teachers and students to be expressed and considered. It was to exist for social as well as educational activity among its members. It was to be for women as well as men—for 'men and women belonging to the working classes'. And it was to aim above all at the 'advanced study' of subjects 'not directly connected with or applied to any handicraft, trade, or business'—the subjects which in the educational jargon of today would be called 'non-vocational'.

The meaning of all this was clear enough, except possibly the phrase 'belonging to the working classes'. Class divisions were much more clearly marked in Victorian times than nowadays, but even in 1889 it would have been very difficult to say exactly where the upper working class stopped and the lower middle class began. Heavy manual labour on the one hand, the possession of a servant on the other, might be obvious points of difference, but between these points the grades were infinite. Clearly it was not intended to define 'working class' as 'manual labouring class', for from the first 'white-collar' workers such as

94

clerks and shop-assistants were admitted as freely as the hornier-handed sons of toil. In its very first annual report the College appears under the style of 'Morley Memorial College'—and then, in parenthesis and in small letters on the line beneath, 'For Working Men and Women.' This usage, which continued for many years, really seems to describe those for whom the College was intended better than does the phrase 'belonging to the working classes'. It was a College for those who had to work for a living, not for the leisured class which was then still fairly numerous and which in fact supplied, in women like Caroline Martineau and Ethel Everest, and voluntary teachers like Leonard Noble and Edwin Drew, much of the initial support and impetus which brought the College into being. The founders, of course, were in no doubt for whom they were providing the College—they were providing it for the local population of Lambeth and Southwark, which as we have seen from Charles Booth's survey was nine-tenths 'working class' and only one-tenth 'middle class'. If they did not express themselves with an exactness of definition which would satisfy the latter-day professors of semantics, that, after all, applies to everyone else who has employed these convenient and imprecise labels.

Such, then, were the objects enshrined in the foundation Charter of the College—objects to which it has, allowing for inevitable reinterpretations in changed circumstances, remained remarkably faithful. Wherein lay the novelty, if any, of the founders' conceptions?

It will be apparent that there was nothing new in the provision of 'elementary instruction'—reading, writing and arithmetic—for those who were too old to have benefited from the Education Act of 1870. Such classes were

95

indeed necessary, and particularly because the elementary instruction in evening schools was rate-supported at this time only for the younger adults. Nevertheless instruction of this kind could be obtained in many places. In Morley College it was from the start regarded as a purely temporary measure: the real objective was always work of a more advanced character.

There was also nothing new in the conception of a College for working people. The People's College of Sheffield, the Working Men's College, the Working Women's College, and the Regent Street Polytechnic had already shown the way—and so too, originally in a somewhat different field of interest, had the Mechanics' Institutes. All these places, too, had had a democratic element in their government and an active social life. In the conception of 'advanced study' of non-vocational subjects by working people there was again nothing new, for the Working Men's College had throughout had this in mind, while the university extension lectures had already made the idea familiar in a score or more of British towns.

Yet if there was nothing new in all these ideas, it can at least be said that the combination of them in one endowed and enduring institution was extremely rare. A permanent college, with an active corporate and social life, and devoted in the main to the humanities, was a very different thing from a polytechnic on the one hand or a set of university extension lectures on the other. Of living entities in the London of 1889, only the Working Men's College and its shorter-lived offshoots, the Working Women's College and the College for Men and Women, provided really close parallels. If not for the

96

most part creating something entirely fresh, the founders of Morley College were certainly establishing an institution that bore little resemblance to the broad run of night school work at the time.

Moreover in one respect their conception appears to have been even more novel. The foregoing chapters will have made it clear that Morley College was far from being created by a single act at a single date: it grew up from the class and club activity in the spare dressing-rooms at the Vic, and to a large extent the official foundation of 1889 was only the formal and permanent embodiment of what already existed. The foundation members of the Council, for instance, were almost the identical 'working committee' which had supervised the Vic classes. Yet when the decisive moment came, and classes and clubs became College, one great change at least was made. In discussion with the Charity Commission, the matter was thrashed out beforehand. The opinions of Emma Cons, who was later to become one of the L.C.C.'s first aldermen, and of Caroline Martineau, who had undertaken the main work of organizing the educational work at the Vic, prevailed. They were both deeply conscious of the inferior position occupied by women in public life, and both resolutely determined to do all in their power to elevate it. The result was seen in the foundation charter. From the first the new College was to be open to women on equal terms with men.

Again, there was nothing new in the idea of women attending evening classes—though the very long hours of labour then endured by working women both in the home and the workshop made attendance at subsequent classes extremely difficult. There was also nothing new

97

in the idea of women attending the same classes or lectures as men: they had done so in several of the Mechanics' and other Institutes, as well as in the university extension courses. That they should be admitted, however, on equal terms to a College, with all its corporate life: that the College should be distinctively founded and endowed for men and women jointly: that its first executive head, and a stated number of its Council, should be of the female sex, though the great majority of the initial students would be male—all this added up to a rarity, if not an absolute novelty. By 1889, women had indeed secured a substantial bridgehead in the university world, but few were the Colleges on which they had as yet planted the banner of complete sex equality.

The foundation of Morley College, then, while representing nothing that was absolutely fresh, was still something of a landmark in the history of the women's movement, as well as in that of British adult education. In case there still survive any of the Old Guard, either in the form of Mrs. Grundies or upholders of Male Prerogative, it should be stated at once that the decision to mingle both sexes in the comradeship of a single educational institution has never, so far as the records reveal, confronted any Principal of the College with any problem more embarrassing than that of securing, in the old days, enough women students for the men, and, in more recent times, enough men students for the women.

98

VI

The First Decade: (1) Work

THE history of Morley College after its foundation falls into four fairly well-defined periods. The first, the period of establishment and consolidation, covers the years up to the death of Caroline Martineau in 1902—the years when the College was still under the guidance of one of its founders. The second, a period of sustained expansion, runs from 1902 to 1924, when the College was obliged to quit the Old Vic. The third, again a time of expansion, stretches from the opening of the premises in the Westminster Bridge Road to the autumn of 1940, when a German bomb destroyed the greater part of them. The fourth witnesses the battle against the war-time and post-war difficulties, the re-creation of the work and atmosphere of the College in damaged and alien premises, and finally the long and successful struggle to obtain a new building. In this chapter it will be sufficient to

99

consider the first of these periods, when the College was establishing itself and its traditions, when the chief educational emphasis was on scientific studies, and when the main problems were how to equip the College properly and secure enough money to carry on.

When the College opened in its incomplete state in September, 1889, its governing body was still the 'class committee' which had already been in charge of the educational activity at the Vic—for the official constitution of the College, referred to above, took an inordinate time to pass through the governmental machine and although drawn up during 1889 was not promulgated by Order in Council until the spring of 1891. The leading members on this committee were Emma Cons and her two devoted friends Caroline Martineau and Ethel Everest, together with Lady Frederick Cavendish, Constance Martineau (elder sister of Caroline), Charles Morley and Leonard Noble. Their choice for the vital post of Principal in the new College was Miss Goold, whose previous experience as Principal of the Working Women's College seemed to fit her exactly for the task.

Bare and incomplete as it was, the new College began with a rush of enrolments. The classes in 1888 before the foundation of the College had been attended by some 200–250 students; but 600 or more presented themselves for enrolment during the first year of the College, and by December, 1890, 1,270 names had been entered on its books.

Who were these 1,270 students of the College during its first four terms? The great majority were men, for the women of the neighbourhood worked too late to fit in with the advertised time of the classes—most of which began at 8 p.m. In age they were a youngish body, much below the average age of the students today. Of the 1,270, all except 136 were under thirty-one, and not far short of a half were under twenty. The three oldest students were all aged sixty-four. Occupations varied widely, but both the 'white-collar' and the 'overall' types of workers were well represented. The largest single group was that of the clerks—199 in number—and after that the 'engineers', with 87. There was a sizeable group of 77 from the printing trades—William Clowes's works were near by—and 45 from the carpentry trades. There were 30 warehousemen, 19 general labourers and 10 teachers. There were 15 porters and miscellaneous numbers of maids, waiters, 'clickers', piano-tuners, dentists, cab-drivers, milliners and tailors. Scores of other trades were also represented. Among those who were the single representative of their occupation were a quill-dresser, a pawnbroker, a detective, a dustman, a publisher, a counter of postcards, a governess, a lady, and one who entered himself (or herself) as 'fancy business'.

What was the choice of subjects available to the 600 or more students who entered the College at the beginning of each of these first two sessions? In September, 1889, it was severely limited: only eight subjects were taught, including the technical classes which had been earning a grant from the Science and Art Department since 1885. Apart from the technical subjects, students could enrol for reading and writing, arithmetic, and French, and for a course of university extension lectures on astronomy. There were also active gymnastic groups, but these did not rank as classes. For the eight scheduled subjects, when September came only five teachers, including two unpaid,

101

proved to be available. In consequence one teacher found himself taking four separate divisions in arithmetic, totalling 120 students, all at the same time, while another found himself taking an elementary French class of 96.

These difficulties did not damp the spirit of the students, any more than did the fact that the walls were still unplastered and bare, and that even such necessary items as chairs and tables were all too few. Many students of course joined their first class without realizing the difficulty of the subject they were undertaking; some, for instance, imagined that they would master French in three months—a degree of optimism not entirely unknown today. But almost all proved to be keen and willing workers. Despite the fact that the gymnasium and the club-rooms—which included a billiard table generously presented by Leonard Noble—might have attracted some of the rougher elements of the neighbourhood, Miss Goold was able to report after four terms that very few 'black sheep' had gained admission to the College, and that there had been very little trouble in keeping order. As a result there had been 'only four expulsions'—inflicted because the men concerned had tried to use the College 'as a mere place of amusement by coming to the gym and other recreations while failing to attend their classes'. On the intellectual side, possibly the College's greatest pride was J. D. McClure's university extension class in astronomy; fourteen students had taken the examination at the end of the course, and all had passed, including three with distinction.

Moreover, in the course of this first session Miss Goold was able to attract several more teachers and start other classes, so that when the second session opened in Septemper, 1890, the choice of subjects had grown from eight to no less than thirty. Besides the subjects before mentioned, they included more advanced mathematics (algebra and Euclid) more foreign languages (Latin and German), elocution, physiology, music (singing, violin, and orchestra), commercial subjects (shorthand and book-keeping), and a further range of technical classes recognized by South Kensington (applied mechanics, chemistry, and electricity and magnetism). Apart from the commercial classes—a concession to student demand—the College was thus already fast advancing towards the sort of curriculum presaged by its foundation charter.

Throughout these two years the problem of finance remained acute. The fees paid by the students were deliberately set very low, and in consequence did not nearly cover the cost of running the College; the registration fee was only 1*s*., and the class fee 1*s*. 6*d*., for the first subject (or 6*d*. for each additional subject) for the first term, plus 6*d*. for each subsequent term. The grant earned from South Kensington was also very small, and the College in fact depended mainly on the generosity of a few supporters, the devotion of a dozen or more unpaid teachers (including Caroline and Constance Martineau and Leonard Noble) and the endowment of £350 p.a. from the City Parochial Foundation. Unfortunately, although entitled to this sum from September, 1889, the College did not receive the first payment (with arrears) until the formal promulgation of the scheme in 1891. During this time it could not have survived but for its close connection with the Victoria Hall at the other end of the building. Emma Cons usually found the time from her duties

103

as manager of the Hall to slip into the College for a few minutes every night, and to watch with a parent's eye over its infant fortunes. Thanks to the fact that she was the leading spirit on both committees—the Hall and the College—and that Lady Frederick Cavendish and Caroline Martineau were also members of both, the Hall readily came to the rescue of its progeny. Out of its own scanty resources for two years it advanced to the College the City Parochial Grant. Moreover when the two instalments due under the foundation scheme were at length paid in 1891, the Hall refused to accept repayment from the College, which thus enjoyed an unexpected windfall of £700. It was put to good use for plastering, decoration and furnishing, and for the creation of a small reserve.

In other ways, too, besides financially and structurally, the College was still very closely associated with the Vic. The pattern of entertainment at the theatre had now become fairly settled, and among its patrons the Morley College students had their regular place. For all entertainments other than the Saturday night variety they were admitted at half-price—a privilege they shared with soldiers, sailors and firemen in uniform. Since the full price of admission even on the 'top nights' was never more than *2d.* and *3d.* in the gallery and *4d.* and *6d.* in the pit, cheap and frequent entertainment was placed well within their means. Moreover on Mondays and Wednesdays, the nights for orchestral concerts or practices, and on Fridays, the night when a temperance meeting was followed by an hour of variety, the full price for admission to the gallery was only *1d.* and to the pit *2d.*, so that the College students could enjoy a night out for a halfpenny. On Tuesdays, the public lecture night, they were admitted

104

quite free, while others paid sums from 1*d*. upwards. This policy produced during the seasons from 1889 and 1891 a regular Tuesday night audience of some 600, to listen to accounts of such subjects as the Stanley Expedition, the Paris Exhibition, the Water Supply of London, the Colours of Animals, and How a Photo is Taken. But the most popular of all of the mid-week performances, with 'to a certain extent a distinct audience of their own', were still the Thursday ballad and operatic concerts, in which during this period stars of the magnitude of Antoinette Stirling frequently gave their services. All told, the two institutions, Hall and College, though now differentiated, were still complementary, and as long as Emma Cons lived they were to remain so. The division of labour was quite clear. 'Recreation,' she wrote in 1891, 'is the first object of the Hall; work is that of the College.'

The first meeting of the new governing Council of the College, to replace the old class committee of the Hall, took place on April 17th, 1891. The seven nominated members had co-opted a number of others, including Dr. J. A. Fleming, one of the scientists who had given great help with the lectures in the Hall, and who now became the Council's first chairman. The other co-opted members included R. W. Bowers, the printer and ex-student of the hall classes who had helped to lead the deputation of working men to the Charity Commission in 1888, and who by his tireless work, had become a pillar of the College—the first of a long line of remarkable 'local products'[1]. Another co-opted member, the youngest, was a student in his twenties named John Keane who had taken part in the same deputation, and who in turn

[1] He later became Senior Alderman of Southwark.

105

was to become one of the great Morley succession as student, voluntary teacher and councillor. The honorary secretary of the Council, and of the College—for which there was also a paid part-time assistant secretary in the form of Percy Eyre—was Emma Cons. Until the year of her death in 1912 she was to be the mainstay of the Council, persistently active in her interest, unfailingly regular in her attendance, and—considering the whole institution stemmed from her own work—with a singular absence of the proprietary attitude.

Almost the first task which the Council faced was that of choosing a successor to Miss Goold, whose health was beginning to suffer from the strain of continuous evening work. The right person was hard to find, more especially because the Council were anxious that the position should continue in the hands of a women. Two or three months of search finally produced a compromise solution. Caroline Martineau would temporarily act as Principal in an honorary capacity, while a young voluntary teacher in the College, Miss Ella Sieveking, would be appointed Vice-Principal at a salary of £50 a year.

This arrangement obtained from the beginning of the 1891–2 session. While it lasted, it proved of exceptional benefit to the College. Caroline Martineau's position was honorary only in name: in fact she was in the College almost every night, and was certainly its guiding spirit during the remaining ten years of her life. A large but quiet and self-effacing woman of notably generous and unselfish disposition, an ardent scientist and convinced Unitarian as befitted the niece of the great Dr. James Martineau, she was admirably fitted for her task. Her high intellectual qualities, kindly nature, and keen sense of social purpose set an example to the whole College, and rapidly helped to create within it a distinctive atmosphere of friendliness and earnest endeavour. She was soon felt to be so indispensable that persuasion was put upon her to accept her position permanently—which at last she did. Until her death in 1902 she remained the Principal, constantly in attendance, yet remaining entirely unpaid. Indeed, so far from drawing a salary, she continued to make gifts of money to the College, as she had done to the educational work which preceded it. Over and over again the Council records of the first few years show such entries as 'Donation of £100 by Miss Caroline Martineau to start a College bank account' or 'Donation of £50 by Miss Caroline Martineau to start the year with something in hand'.

If Caroline Martineau had one deficiency, it was perhaps that her solid virtues were not accompanied by an equal measure of feminine vivacity and charm. These, however—together with devotion and high purpose—were exactly the qualities which distinguished Ella Sieveking. As the salaried Vice-Principal she bore the main burden of the executive work, and she quickly became the best-loved figure in the College. Her health, however, soon suffered from the continuous evening duties, and in her first session she was obliged to take three months' leave of absence—during which Ethel Everest generously provided the money for a deputy. Despite these absences, her success with students and tutors alike was such that the Council elected her Principal in December, 1892, only for her to decline the post on the grounds of ill health. Meanwhile from the October of that year she was greatly helped by the appointment of an

107

assistant in the person of Miss Florence Acton, who was soon to become Director of Studies.

Ella Sieveking's ill health nevertheless continued, until in September, 1894, her doctors ordered complete and prolonged rest. Miss Acton thereupon became Vice-Principal and working head of the College under the Principal, and Miss Sieveking retired to the unexacting dignity of a Vice-Presidentship. The story behind this shows the peculiar esteem in which she was held. Thus far the College had had neither President nor Vice-President. The Council now resolved to create the former position, and two or three of the latter, all in order that there should be some purely honorary post which this modest and attractive young woman would agree to accept.[1]

Caroline Martineau had thus far contributed high moral purpose and enthusiasm for science, Ella Sieveking all those softer qualities which fostered a friendly atmosphere. The advent of Florence Acton, another good-looking young woman but also the first female graduate of the Victoria University, brought greatly enlarged intellectual interests. Within a few months of her appearance she took the main part in framing, in response to a request from one of the students, an ambitious 'plan of studies'. About this there was nothing compulsory: but it held up the ideal of systematic and continuous study on a coherent plan in opposition to the easier practice, into which the students would naturally fall, of attending unrelated lectures and classes.

The plan was certainly conceived on the grand scale.

[1] As Mrs. W. E. Crum she remained a Vice-President for many years, attending meetings of Council and taking an active interest in the classes and clubs. Her close connection with the College ended only in 1913, after she had moved from London.

108

In the first year the students, as yet ignorant in what direction their tastes would lie, would broach all 'the four great branches of education'—viz. English (represented by English Grammar), Mathematics (represented by Arithmetic), Languages (represented by French or Latin) and Science (represented by Physiology, Botany or Chemistry). In the second year, English Grammar having been mastered, English History would take its place. Arithmetic, too, being by now fully at the students' command, would be superseded by a more advanced branch of mathematics, such as elementary algebra or Euclid. The study of the chosen foreign language would of course continue; and the fourth subject could be either another language (possibly Greek or German), or a subject allied to mathematics (mechanics or physics), or another science. By the end of the second year, it was thought, a student might 'fairly expect to have tested himself thoroughly, and to have found his favourite subject'. During the third (and final) year of the plan, students would therefore drop all subjects for which they had no taste, and devote themselves to good work entirely in literature, or mathematics, or science.

For each of these subjects at each grade examinations were arranged, and the student was required to pass the examination in every subject before proceeding to the next stage. He was not, however, necessarily expected to take all four subjects of the first year within twelve months: if he cared, he could spread them out over two, three or four years. Similarly the four subjects of the second year could be taken in anything from one to four years; and the single subject of the third year, being prescribed in three sections, could be taken in anything from one to three years. The entire plan thus offered a scheme—openly declared to be quite provisional and subject to future amendment in the light of the students' criticisms—by which a student could work on systematic lines for anything from three to eleven years (or longer still, if he failed at any point). It says much for the Morley student that in the first year nearly a hundred men and women embarked upon the scheme, and that one member wrote to the College Magazine suggesting that in the third-year stage an extra section should be added, 'which should comprise the blending of Science with Literature'. It says perhaps even more for Caroline Martineau that in her official explanation of the scheme in the Magazine she should have been at pains to apologize for its 'narrow range of subjects', and to explain that the student must learn to renounce the desire to master everything if he is to master anything. 'Few will venture to deny,' concluded this grave and high-minded woman, 'that the days of encyclopaedic knowledge are over. It is useless to deplore what is a necessary condition of progress; but though we may be compelled to renounce, let us never renounce with scorn'.

Most of the students in fact found the plan too exacting to follow in its entirety, and only one or two brave spirits—J. G. Sparkhall was one—toiled almost to the end. Whether following the plan or not, however, the Morley student of this period was already offered a remarkable range of subjects. To those available in 1890,[1] Natural History, Botany, Drawing, Wood-carving, 'Ambulance' (First Aid), Cookery, and Dressmaking (two concessions to student demand) were added in 1891; Spanish, History,

[1] See pp. 101 and 103.

110

Geography, Logic and Hygiene in 1892; and Italian, Greek, Heat and Steam, and Political Economy in 1893. By this time the subjects were listed in the annual syllabus in five divisions—Literary, Science, Art, Technical, and Occasional (gymnasium, etc.). Still the choice continued to widen, and 1894 saw the addition of Physiography, Geology, Art History and Appreciation, and Swedish Drill—the last-named paid for by the scientifically-minded Principal, who had some difficulty in foisting its tedious manœuvres on young women already keen on 'the more showy and perhaps more entertaining' forms of gymnastics. In the next two years the list was extended to include special practical classes in heat, sound and electricity; and the last four years of the century saw great developments in Biology, and the introduction of Poetry, Psychology (1896) and Ethics.

These classes brought into the College several teachers, paid and unpaid, who gained a great hold over the affections of their students and became very much a part of the Morley scene. Among the linguists, for instance, Henrietta Baatsch began teaching in 1897 and gave up only in 1939. Frederick Black—later Sir Frederick—a voluntary teacher, a civil servant in the Admiralty, and one of the finest and most outstanding figures in Morley's history, began his long association with the College in 1894, when he took classes in English Grammar, English Composition and Latin. Within a year or two he was also taking the late class in Arithmetic—which began at 9 p.m.[1] Still more eminent and soon to be equally devoted, Graham

[1] Sir Frederick W. Black, K.C.B., b. 1863, d. 1930. Director of Naval Stores, 1903; Director of Naval Contracts, 1906; Director-General of Munitions Supply, 1917; Acting Chairman of British War Mission to U.S.A., 1917–18; President of the Institution of Petroleum Technologists, 1919.

Wallas first came to the College in 1893, when he began a series of university extension lectures on 'The English Citizen, Past and Present'—to a class of 81 students. The following year he lectured again, on 'The Making of the English Constitution'. Almost a generation later he was to become the College's third President.[1]

That scholars of the calibre of Graham Wallas should be willing to take classes at the College was indeed a happy omen for its future. The next few years were to show that he was no isolated figure. In 1897 Professor E. J. Urwick, the philosopher and lately the sub-warden of Toynbee Hall under Canon Barnett, introduced the study of Ethics into the College with a series of lectures on the 'Nature of Right and Wrong'. Like Black and Wallas, he was to be caught up in the atmosphere of the place, which he was to serve for long years both as President and as Chairman of Council. The following year Mrs. Bernard Bosanquet contributed another course on Ethics; and the turn of the century saw a blaze of intellectual brilliance, with Chalmers Mitchell giving several courses on biological subjects, Holland Rose lecturing on English History, and Lowes Dickinson running a discussion class in Ethics.

Among these early classes, two were to establish for themselves a very special and long-enduring position. In 1895 J. J. Denton, a more or less self-educated man and himself a student of the technical classes, began to take his own first class in the College—that on practical elec-

[1] Graham Wallas, b. 1858, d. 1932. Schoolmaster, 1881–90; Extension Lecturer, 1890 onwards; Lecturer at London School of Economics, 1895; Professor of Political Science in London University, 1914; early Fabian and part-author of Fabian Essays, 1889; Member of London School Board and later L.C.C.; Author of *Life of Francis Place, Human Nature in Politics, The Great Society,* etc.

tricity. The intention was that he should supplement, by practical work, the lectures of those theoretically better qualified than himself. In actual fact, by force of his energy, devotion, and genuine scientific gifts, he soon came to stand for all that was best in Morley's scientific work. Perhaps his most remarkable quality was his forward-looking mind, which kept him abreast of the latest scientific developments, and prompted him to conduct at the College practical experiments in wireless telegraphy by 1899, in wireless telephony by the early 1920s, and in television by 1933. Almost equally remarkable was his ability to inspire his students with his own enthusiasm for this kind of scientific experimentation.[1] Among his earliest and most gifted pupils was William Rivers, a young scientific journalist who soon became his principal unpaid assistant, and who was himself, as student and councillor, to play an outstanding part in the College life for over fifty years.

The other class of which no student at Morley in the nineties could remain unaware was that taken by Professor Pritchard on 'The Care of Horses'. The professor, a colourful character, was an ex-President of the Royal Veterinary Society, and the expenses of the class were met by the R.S.P.C.A. Started as an experiment, the course proved an instant success, no less than 130 students enrolling. Most of them were vanmen, cab-drivers, ostlers, farriers, and others with a technical interest in the subject. They made a welcome addition to Morley's student population: for—in the words of the annual report—they were 'quite a different set from what are attracted by our other

[1] His greatest work was in television, on which he laboured with J. L. Baird from 1923 onwards.

classes'. Different or not, they soon became devoted to their class and in many cases to the College. The class secretary, a farrier appropriately named Faithfull, became a particularly ardent champion of its merits, and attended year after year. Before long there was a pleasant little ceremony when the students presented the professor with an ebony walking-stick which could be extended to measure horses, and for some years the same keenness prevailed. At the end of the century, however, there was opposition from veterinary circles on the ground that a little knowledge was a dangerous thing, and the class was reluctantly discontinued. While it had lasted it had not only enlightened many hundreds about the animals in their care, but had also brought within the orbit of the College in large numbers just that type of labouring man who has generally proved least responsive to the calls of adult education.

Among the means favoured by the College Council to foster keeness in class were the holding of regular examinations and the award of scholarships and certificates of proficiency. Students in the extension courses, for instance, were examined under university auspices, often by scholars of the highest repute. It was asking not a little of the Morley student, who it is to be hoped was conscious of the privilege and compliment, that his work under Graham Wallas should be examined by F. W. Maitland. That great man professed himself 'well satisfied' with the results; and so, examining the class of another tutor, did Professor Tout. F. C. Montague, however, in examining Wallas's students, detected a common failing—that of inability to marshal information adequately and direct it to answering a particular question. 'The answers were such,'

114

he wrote in 1894, 'as might be expected from intelligent persons who had taken a real interest in the lectures, but had little general knowledge, and less intellectual discipline. . . . Questions requiring a knowledge of history or of institutions naturally were not so well answered as questions relating to the special interests of the working class, which often elicited answers showing considerable knowledge, if not an absolutely philosophic temper.'

Of the other classes, those run under the Science and Art regulations were examined by that Department until 1900, when it was combined with the Education Department at Whitehall to become the Board of Education. By that time its grant had at last ceased to depend on 'results'. From 1895 certain classes were also run under the regulations of the Technical Education Board of the L.C.C.[1] Here the criterion for grant was attendance and not examination, but most of the students nevertheless sat for one. In fact even the most purely domestic College class normally underwent tests set by someone other than its tutor: William Poel, for instance, was the voluntary examiner in 1900 for the elocution class. After 1907 it became the practice to submit classes to the verdict of the Cambridge Examination Syndicate; but whatever the examining body, from university to private individual, a certificate was the prized reward—and the annual presentation of these in the Victoria Hall one of the great events of the College year.

On the results of these examinations depended the awards of scholarships to the summer extension meetings at Oxford and Cambridge—an object particularly dear to

[1] County Councils had been empowered to provide technical education since 1889, when the Technical Instruction Act was passed.

the founders of the College. In its early years very great efforts were made in this direction: subscriptions were invited, and Caroline Martineau herself contributed enough for several bursaries. As a rule the main difficulty was not so much the money, for an award of £5 was usually sufficient, but the fact that in many cases the recipient was quite unable to secure the free time to take advantage of his success. Nevertheless many students did contrive by these means to put in two or three weeks at one of the older universities. In the summer of 1899, for instance, no less than ten students went to Oxford for periods varying from a fortnight to a month. The group consisted of three clerks, a schoolmaster, a music teacher (the only woman), a draughtsman, a compositor, a hatter's apprentice, a laboratory assistant, and a horse foreman. 'It was a pleasure to be in the College,' wrote Caroline Martineau, 'when these students came back from Oxford, to see the brightness and enthusiasm with which they talked over the events of their outing. . . . They bring back with them a fresh interest in life, and a conviction not only that there are better things in the world than money-getting, but also that there are some people who live up to that conviction. . . .'[1]

In addition to these extension scholarships, another award was available from 1892 onwards. In that year the Council decided to nominate a few selected students as Associates. Those chosen were to have been students for

[1] The university authorities who were interested in the Extension movement were extremely generous of their time and hospitality. A student who spent ten days at Cambridge in 1891, besides receiving invitations to tea almost every day, was invited to luncheon by the Master of Peterhouse and a don at King's, to a reception by the Master of Trinity, to dessert by the Master of Selwyn, and to a garden-party at Downing.

116

at least three years, to have distinguished themselves in their studies, and to have brought credit to the College. They were privileged to attend all classes for one year without fee, and to have their names inscribed on an honours board in the Common Room. The first students nominated under this scheme were Percy Eyre, Frederick Jacob and Charles Levett; and before the century was out the board displayed the names of the brothers E. J. and C. H. Hartley, J. G. Sparkhall, James Clough, and many others whose untiring efforts in class and club had made them pillars of the College.

Examinations, certificates and honours boards have long since been discontinued at Morley College, and the falling value of money has brought about an almost total lack of interest in the bursaries. The whole apparatus of test and reward created in the early days has thus been laid aside, without noticeable effect on the keenness of the students. Nevertheless, it is not to be inferred that the College Council of the 1890s were mistaken in their policy. Examinations were very much the order of the day, and without them the best students of the time might well have felt a lack of seriousness in the College classes. In any case, no student was compelled, though all were encouraged, to go in for them. Undoubtedly, however, many of the best among these men and women welcomed the opportunity to measure their work against the impartial standards of an outside examiner. In this period at least, they were justifiably proud of the certificates which assured them that they, too, were not unfitted for the ardours and the joys of study.

In any case, whether quickened or not by the spur of examinations, the Morley student of the nineties soon

117

established an enviable reputation for intelligence and hard work. Chalmers Mitchell was only one of many distinguished men who came to take extension lectures, found that almost everyone stayed to the supplementary class afterwards, and professed himself 'repeatedly surprised by the enthusiasm and interest displayed'. Many glowing tributes, too, came from the inspectors of the three ill-co-ordinated organizations—the Science and Art Department, the L.C.C. Technical Education Board, and the Education Department—with which the College had to deal, and from which it earned grant. Inspectors in those days were not encouraged to believe that their most valuable function lay in making helpful suggestions: they were there, primarily and plainly, to see that regulations were observed and that the taxpayer's or ratepayer's money was not wasted. They were not easy men to impress, but they were nevertheless frequently impressed by what they saw at Morley College. In 1894, for instance, after the College had first applied for grant as an 'Evening Continuation School', under the new 'Acland' Code, it was made the subject of frequent 'surprise visits' by Her Majesty's Inspectors. Some apprehension was felt by the College authorities as to how the voluntary teachers would take to this, but they accepted it cheerfully in the interests of the College, and were later gratified by the terms of the inspectors' report. 'The educational work of the College,' it stated, 'is of a most thorough and practical nature. The list of subjects taught is extensive, and good progress has been made by the pupils under the efficient guidance of an admirable staff of lecturers and teachers.'

Year by year, whether the inspectors were those of the Education Department or the L.C.C., the College continued to earn reports of a similar character. The 1898 report by the Education Department may stand for many: 'It is difficult to speak too highly of the work done in these classes, or to express adequately the pleasure it gives to see the earnest way in which the students set about their studies. The teachers, also, are deserving of the very highest praise for their lessons, which show infinite care in preparation.' With such words even Caroline Martineau could be content—'though only,' as she once put it, 'with the kind of content which encourages to fresh effort'.

Perhaps the most remarkable tribute of all, however, came from Dr. W. Garnett, the head of the L.C.C. Technical Education Board. In 1895, soon after the College began to run classes under L.C.C. auspices, two L.C.C. representatives were added to the College Council. One of these was Dr. Garnett, who in his first year of membership made not a single appearance. When the L.C.C. again nominated him the following year, Emma Cons wrote to point out that members of the College Council who were not present at least once during the twelve months normally forfeited their seat. Dr. Garnett replied that he intended to remain one of the L.C.C. representatives, but 'had not time to attend meetings of institutions which were working smoothly'.

119

VII

The First Decade: (2) Play

By 1901 the College was running 55 classes in 32 different subjects. All these were but one side, though of course the most important, of its ever-increasing activity; for the foundation scheme had also enjoined another objective—'the promotion of social intercourse' among the students.

The tradition and some of the facilities for this were inherited from the Working Men's Club and recreation-rooms in the Vic. The gymnasium, for instance, was older than the College. Despite frequent requests from the students, it was not until 1902 that gymnastics were allowed to count as educational activity; until then—'to prevent rowdiness such as formerly prevailed in the Vic gym'—they could be indulged in only by those who had already joined an official class. Throughout the 1890s the gymnasium accordingly remained one of the main centres

120

of College social life, patronized (though on different nights) by men and women alike. And a gym display with the men performing on the parallel bars and the women marching and counter-marching in voluminous skirts and blue sailor blouses, was an ever-popular feature of the annual speech-day and prize-giving.

Next door to the gymnasium in the basement was another centre of social activity—the refreshment-room (Room M). This was at first very bare, and regarded as an all-male stronghold. In the early days it was operated at his own risk by Pearce, a local man who had taken a lease of the Coffee Tavern in the Vic and who later succeeded in establishing the 'Pearce and Plenty' eating-houses. Many were the complaints, however, against the quality of his refreshments, and from 1893 the College assumed more responsibility. Some of Pearce's equipment was bought up and the caretaker West and his daughter were prevailed upon to run the service—at West's risk. This arrangement lasted until West's retirement in 1898, when the College took over completely. Meanwhile the ladies, barred from the refreshment-room lest the figures of the male gymnasts in their athletic vests should offend their eyes, and an occasional unacademic word their ears,[1] had their refreshments sent upstairs, either to the Women's Room or later to the Common Room. To save them the embarrassment of descending even briefly to the basement, they were soon able to place their orders from the ground floor through a speaking-tube.

[1] The gymnasts, usually regarded by the Council as liable to include a rough element unless care was taken, were apparently purer in vocabulary than was officially believed. West's daughter, who served in the refreshment-room for many years, declared to Miss Sheepshanks that during all her time there she 'never heard a nasty word'.

A third centre of social life was the Library, an excellent long room at the top of the building. Very little if any money was available to purchase books, and the collection was built up almost entirely from gifts. Here again Caroline Martineau, her sister Constance (now one of the teacher's representatives on the Council), and Ethel Everest displayed their customary generosity. By 1895 there were some 3,000 volumes, but this growing number, in which fiction occupied little place, could not be freely issued to the students until there was a librarian in attendance five or six nights a week. At first volunteer labour was tried, but proved too irregular. By 1895 the principle of a paid supervisor was accepted, and thenceforth the position was held until 1912 by a succession of ladies of academic distinction, most of whom added something of value to the College but departed after two or three years for reasons of health. It is probably not, however, strictly as a library that survivors from the period will best remember this room—for the College authorities frequently proclaimed their desire to see more students studying there. What they will remember is the part it played on Saturday evenings, when it became the setting for soirées, debates, concerts, special lectures and many other important functions of the College year.[1]

Of these various events, the most regular and the most important held within the College were for long the 'opening soirées', on the first Saturday of each term, and the students' 'socials', held on Saturday evenings once a month. The soirées, organized by the College authorities, usually took the form of an exhibition and demonstra-

[1] Among those who held the position of Librarian between 1895 and 1912 were the Misses Parnall, Meade, Kane, Bernard and Browne.

tions—at this period, mainly of scientific subjects—followed by a short talk from some well-known man. Bernard Bosanquet and Michael Sadler, for instance, came along for this purpose in the mid-nineties. Tea and cakes were then served—in West's time at a cost to the College 3*d.* a head—and the proceedings concluded with a concert in the Library. Every student in the College was invited by post, and for the opening soirée of the year all ex-students as well—a practice which by 1897 involved sending out more than three thousand invitations. This of course could not continue, for ex-students were increasing at the rate of some hundreds each year. By the 1900s among the ex-students only the regulars and those who specially requested a ticket were invited, together with all students of the current year.

No such problem occurred with the Saturday socials organized by the students under their able chairman, Fred Monro. These attracted the keen social element of the College, but were never in danger of being overrun. They consisted largely of a concert with refreshments, at which songs such as '*Queen of the Earth*', '*The Mighty Deep*' and '*True Till Death*' and humorous recitations such as '*Bill Adams*' and '*Rubinstein's Piano*' were rendered with varying skill. There were few occasions on which the performance began punctually, and many times when it went on too long, but in general the evenings were much enjoyed and greatly helped to foster a community spirit within the College. When in 1896, however, the students requested socials twice a month instead of once, the College Council unhesitatingly refused. Its members feared that fortnightly socials would compete with other forms of Saturday evening activity, such as club meetings

123

and debates, and no doubt they were apprehensive about the supply of talent.

If the Library saw the larger social gatherings, very much the heart and soul of the College life was the Common Room (Room H). By 1892, thanks to gifts of rugs and chairs from Lady Frederick Cavendish and others, this had become reasonably comfortable, and in it gathered not only those who wished to read a paper, or enjoy a game of draughts or chess, or indulge in conversation, but also, in various corners, the committees of the clubs. The remarkable feature, however, was that the Common Room was also the centre of the College administration. At one end was the 'desk'—soon to become 'desks'—occupied by the Principal or the Vice-Principal and the Secretary, so that the students could enjoy the freest possible access to the College authorities, and they in turn could keep intimately in touch with student activities and opinions. 'The official work of the College' —reported Caroline Martineau in 1897—'would no doubt be done more quickly in another room less liable to interruption, but the change would destroy a most valuable opportunity of natural and unrestrained intercourse between officials and students.' This unique arrangement, which did much to create a distinctive spirit within the College, lasted uninterruptedly until 1927, by which time telephones and the increasing pressure of business drove the Principal (though not yet the Secretary) to take shelter within a room the doors of which could be, but were not often, closed.

Many, no doubt, will remember conversations in this Common Room on the first floor of the Vic building. Caroline Martineau, herself nothing if not earnest, writes

124

in the annual report for 1893 of the 'informal but very earnest conversations, into which commonly one or other of the ladies occupying the "desk" is drawn. Socialism, Politics, the priority of mind or matter, the composition of a comet's tail, the origin of virtue, the position of women, the philosophical views of Kant, Schopenhauer and Aristotle, the poetry of Browning, the nature of Beauty, the utility of war, have all been eagerly discussed here within the last few months. . . .' Possibly the picture is a little one-sided, but at least it shows something of the intellectual excitement generated by their new studies among these keen-brained men and women.

Others will perhaps retain more vivid recollections of the whispered discussion of club committees in the corners of the room. The clubs which flourished during the nineties included, in approximate order of foundation, the Gymnastic Society, the Cricket Club, the Debating Club, the Swimming Club (with separate sections—and nights—for men and women) the Natural History Society, the Football Club, the Chess and Draughts Club, the Women's Games Club (with croquet as the main activity at first and tennis beginning in 1895) and the Cycling Club. Nearer the end of the century the Archaeological Society, the Photographic Society, the Faraday Society and the Dramatic Society were formed, and the Women's Games Club gave way before the progress of a mixed Lawn Tennis Club. An Essay Club, a Book Club and a Literary Society were shorter lived, for the College was not yet as much interested in the arts as in the sciences. Even a short life, however, was an improvement on the state of affairs round about the time the College was founded. 'A notice was put up,' recorded Emma Cons in 1891, 'Inviting students to put down their names for a Literature Class. Someone scribbled under the notice the query "What is Literature?" to which someone else added the answer "Bosh".'

Those clubs which could do so, naturally met within the College. The gymnasium, which was under College organization, functioned during the week, but most of the others only on Saturdays. Billiards could be played in the basement during the week, as could bagatelle in the Women's Room. The athletic club had of course to meet outside the College; during this period the Cricket Club enjoyed practice facilities in the grounds of Lambeth Palace and played matches at Raynes Park on a pitch paid for by Ella Sieveking, while the Women's Games Club met for croquet in the garden of Mary Martineau (a cousin of Caroline's) at Clapham and later for tennis at Streatham. In the winter, from 1895 onwards, the Women's Games Club also played badminton in the gymnasium. The notice in the Magazine announcing this stated that 'for those who are waiting their turn at Badminton, or prefer a quieter game, there are Halma, Reversi, or Tiddledywinks'.

Among the more intellectual clubs the Natural History Society, mainly guided at this time by the voluntary teachers Dr. and Mrs. Rose, easily led the field—even if there were occasional comments that it might, from the nature of its excursions, be more aptly called a 'Picnic Club' or a 'Flirtation Society'. Against any accusation of lack of seriousness, however, the strong interest taken in it by the Principal was more than adequate defence. During the nineties the Society persuaded many distinguished

126

men and women to give talks at the College—among them a young biologist named H. G. Wells, who on November 17th, 1894, lectured on 'The Shapes of Leaves'. At the end of the century the Society combined with the Photographic Society to form a Field Club organized in three sections—Natural History, Photographic and Microscopic. Of this combined club, for many years the most important in the College, the tireless, genial and enterprising secretary was William Rivers.

From 1895 onwards a new social function took its place in the College calendar—the annual dinner of the United Clubs. This function was held outside the College and for long confined to the men. At it a succession of those longest connected with the College and its preceding classes, such as R. W. Bowers, John Keane, James Clough and Fred Snelling contributed suitable reminiscences, and sufficient amity was exhibited fully to justify the motto of the organizing body—'Unity and Good Fellowship'. No one generated the latter quality more unfailingly than (Sir) Frederick Black, who for many years occupied the chair, and whose genial presence and entertaining speeches were the surest guarantee of the evening's success.

Two other innovations in the life of the College between 1895 and 1900 also took lasting root. The Principal, on the nearest Saturday to her birthday, invited all the new students to tea. After her death the practice was generously continued by her sister and it still goes on—though the Principal no longer meets the bill and it has nothing to do with his birthday. This function gave an opportunity for all the club secretaries to speak on the advantages of joining their societies, and brought the

127

senior students into touch with the newcomers. To the same end, a students' reception committee was also formed, devoted members of which attended the College every night during the fortnight preceding the opening of term and the first month afterwards in order to establish friendly relations with new students and 'show them the ropes'. Substantially the same thing still goes on today, in a less extended fashion, when members of the student executive committee and the clubs attend during enrolment week and take much of the burden of that period from the shoulders of the harassed staff.

The corporate spirit was also fostered, for a more limited number of people but perhaps in an even deeper way, by the generosity of members of the Council and their friends in entertaining the students at their houses and lending them cottages for the summer holidays. Among those who regularly invited parties of students, of one interest or another, to spend a summer's day with them—usually from lunch to supper with concluding songs and 'party pieces'—were Dr. Longstaff (a voluntary science teacher with an observatory at Putney), Frederick Black and his wife (on more than one occasion he took the chair at the clubs' dinner on a Saturday night and entertained the Cycling Club to breakfast at his Sutton house the following morning), Leonard Noble (who had a private cricket ground at Henley on which the Cricket Club infallibly failed to strike their best form), — Vaughan (a master at Eton and a strong supporter of the Vic project from the beginning), Ella Sieveking, and Dr. and Mrs. Rose. Most extensive of all in their hospitality were Emma Cons, Caroline Martineau, and Ethel Everest, who invited parties of students not merely for the day but for the week-end, either to Caroline Martineau's houses near Maidenhead and Bury St. Edmunds, or to Miss Everest's lovely home (Chippen's Bank) and model farm at Hever, in Kent. At Chippen's Bank were held what for the students were the most memorable parties of all, with impromptu sleeping quarters in barns, glorious walks in daffodil woods, and much petting of piglets and calves of unexampled cleanliness and domesticity. Often, too, study was combined with play. One Saturday in July, 1900, for instance, several members of the Faraday Society were invited with J. J. Denton to conduct experiments at Hever in wireless telegraphy. Other friends of the College, such as Dr. Rose, with houses at high points along the North Downs, invited similar parties, posts were also set up in and near London, and attempts were made to signal between all these stations at fixed times. 'It cannot be said that decided results were obtained,' recorded the annual report, 'but there were enough hints of possible success to excite great interest and a desire to repeat the attempt after . . . more . . . laboratory work.' Fifty-seven years later the impression made by these experiments and the party on a cousin of Ethel Everest's, then a sixteen-year-old youth staying in the house and afterwards to become a distinguished scientist, was sufficiently vivid for him to recall the incident to the author of this volume, even to the name of Mr. Denton.

These parties did much to open fresh horizons to the students, and to contribute in their small way to that grand object which inspired all these kindly hosts—the lessening of the gulf between the social classes. They also promoted friendly relations among the students. In

129

this respect the visits to houses lent by members of Council and their friends for the summer holidays were perhaps of even greater value. Once more Caroline Martineau set the example: having ceased to occupy her house (The Walnuts) on Maidenhead Thicket she lent it for the summer of 1897 to the students. Furniture was borrowed, and two married couples among the students—the Monros and the Cloughs—each agreed to look after the housekeeping for some weeks, despite the fact that for part of the time the husbands would have to travel back and forth to their normal work. In this summer residence students were able to pass a week or two at merely the cost of their food, or to enjoy a brief week-end or even a few hours—as large numbers did—if they felt like cycling down from London. Some enjoyed most the beauty of the countryside, others the fun of the makeshift arrangements, others the novel experience of living in a house complete with paddock, orchard and a garden equipped for croquet and lawn tennis. As one student put it: 'While you are down here it is like having a country-house of your own, and £500 a year.' 'For the time being,' wrote Clough afterwards, 'we lived in Arcadia, we formed an ideal republic.' Similar sentiments filled the bosoms of those who occupied the house in succeeding summers, or who later enjoyed holidays in a house lent by the Roses in Kent and a cottage lent by Miss Mocatta and Miss Llewellyn Davies near Reigate. It was indeed a fact that for many students the memory of these holidays never faded. The first party at The Walnuts then and there vowed to meet together ten years later on the steps of St. Paul's Cathedral and proceed to a celebration supper. It says everything for their enthusiasm, if not

130

so much for their arithmetic, that some of them turned up a year too early.

Two more institutions—the Magazine and the Debating Club—which established themselves during the earliest years of the College also deserve some detailed mention. The Magazine, begun in 1892, appeared monthly during term and helped to keep the College together by acquainting the students with all the various activities. It was edited at first by a younger member of the Council (for some time Frederick Black and then John Keane), and was only gradually entrusted entirely to the students. It was for some time of extreme sobriety, mingling its reports and announcements not with 'creative writing' but with learned and factual essays on such subjects as 'May Day' and 'The Evolution of Words'. Later 'poetry' began to creep in, but of negligible merit until the end of the century, when a real master of the craft settled in as resident versifier. His witty rhymes were published under the pseudonym of Skrep, which was his own name (Perks) backwards. He owned a bookshop, and was a brilliant student of botany. One of the first, but by no means the last, of the many eccentrics who have lent variety to the student body and found in Morley a platform for their talents, he was a strange, unkempt, bearded figure, who lived at home in the utmost squalor. On one occasion the infallibly helpful William Rivers spent two days clearing up his rooms after the sanitary authorities had threatened eviction.

The Magazine, though nowadays appearing in duplicated form rather than print, has continued uninterruptedly from the year of its birth. Not so the Debating Society, which has for many years been defunct. It

131

warrants mention not so much for its size—thirty or forty was an average 'house'—as because from its debates one may reconstruct the opinions of these long-since departed students. It met at first under the chairmanship of an M.P., Walter McLaren, and then under so distinguished and quixotic a figure as the young C. P. Trevelyan—brother of G. M. and later to become Sir Charles and a President of the Board of Education. From the records of its divisions one may form one's picture of the Morley students (or the more vocal among them) in the nineties: students who were predominantly Liberals (but at first far from Socialists), moderate champions of 'women's rights', abstainers or near-abstainers from strong drink, enthusiastic consumers of meat, and more than half non-smokers. Believers in imperial federation (but anti-militarist), they resented the powers of the House of Lords, considered that M.P.s and local councillors should be paid, demanded universal suffrage, and maintained that public elementary education should be purely secular. In their opinion, the formation of an Independent Labour Party was 'neither necessary nor desirable' and the extension of state control must be zealously resisted; but at the same time any abridgement of the powers of the L.C.C. would be 'contrary to the best interests of the Metropolis'. At the end of the century, by a majority of one in a small house, they voted that the Boer War was 'unnecessary and grossly immoral'. A year later, by a majority of eight, they passed their first resolution in favour of Socialism.

To this list of social activities many more could be added. There were the annual Flower Shows, organized from 1900 onwards, and the great draughts matches,

132

North London versus South London, played with a hundred boards a side. There were the parties to see performances at the Vic, or to hear the Tuesday lectures, when Professor Ramsay lectured on argon or Flinders Petrie on Ancient Egypt to houses packed from floor to ceiling. There was a Convalescent Aid Society, with special rights in a convalescent home at Broadstairs run by an ex-student and known as Morley House. In sum, the College social rooms, the clubs and the extraneous facilities together made possible a wealth of useful and enjoyable activity, which in turn helped to hold the College together, and establish it firmly in the affections of the students.

How strong were the bonds forged between students and College by all this personal hospitality and social activity may be seen from the many reminiscences sent to the author of this history. Men and women now in their eighties and nineties still have vivid recollections of this side of the College life. Mr. A. W. Arnold, a stalwart of the Debating Society from 1895 onwards, recalls the great kindness of his French teachers, Miss Joachim and M. Descours, and how he and Descours would enter into amicable arguments. 'I was an active Socialist propagandist, and I got Descours to the point where he would translate notes from foreign journals for *Justice*, the Social-Democratic weekly.' Such friendly relationships were by no means rare, and followed naturally from the example set by the ladies at the head of the College. Mrs. C. Garnon, who joined the College in 1894, recalls many instances of this. 'I was to be married in 1900,' she writes, 'to one of the students. I did not know Miss Martineau knew anything that was happening in our private lives,

133

but one night she sent down to the Gym. for me to come and see her in the Common Room. To my great surprise she presented me with three lovely Wedgwood jugs. I have valued them so much that I never used them, but kept them in a china cabinet—I learnt afterwards that she presented a set to all those who met and married through the College.'

Mrs. Garnon's memories of the 'lovely outings' and the holidays are also very keen. At the Walnuts, the furniture being short, 'it was straw beds for the men and boxes for chairs when we had a crowd, but oh! how we enjoyed ourselves!' At Chippens Bank 'we slept on hay in the barn, and I can remember, though it's nearly sixty years ago, Miss Everest and Miss Cons visiting us in the middle of the night with storm lanterns to see if all was well.'

From all this it will be apparent that relations between the students and the College authorities were exceptionally warm and close. They were not, however, invariably unruffled. Morley College has never lacked students prepared to voice a grievance, and several times in the 1890s the views of the Council and of the student representatives on the Consultative Committee were by no means identical. Few feelings were seriously hurt when the Council declined the students' request that roller-skating should be permitted in the gymnasium, but several other matters of difference persisted a long time. Some of the students wanted dances and a Dancing Club: the Council refused to allow the formation of a club, and any dances had to be held outside the College. Other students desired to act scenes from plays: for long the Council withheld permission, and then agreed only on condition that there was no dressing-up. Round about 1894 a serious conflict

134

developed over the custom that the Principal, or her representative, was *ex officio* a member of all club committees, even if she did not normally choose to attend meetings: several students objected to this on the ground that it defied the democratic principle of election, and the secretary of the Swimming Club even threatened to adjourn forthwith any committee meeting at which the Principal appeared. Only a very conciliatory formula devised by the Council resolved this difficulty. Worst of all, perhaps, was the row in 1894 about the dismissal of one of the College clerical assistants; after Walter McLaren had resigned from the Council because he thought the lady unfairly treated, nearly a quarter of the students petitioned for her reinstatement. They were roundly told by the Council that a deputation on the subject could not be received. 'The Council desire to point out to the students that it is obviously impossible for them to enter into any discussion with the students on questions affecting the appointment of the College Staff, for which the Council alone are responsible. The Council need hardly say that they always seek to act only with a view to the best interests of the College.'

Such incidents were fortunately rare. In general the only serious causes of tension were the occasional difficulty of reconciling the claims of educational work and social activity—Council members sometimes expressed the view that the clubs were getting a little 'out of hand'—and the natural clashes of the young against the old, the more advanced against the more conservative. At a time when many long-cherished beliefs were beginning to be challenged, it was natural that feelings should sometimes run strongly, and friendships suffer strain.

135

A striking, and not surprising, example of this arose in connection with an unexpected choice of subject by a visiting lecturer. The incident is related by Mrs. Marvin, who as Miss Deverell joined the College in 1896 to help with the administrative work. It illustrates also the feelings on 'women's rights' which were entertained by many high-minded and progressive women of that time who were not of the younger generation:

'Miss Martineau asked me,' writes Mrs. Marvin, 'to arrange a lecture which was likely to be of interest to newcomers to the College as well as to the older students. Through the kindness of the secretary of the Fabian Society I was able to get Mr. Charles Charrington, the actor, to speak to us. He came with his wife, who on the stage was Miss Janet Achurch. The intention had been in the first instance that he should speak on some aspect of Socialism, but he wrote to me that he would speak on Ibsen. Ibsen was in those days still new to the English stage and regarded by many people as dangerous and immoral. So a notice was put up in good time in the College in case anyone should think it necessary to protest against the subject chosen, but no criticism was forthcoming. On the evening of the lecture I met Mr. Charrington at the door of the College to beg him to remember that our Principal, though a most broad-minded woman, belonged to an older generation and might find some of Ibsen's plays unacceptable. But he said he had changed his mind; he was going to speak about a greater than Ibsen—Bernard Shaw. At this time Bernard Shaw was little known as a playwright and certainly not appreciated, and I begged Mr. Charrington to

136

tell Miss Martineau at once of his proposed change of subject and get her approval.

'At the lecture Janet Achurch sat beside me and I felt she was nervous for she held my hand throughout. I hoped for a talk on one of the lighter amusing plays, *John Bull's Other Island* for choice, and was distinctly anxious when Mr. Charrington announced he was going to speak on *Mrs. Warren's Profession.* Miss Martineau was present at the lecture and my whole concern was that there should be nothing to which she would object. Mr. Charrington was a good speaker with a beautiful voice and as he spoke on the connection of low wages and prostitution, to which far too little attention was paid in those days, I felt sure no one could see anything unsuitable.

'Immediately his lecture was over I went across the room to ask Miss Martineau if she thought it was all right. "He was a very good speaker," she replied, and she did not think that what he had said could do any harm. "But I don't like any *spoken* protest against the position of women," she said; "you and I," she added, "are far more effectual protests than any mere speaking can be. When people see that we will not marry while the position of women is so unsatisfactory, they will begin to take action." It was characteristic of Miss Martineau that she gave me credit for sharing to the full her serious purpose in life, and could think of a girl in her early twenties as having forsworn marriage rather than take part in the out-spoken warfare against sex inequality which began a few years later.'

'I had hardly finished speaking to Miss Martineau on the conclusion of the fatal lecture before one of the students

137

came to speak to me. "This is the first helpful word I have heard at the College," he said; "we ought to have heard this long ago. You ladies at the desks don't know anything about our lives. This thing concerns our sisters! We ought to be able to get advice about it here." But when I went back to the Common Room where the members of the staff had their desks I found opinion going in the other direction. A number of the students and one or two members of the staff who had not been present at the lecture were shocked, and I heard it described as an attempt to introduce free love into the College.'

Mrs. Marvin goes on to relate how she left soon afterwards to take up a research studentship, and how Miss Martineau told her that she still belonged to Morley, and must come back and succeed to the Principalship. The death of Miss Martineau a little later drove any such thoughts from Mrs. Marvin's mind. 'But years afterwards when I told Miss Everest and Miss Cons of my approaching marriage, I found that these kind people were still expecting me to return to the College. However, the prejudice stirred up by the Bernard Shaw episode would have made my return there very difficult, if not impossible.'

Incidents of this kind, with their sharp clashes of opinion and feeling, were of course only to be expected in a place which attracted keen-witted and thoughtful men and women. That there were occasional rows did not prevent the College from being a family that was happy and at heart united. In sum, by the end of the century a wealth of useful and enjoyable activity had been built up to complement the basic work of the classes, and

138

to give reality to the College's declared aim of 'promoting social intercourse' among the students.

Soon after the opening of the College, Emma Cons had explained in the annual report the justification for this aim. 'Those who have been brought up from childhood in cultivated homes, surrounded with intellectual society, may perhaps find it difficult to imagine what life would be without these blessings, to the girl or young man in a lonely lodging, or the dwellers in a crowded room where quiet is impossible. "We can't make friends in our rank of life," said a shoemaker with ten children. "How can I tell my boys to bring home a pal in the evenings? We've not room for it!"

'If,' concluded Emma Cons, 'we can bring into the lives of our students books and an intelligent interest in the affairs of the world and the beauties of nature, we do much for them. If we make friendship possible to them, we do perhaps still more.' Ten years had now elapsed, and as she surveyed the College at the close of the century she must surely have felt that by its work in both these fields it was already no unworthy memorial to Samuel Morley.

139

VIII

The New Century

THE opening of the twentieth century, with the death of the Queen and the exasperating prolongation of the Boer War, was a depressing phase in British political and social life. The rising sap in the tree of education, too, was for the moment arrested. In 1899 Cockerton, the London district auditor, successfully challenged, on grounds of illegality, the growing practice of the London School Board of financing post-elementary education from the rates. Considerable confusion resulted, and it was three years before Balfour's great Education Act could sort out the tangle, set up a national framework for secondary instruction and release fresh stores of educational energy.

Only two people connected with Morley College appear to have been directly involved in the war in South Africa—Leonard Noble, Councillor and ex-voluntary

140

teacher, who served as a combatant, and Joseph Ash, student, who volunteered for ambulance duties. Nevertheless the national depression was reflected in the College, which for a brief spell seems to have lost some of its former vitality. This was reflected in the numbers: in the mid-nineties the membership had risen to more than eleven hundred students, but by 1902 it was down in the seven hundreds, where it had started a dozen years beforehand. Much of this loss was brought about by the opening of the Borough Polytechnic less than a mile away and by the great expansion of London School Board evening classes, which from 1893 began to offer a much wider range of subjects, including recreative ones, and from 1898 were free to all comers. But some of the loss was no doubt also caused by the absence or departure from the College of its earliest leaders.

The departures occurred in rapid succession. In 1894, to the regret of all within the College, ill health had compelled Ella Sieveking to give up the post of Vice-Principal. Fortunately her successor, Florence Acton, also combined great ability with an attractive appearance and manner, and for a few years the College continued to enjoy the leadership of two outstanding women. But in 1898 circumstances at Miss Acton's home demanded that she should look after her parents, and she too was compelled to depart. Within a few months Edith Deverell, the young assistant of whom Caroline Martineau thought so well and who had been awarded a research studentship at the London School of Economics, also left.

To offset this double loss the College was again fortunate in securing, in 1899, a Vice-Principal of great intellectual and administrative ability. Mary Sheepshanks, a daughter of the then Bishop of Norwich, was not yet out of her twenties, but she already possessed exceptional breadth of culture and determination of character—qualities which were soon in evidence at the College. According to her recollection she was asked only three questions at the Council meeting which appointed her. Had she a sister at home to look after her parents if they fell ill? Could she stop an over-vigorous glove-fight in the gym? Could she tell if a vet was too drunk to take the horse class?

Mary Sheepshanks, however, had barely taken up her duties as Vice-Principal when the Principal fell gravely ill. For the rest of 1899 Caroline Martineau was away, and though she returned during 1900 her health was clearly far from restored. In fact cancer was already at work. For some time she struggled on, until at the end of 1901 she was forced to take to her bed. By January, 1902, she knew the worst and wrote to Frederick Black. 'It is no use shutting our eyes to facts, I shall never come to my dear old College again.' A month later, at the age of fifty-eight, she died. Her last letter, unfinished, concerned College affairs; and her death occurred on a day when several students were invited to tea in her bedroom.

Apart perhaps from that of Emma Cons, Caroline Martineau's was the greatest contribution made by any individual to the successful establishment of Morley College. In the very earliest days she had been Miss Cons's right hand in the organization of the pre-foundation classes and the penny scientific lectures. On the unexpected departure of Miss Goold, she had reluctantly accepted the chief executive position in the new College, and night by night, for more than ten years, had made her way during term-time from Bayswater to Lambeth. Entirely unpaid, she had devoted a substantial proportion of her income to bolstering up the College finances, her last and most generous gift, made in conjunction with her sister Constance, being nothing less than a physics laboratory built on the top storey of a new tenement house attached to the College. This house—'College House'—she left to the College, together with a legacy of £300.

Because she was somewhat retiring and withdrawn, and because her quiet insistence on the highest moral values was entirely inflexible, Caroline Martineau was considered by some of the students to be unduly 'strait-laced'. Others, including some of the hardest workers, found it difficult to accept the fact that she rarely thanked them for their services: to serve others, and in this case the College, was in her opinion not a task for which thanks should be received but a privilege for which thanks should be given. All this had led at times to serious misunderstandings. The grief at her illness and death, however, and the many moving tributes to her in the memorial number of the College Magazine, leave no doubt that in general her character and her unique services to the College were appreciated at their true worth. Many of the oldest students and ex-students—James Clough, F. W. Jacob, Fred Munro, A. W. Arnold and others—emphasize her unfailing generosity, her kindness and sympathy, and her unswerving sense of duty. And three or four others, asked to contribute some message, could only reply in effect with Emma Cons, who wrote: 'I can find no words to express my deep sorrow

143

for the loss of her, which is indeed irreparable to me and to our work. There are few such as her in this world. She devoted her life and her all to her work for others.'

Some indication of the quality of this selfless, Quaker-like woman may perhaps be glimpsed from what proved to be her three final messages to the College. Towards the end of 1900, when several students became unemployed, she wrote to the Magazine suggesting that the College should act as an informal labour bureau: those who desired work and those who knew of vacancies should put up details on a special notice-board. A few months later, as assassinations shook the thrones of Europe and the Boer War dragged on relentlessly, she wrote deploring the increased resort to violence for political ends, and the fact that arbitration on the lines of the 'Alabama' award had not developed into the regular method of settling international disputes. Her last message of all was delivered in December, 1901, at the Principal's tea to the new students. Despite her manifest weakness and her lifelong antipathy to public speaking she addressed some remarks to her guests, and among them spoke words of abiding truth in relation not only to Morley College, but to many another place of adult education: 'No matter what the Council may do, the smooth and efficient working of the College depends after all on the students . . . students may become selfish and narrow by breaking up into antagonistic cliques, or they may, on the other hand, determine to cultivate a general sympathy with the whole life of the College, and so promote harmony and all-round efficiency.' In its calm assertion of the facts as she saw them, addressed without fear or flattery to students

144

whom Mary Sheepshanks found for all their virtues to be generally class-conscious and 'touchy', that statement is entirely typical of the woman.

For the innermost springs of her mind, however, perhaps nothing is more revealing of Caroline Martineau than a passage from her last scientific paper, quoted in a memorial tribute by the Rev. P. H. Wicksteed, the Unitarian minister who was one of her oldest friends and counsellors, and one of the first to act as a voluntary teacher in the Old Vic. The paper is entitled 'Shapes and Sounds: An Account of Compound Pendulum Drawings and Musical Intervals'. It shows her fundamental equation of religious order, morality and beauty, and explains why as a scientist she found it inconceivable that the theories of Darwin could in any way conflict with Christianity:

> Beauty and simplicity of sound, corresponding with beauty and simplicity of form, and both caused by simplicity of numerical relation! It is a connection of ideas which takes a strange hold on one. When first I made the acquaintance of the compound pendulum apparatus, I felt a sort of breathless excitement, and I have often watched it till my eyes were moist, I should have been puzzled to explain why. But I am not the only one who has found the production of these curves a strangely *touching* sight. One friend, quietly watching the pen at work, said 'I feel as if there were something religious in this'. Another said 'This instrument alone would go far to make one believe Atheists mistaken'. It is not easy at first sight to tell what it is that excites thought of this sort in very different people. I believe

145

it is no mere coincidence but a half-conscious perception of the fact that *Law and Order*, when they have free play, *result in Beauty*. To most minds few things seem more dry than the relations of numbers to one another. Yet here we see that motions which are accurately governed by these relations produce beauty of form and the still more impalpable beauty of harmonious sound. In these diversities of operations we dimly perceive the same spirit. We have on the one hand simple beauty of form, which appeals to the eye, simple harmony of sound which is perceived by the ear, and the simple relations between numbers which the thinking brain can grasp and understand. On the other hand we have confused curves, discordant sounds, and arithmetical relations too complicated for the mind to follow.

Does not this hint at another fact, that beauty is not a mere conventional idea invented by man? Of course I do not mean to deny that our ideas of beauty are apt to be led astray by fashion and other causes, so that we often for a time think of something as beautiful which we do not care for permanently. But surely the facts we have been considering seem to show that there is a true and lasting idea of beauty outside of us, besides the ideal within our own minds, which may go astray for a time but comes back in the long run to recognize the truly beautiful. It seems to me that what makes us take a delight in these curves is some dim, unrecognized perception, which is, perhaps, more emotional than intellectual. Here we have Order making for Beauty and Harmony in the physical world. Is not that a step towards perceiving that truth and

146

duty tend to harmony in our own lives? We are very well aware of disorder and want of harmony and ugliness in our own lives and the lives we see around us. Do not these curves say to us, 'Go on struggling for the triumph of Law and Order till they reign over human life as they reign in the physical world. See what beauty and harmony they bring with them!'

* * *

To find another Principal of distinction (and private means) who would bring to the position the devoted labour of a Caroline Martineau was no easy task. For nearly three years the College Council pursued this quest in vain, the burden of administration meanwhile resting almost entirely on the shoulders of the young Vice-Principal. During this period the Council itself underwent considerable changes. In 1902 the College President, Professor Stuart, who had treated the office as largely nominal, resigned and was succeeded by Professor E. J. Urwick. The latter, already active in the College as a teacher of ethics, took a different view of the position—and attended Council meetings regularly. Frederick Black, chairman of the Council since 1899, thereupon stepped down to vice-chairman on his own suggestion, and from 1903 Urwick presided over the Council. In the same year Emma Cons laid down the honorary secretaryship of Council and College—a task which devolved for a year or two on Mrs. Crum and then on Miss E. St. John Vaughan. About this time, too, R. W. Bowers and Dr. R. D. Roberts ceased to be active councillors and became Vice-Presidents, and William Rivers first joined the Council as a co-opted student member.

None of these changes was as important as the next.

147

In 1904 Professor Holland Crompton resigned from the Council and Charles Roden Buxton, son of Sir Thomas Fowell Buxton and great-grandson of the slave emancipator, took his place. Buxton had already been working in the College for a year as a voluntary teacher, taking a class in 18th-century English literature. He was young, active, good-looking, deeply religious and idealistic, talented, likeable and leisured. Not surprisingly, within a few months the Council had invited him to take on the vacant Principalship, and in January, 1905, he accepted. He was the first male to be entrusted with the destinies of the College, and the break from tradition was made with some misgiving. Women had been appointed, Caroline Martineau had once explained, because what Morley College needed was an 'influence' rather than a 'power'. Apparently the Council now felt that the College could do with a 'power'—or else that Miss Martineau's antithesis was unjustified. Or perhaps it just felt with Miss Deverell, who more than fifty years later was to write of the Martineau period: 'Looking back on those days, I am very sure that the students would have gained, perhaps have gained greatly, by having men on the staff as well as women.'

The character and personality of Roden Buxton have been movingly described in a memoir by his sister.[1] His generous championship of the working classes, his utter rejection of appearance and comfort, his unaffected friendliness, his breakaway with his still more quixotic wife from the haunts of aristocracy, and his establishment in a house in Kennington Terrace, all endeared him

[1] *Charles Roden Buxton*: by Victoria de Bunsen (Allen and Unwin, 1948).

148

to the College. His ardent love of literature, too, communicated itself to many of the students, and brought the College new interests and strength. But he had scarcely been Principal for more than a few months when his burning desire for social reform carried him into politics. He became the Liberal candidate for East Herts, and when defeated in the election of 1906 accepted the candidature for mid-Devon. To nurse this constituency he took a house at Bovey Tracey and from 1907 onwards his appearances at the College became comparatively infrequent. He still attended Council meetings and the occasional social, still entertained students, still introduced his friends to the College; but he was no longer a guiding force. Throughout the whole period from her appointment in 1899 to her departure in 1913, the helm in fact rested mainly in the hand of the Vice-Principal, Mary Sheepshanks, and it was largely due to her that the troubled waters of the early years of the century were safely negotiated, and the College vessel borne forward into smoother seas.

The central problems facing the College at the beginning of the century were the decline in numbers, and the relationship of the College with the L.C.C. and the Borough Polytechnic. These three matters were closely inter-related, and not only because the opening of the Borough Polytechnic had drawn off prospective technicians among the students. Towards the close of the 1890s the College had been earning small grants from three different sources—the Education Department in Whitehall, the Science and Art Department at South Kensington, and the Technical Education Board of the L.C.C. It had found from experience that, in the words

149

of the Council minutes, the L.C.C. were the 'best paymasters', and it had accordingly resolved, wherever there was a choice, to work under the L.C.C. regulations rather than those of the other bodies. This decision accorded closely with the spirit of Balfour's Education Act of 1902, which allotted general responsibility for secondary education to the county councils and county boroughs. By 1906, in place of a total of £285 earned ten years earlier in roughly equal amounts from the three different authorities, the College was attracting a grant of £640, of which £140 came from the Board of Education and all the rest from the L.C.C.[1]

This greatly increased support from the L.C.C., however, involved certain obligations, and prominent among these was the duty of 'co-ordination' with the Borough Polytechnic. The policy of the L.C.C. was not only to expand London's educational facilities but to tidy up the picture by cutting out overlapping or competing provision in any given neighbourhood. In pursuit of this aim it naturally wished the various institutions it supported in any district to have a specialized character. Morley College and the Borough Polytechnic were within less than a mile of each other, and the L.C.C. administrators were well aware that one was primarily a centre for the liberal and humanistic studies, the other primarily a centre of technical education. They therefore strove, since Morley had some scientific and technical classes, and the Borough Polytechnic some literary and artistic ones, to eliminate these subsidiary interests in each place, and to make the one institution more

[1] The Board of Education was formed in 1900 by the coalescence of the Education Department and the Science and Art Department.

exclusively humanistic, the other more exclusively technical.

With the thesis that institutions should broadly speaking have a special character, the College Council had of course no quarrel. It was also well aware that where elaborate or costly scientific or technical equipment was involved, unnecessary duplication of facilities would be foolish and wasteful. It understood therefore, though it regretted, when during the 1890s the Chemistry and the Applied Mechanics classes failed to attract grant and had to be closed; and it still understood, though it regretted still more, when in the early 1900s, first the Machine Construction and then the Building Construction classes, which had been running successfully since the pre-foundation days of 1885, ceased to be recognized and on L.C.C. insistence were transferred to the Borough Polytechnic. But it soon came to feel that the process was being carried too far, and was working out largely in the interests of the other institution.

The first steps in the direction of co-ordination were thus marked by more enthusiasm than the last. When the Borough Polytechnic was founded in 1892 there were many projects for fraternization between the College and Polytechnic students, and goodwill abounded on both sides. By 1906, however, this goodwill began to come under some strain as the L.C.C. inspectors developed a scheme for the complete integration of the two institutions, and their taking over by the L.C.C., with Morley College figuring as a literary branch of the Polytechnic. Several meetings to explore these possibilities were held between representatives of the College, the Polytechnic and the L.C.C.; and Roden Buxton, whose interests unlike those of Caroline Martineau were all on the literary and humanistic side, went very far in the direction of agreeing to the abandonment by the College of all scientific and commercial subjects. Breaking-point was reached on the broader aspects of the scheme, however, when the L.C.C., whose support had now become vital to the College, refused to continue the grant for the practical mathematics classes, and insisted on their transfer to the Polytechnic.

This proposal was strenuously resisted by the College Council, but without success. They objected to it on several scores. The practical mathematics classes were taken by Frank Castle, who had taught continuously in the College since the first scientific classes began in 1885, and whose other classes on building and machine construction had already been transferred. Castle was an extremely popular and able tutor and a devoted friend of the College in every way: a virtual order to part with him entirely was not one which the Council could accept without protest. The 100-odd students of the practical mathematics classes, too, were largely of the mechanic and artisan type, who by the combined pull of the Polytechnic and the trend of L.C.C. policy were already being drained away, and who by this decision would almost disappear from the College. The College Council thought it completely wrong that this artisan element should thus be in effect segregated from the office-worker and clerical element. Moreover several Council members were deeply conscious of the links which bind science and art, and distrustful of any plan which by separating scientific and humanistic education would tend to produce a breed of technicians ignorant of the humanities and

152

humanists ignorant of science. They therefore clung with determination to every science class which could be conducted on broad rather than technical lines, and in which effective instruction did not depend on elaborate apparatus. In this the general verdict of their own and the next generation was against them, but the verdict of today and tomorrow may well be on their side.

The mathematics classes needed no apparatus, and to have them transferred *en bloc* to the Borough Polytechnic against the wishes of the College Council virtually ended any chance of the College's agreeing to more radical plans of integration. Nor were matters improved by the *quid pro quo* by which the Borough Polytechnic music classes were transferred to Morley College: for the classes, including one in harmony, were transferred in name, together with their tutor, H. B. Dart, but few if any students came along with them. Meanwhile the popular College instructor in vocal work, Seemer Betts, had perforce been dismissed. It was therefore little wonder that in the annual report for 1906–7, while there was warm reference to the 'friendly feeling' existing between the College and the L.C.C., the whole scheme of co-ordination with the Polytechnic was openly described as 'one-sided' and the compulsory abandonment of the mathematics classes as 'a serious injury to the College'. Nevertheless some further (and minor) steps in the direction of co-ordination were accepted with good grace between 1907 and 1914, and a co-ordinating committee, amicable but somewhat distrustful on both sides, was set up by the two institutions. Nothing much resulted, except some arrangements for mutual advertisement in prospectuses and a basic preservation of the *status quo*. The College managed to keep its remaining science classes; it was not rebuilt, as L.C.C. officials suggested it should be, in the Borough Road; and it never became the Polytechnic's literary department.

* * *

Apart from the loss of the original technical classes, the most striking feature of the class work during the first decade of the new century was the growing enthusiasm for music. With this, and equally encouraged by Roden Buxton and Mary Sheepshanks, went an increased appreciation of literature. Buxton's own classes were important here; and so too were those of a young woman named Virginia Stephen who took classes in composition and poetry from 1904 to 1908, and whom posterity knows better as Virginia Woolf. Other literary ventures of the decade included the College's first courses on Shakespeare—a Shakespeare reading circle run in 1907–8 by G. M. Trevelyan, and a lecture-series given the following year by C. Delisle Burns. The College was fortunate, too, in attracting distinguished visiting lecturers to speak on literary topics—Dr. Hugh Dalton, for instance, and 'the rising young novelist' E. M. Forster.

Of other classes, among the most outstanding were those in philosophy and history. Philosophy, as distinct from ethics, was introduced to the College in 1910; the voluntary tutor was no less a philosopher than G. E. Moore, already a distinguished figure in Cambridge.[1] In history, the most distinguished courses were those given

[1] Moore's lectures in this series, with a dedication to his students, were later published under the title *The Main Problems of Philosophy*.

154

between 1904 and 1907 by G. M. Trevelyan (a schoolboy friend of the Principal's) on the French Revolution and Napoleon—topics also explored a few years later by Sydney Herbert. In constitutional studies, considerable interest was aroused by the lectures of Percy (later Sir Percy) Ashley on 'English Government' and on 'Modern Statesmen', and by those of Graham Wallas on 'Nineteenth Century Democracy'. For this last course, begun in 1907, a special reading group was formed under the guidance of Roden Buxton and a young voluntary teacher named H. F. Chettle, whose connection with the College was to be severed only by his death more than fifty years later.

Even the interest in these subjects, however, was soon eclipsed by that in economics. This was virtually a new study at the College, and its growing hold can be ascribed partly to the rising wave of industrial unrest which marked the later years of the decade and partly to the foundation in 1903 of the Workers' Educational Association. Roden Buxton was exactly the man to give the warmest possible welcome to Albert Mansbridge's project, and as soon as the movement spread to London, in 1906, Morley College became a main centre of W.E.A. activity. After Percy Vaughan had taken an extremely successful course in economics in 1908 with a class of 51 students, the following session the first three-year Tutorial began. The subject was 'Making and Sharing Wealth' and the lecturer J. A. Hobson. Special supplies of books were borrowed or even bought, and for the opening lecture no less than 96 students presented themselves—only 30 of whom could be accepted for the full course. No Tutorial class had been held in London before. Few

155

years have since passed in which Morley College has been without one.[1]

Outside the realm of the social sciences another notable addition to the College curriculum came in 1912–13, which saw the first class in Country Dancing. Vaughan Williams, Holst and Cecil Sharp had already brought the College into close touch with the folk-dance and folk-song revival, and this first class had the benefit of a tutor, Miss Walsh, who was secretary of the newly formed Folk Dance Society. The College Council were not yet prepared, however, to allow so entertaining a subject to be taught during the week: the class had to be held on Saturday. Of other class matters during these early years of the century it is perhaps sufficient to mention the departure in 1911 of Mrs. Monroe, dressmaking teacher for the past twenty years, and the arrival of M. Bosc, French teacher for the next twenty-two; the end of capitation fees paid to tutors on the number of their students (1904); the first appointment of class secretaries (1906); the carrying of electric current to the laboratory by Mr. Denton's students at a cost of £5, defrayed by Emma Cons (1905); and the introduction and rapid collapse of classes leading to London Matriculation (1908–12).

With the expansion of the College classes went from 1906 onwards a rapid growth in social activity. Most of

[1] There were several features which distinguished (and distinguish) the University Tutorial classes from the Extension classes. They operate under a joint committee of the local University and the W.E.A., an arrangement intended to ensure both academic excellence in the teaching and responsiveness to working-class needs. The students, limited to 30 in number to form a coherent and manageable group, pledge themselves to regular attendance for three years, and to undertake written work. Formal lecturing occupies only one-half of the two-hour evening, and in the second half the subject is pursued by methods of discussion between tutor and students.

the clubs had by now been formed, but a vigorous newcomer was Le Club Français de Morley College, rashly described by the Vice-Principal in the Report for 1906–7 as 'quite the most successful club in the College'. Another was the Long-Distance Walking Club, which celebrated its formation by a night walk from Purley to Brighton. Not to be confused with this was the Rambling section of the Scientific, Photographic and Rambling Club, which from 1912 replaced the Field Club. Of this the energetic secretary was Felix Webster, who the previous year had distinguished himself by winning a scholarship to the W.E.A. summer meeting at Oxford, and who several years later was to become the College librarian.

Not all the clubs, of course, prospered in equal measure. Several of those which met outside the building found they could survive only by recruiting from the general public—a perennial dilemma—and at one time both the Tennis Club and the Cricket Club were reported to have only three *bona fide* student members. This was despite the fact that from 1902 onwards students who had been members of the College for three years could by a payment of five shillings enjoy membership and College privileges without attending a class. Nevertheless in general the clubs flourished, and the Clubs Dinner, embellished after 1909 by the presence of ladies, continued to provide its annual display of unity and good fellowship.

Of new developments in the College social life during these years one could note an almost infinite number, from the introduction of 'ping-pong' (1911) upwards. Probably the most important, apart from the greater part played by music, was the abandonment of some of the austerities which had marked the Martineau régime. In 1901, against the opposition of Emma Cons, the women were at last allowed to remove their hats in College—an overdue reform when one considers the size and inconvenience of the head-dresses of the time. A new rule, however, was substituted, against the wearing of evening dress. This preserved the declared intention of the hat rule—to stop 'dressing up' and so keep the place open to the poorest. The change was nevertheless a step in the direction of greater informality in relations between the men and women students. A few years later, in 1905, the Cycling Club organized the first College dance—at Caterham; and round about the same time smoking was allowed—in the basement. By 1910 the women were permitted to penetrate this male holy of holies and patronize the refreshment-room. A still greater victory for the libertarians was to follow. In January, 1914, after a two-year campaign waged in the Council by Fred Snelling (student representative) and H. F. Chettle (voluntary teachers' representative) sanction was at last given for a whist drive and dance to be held within the precincts of the College.[1]

Broadly speaking, however, until 1914 the old pattern of social activity established in the nineties still continued. There were still the opening soirées (at which Paul Oppenheimer was still to be found playing the violin); still the monthly Saturday socials (at which a young man named Nelson Keys was soon abandoning drawing-room ballads and scoring much more of a hit with comic songs); and still the visits to hospitable friends in the

[1] One of the M.C.s was Miss Wathen, now Honorary Treasurer of the Old Morleyite Association.

158

country—to Ethel Everest at Hever, Constance Martineau at Bury St. Edmunds, the Carey Fosters at Rickmansworth, the Blacks at Sutton, the Bertrand Russells at Oxford, as well as to holiday cottages at Reigate and Leith Hill. And there were still, of course, debates. After a period of quiescence the Debating Society came to life again in 1904, and from then until 1914 was fortunate enough to attract many distinguished visiting speakers. Together with the free lectures on Saturday evenings in the Library (the books were in 1909 moved elsewhere and the room converted into a large lecture-hall), the debates kept the Morley student in touch with the many controversial questions of the time. It was no small privilege of College membership to be able to hear Mrs. Despard clash with A. V. Toynbee on the provision of school dinners, Cecil Chesterton proclaim the need for an Anti-Puritan League, his brother G. K. C. speak of the 'Sacredness of Revolutions', and G. P. Gooch analyse the mentality of Kaiser Wilhelm II. It was equally instructive to hear R. C. K. Ensor demand the establishment of legally enforced minimum wages, Mrs. E. M. Lowe and Herbert Morrison discuss children's care committees, the Earl of Lytton undergo heckling on imperialism, and a whole series of speakers including Christabel Pankhurst and Margaret Bondfield carry motions in favour of women's suffrage. Among these last speakers none made a more striking impression than the youthful Miss Amber Reeves, who visited the College in 1909 to advocate female suffrage and returned a few weeks later to debate the question of Free Will. She started what the Debating Club secretary described as 'the best discussion we have ever had', a statement

159

readily comprehensible to Morley students who now know her as Mrs. Blanco White.

Together with all the club meetings, the visits and the debates went a new interest in dramatic activity. Undoubtedly the appetites of the students were whetted by developments in the Vic under Lilian Baylis—who had succeeded her aunt as manager at the turn of the century. Drama except in short scenes during variety performances was still forbidden to the Vic up till 1912, when application was made for a full theatrical licence, but from 1900 onwards much more had been done in the way of opera. Emma Cons, presenting opera, had found herself hampered by the licensing regulations and restricted to giving concert performances with intervening tableaux. Under a less strict administration of the laws, Lilian Baylis was able to present complete operas—which soon became so popular that they replaced not only the Thursday ballad concerts but also the Saturday variety shows. To these performances the College students continued to be admitted at half-price, just as they continued to attend the Tuesday lectures free of charge; and many doubtless acquired there an abiding love of the theatre. With the College authorities now disposed to allow dramatic performances as long as they were not in costume, and with an able teacher, Leonard Howard, in charge of the elocution class, scenes from plays accordingly became a frequent attraction at the Saturday socials. This new development eventually culminated in the first presentation of a play in costume—*Much Ado About Nothing*, in 1909—and the formation of a Dramatic Society within the College. The final seal of educational respectability came in 1913 with a presentation of the *Antigone*, in

160

translation, at the annual prize-giving in the Victoria Hall. The cast was all female, and the thirty or forty young women who took part had spent many months under the direction of Professor Richardson in studying not only their parts but also Greek art and culture generally. There were several press notices, including one in the *Daily Mirror*, in terms varying from the kindly to the enthusiastic.

* * *

Transcending all other interests from 1907 onwards, alike on the educational and the social side, was the College's new-found love for music. It was not a question of love at first sight. During the earliest days the orchestra had rehearsed under the Victoria Hall's bandmaster, Alfred Dove, but the general level of musical work had remained low. From 1902, however, under the encouragement of Roden Buxton and Mary Sheepshanks, standards began to improve. The choir under Seemer Betts was adjudged good enough to take part in one of the Thursday Ballad Concerts at the Vic, and a new teacher, P. Stoeving, stimulated the efforts of the violinists. On the listening side, interest was aroused by a series of recitals in 1902–3 given by a trio whose violinist was Mme Solly and whose pianist was Miss Geisler-Schubert, a relative of the composer: of the first concert, which attracted 100 students, the College Magazine wrote that 'never before has the College had the privilege of hearing such perfect rendering of first-class music'. Invited again in 1904, Miss Geisler-Schubert returned with a string quartet to give a performance of Dohnanyi's pianoforte quartet in C minor which left the Magazine bereft of superlatives and exclaiming 'in the famous words of Oliver Twist, we can only say "we want some more!"'

Nevertheless the College was still far from music-minded, and in the same year Seemer Betts announced his intention of resigning unless there were more concerts—a complaint which will ring strangely in the ears of the present music staff. Shortly afterwards, as already recorded, he was compelled to resign for another reason—the demands of co-ordination with the Borough Polytechnic—and the Polytechnic tutor, H. J. B. Dart, took over. He was a good musician, who introduced the study of harmony to the College, revived the defunct orchestra, and eliminated a good deal of the rubbish that had been performed on the few occasions when the music classes appeared before their fellow-students. Early in 1907, however, after little more than one session at the College, Dart met an unexpected death, and the newly recognized position of director of music classes fell vacant. It was at this moment, when the tide of musical interest was already rising, that the College found Gustav Holst.

Holst was not in fact the Council's first choice for the post. A year or two beforehand Ralph Vaughan Williams had lectured in the College as a visitor, and in November, 1906, he had returned with Cecil Sharp to give two lecture-recitals on English Folk-Song. The impression he made was deep and unforgettable, and when Dart died a Council representative at once sounded him about the vacancy. He was too busy to accept, but he strongly recommended his friend Gustav von Holst, then in his early thirties and but recently appointed director of music in St. Paul's Girls' School. The Council, which fortunately included Miss St. John Vaughan, a relative by marriage

162

of Vaughan Williams and herself an ardent musician, interviewed three candidates. It made no mistake, and in April, 1907, Holst got the job. From that single decision has flowed the College's whole subsequent reputation in music.

Holst's first step was to eliminate all the remaining rubbish from the repertoire of the choir and orchestra—a policy which at once cost him several students. But other students soon joined, attracted not so much by his obvious musical gifts as by the loving magnetism of his personality. This apparently quiet man, bespectacled and carelessly dressed, had an engaging habit not merely of coming immensely and overwhelmingly alive and bursting out into all sorts of fun, but of communicating his enthusiasms to others. A musician of the finest calibre, and determined to perform the best at the highest possible level that could be obtained from the given performers, he yet possessed all the qualities of sympathy, consideration and patience which endeared him to amateurs. Within the briefest time he had a complete hold on the affections of his students, most of whom remained his devoted slaves for life.[1]

What sort of impact Holst made on the College may be seen from the Magazine, which in its fifteen years of existence had never before found itself making such frequent and glowing references to a tutor. Before 1907 was out, its musical correspondent was writing of Holst's

[1] Holst laid down no standards of admission to his orchestra but worked upon whoever came along. He even tolerated one second violinist with a semi-paralysed bowing arm—which she rested against the wall. To compensate for the immobility of the bow, the lady shifted her fiddle back and forth underneath.

163

'creative gift . . . his erudite musicianship . . . and over all this a character unswerving in its allegiance to an ideal, that of the pursuit of the good and true in all that pertains to the musician's art, and also his great desire to inspire others with a similar yearning, which few can escape, being bound to succumb, carried along as they are on the wave of his whole-hearted enthusiasm'. And even before this, after his first lecture in the College—a musical survey in which the audience 'was wafted, as it were, from the horrors of the bagpipes to the glories of Richard Wagner'—the Magazine was exclaiming rhapsodically 'How proud we shall all be of our Mr. Holst when we get to know him better!'

In the years from 1907 to 1914, under Holst's loving care, music at Morley College flowered as never before. Straightway he introduced private musical tuition, and obtained so excellent a pianist as Miss Vally Lasker to help with it. When promising students could not afford the modest fees—£1 a term—more often than not Vaughan Williams paid for them, or Holst gave the lessons free. Straightway, too, he introduced regular College concerts—not socials of the old type with drawing-room ballads and comic songs, but performances of first-class music from Tudor polyphony onwards by his choir, his orchestra, and his star pupils—among whom the names of Alice Hazelgrove, Percival Poole, Lilian Twiselton and Dulcie Nutting were soon prominent.[1] Within a year his choir were helping Charles Corri in the Good Friday performance of Rossini's *Stabat Mater* at the Vic, and within two years choir and orchestra together were entrancing

[1] Miss Twiselton and Miss Nutting in due course became College tutors, the former in voice and piano, the latter in voice and choral work.

164

College music-lovers with extracts from a work not heard in London within living memory—Purcell's *King Arthur*. Several professional music critics attended, and were suitably impressed.

How keen the College was fast becoming on music could be seen from the voting in 1908 for the ensuing session's extension lectures. Normally the students voted for which subject they would prefer, and for the first time and by a large majority they now chose music. The decision dismayed A. L. Leon, one of the extremely helpful L.C.C. representatives on the Council: he forthwith proposed that in future the Council itself should decide the subject of the extension lectures, 'choosing what is most educational'. Mr. Leon need not have worried, for the lectures when they began in October, 1908, were even more than educational. They were given by Vaughan Williams under the title 'From Haydn to Wagner', and within a few months the Magazine was recording: 'Dr. Vaughan Williams has endeared himself to all, not only on account of his constructive and inspiring subject matter, but also his unfailing kindness and individual help.'

The musical activity of the next session, 1909–10, was typical of what was to follow. In addition to the normal class and individual work, there were three concerts: at one the choir sang folk-songs harmonized by the harmony class, at another the main work was Bach's *Christmas Oratorio,* and at the third a varied programme included part of Gluck's *Orfeo,* orchestral music by Mendelssohn, Tchaikovsky and Elgar, an elaborate six-part madrigal, and songs by Mozart, Schumann and Brahms. Besides this Holst himself gave two series of lectures. The first series, on Bach, introduced the Bach Choir under Dr. (later Sir) Hugh Allen for some of the illustrations; for the second series, 'The Orchestra and How to Listen to It', the illustrations were provided by, among others, Isidore Schwiller and an orchestra under Vaughan Williams.

The crown and climax of Holst's first years at the College came on June 10th, 1911, when the Morley choir and orchestra performed the musical numbers of Purcell's *Fairy Queen*. It was the first performance for more than two hundred years—the manuscript had been lost and rediscovered only in 1901—and like the earlier performance of *King Arthur* it was one of the events which, following the devoted labours of the Purcell Society, helped to place Purcell once more 'on the map' of English music. For the occasion the music classes had hired the Victoria Hall, which was open to all comers at prices varying from a guinea to sixpence. An immense co-operative effort had gone into the preliminary preparations, the students copying and in some places transposing more than 1,500 pages of vocal and instrument parts. No pains were spared, either, to notify those who might be interested. From Windsor Castle came an encouraging message from King Edward VII; Mr. Balfour wrote expressing 'profound interest' and the 'deepest regret' that he was unable to be present; Sir Hubert Parry, Sir Alexander Mackenzie, Sir Henry Wood and others hastened to send their best wishes. Before a highly musical but far from full house—it is always easier to find performers than audiences at Morley—Vaughan Williams introduced the numbers, and the whole performance went splendidly. The music critics, present in quantity, vied with each other to do justice to the enterprise. In long

166

notices *The Times* spoke of the 'remarkably high standard' of the performance, the *Telegraph* gave 'all praise' to those concerned, and the *Birmingham Daily Post* regretted that the event could not have taken place a week earlier for the benefit of foreign visitors to the International Music Congress. Echoes of the performance even appeared in the press of France and Belgium. Of the contribution of the choir, perhaps the most flattering remark was that of an unnamed listener who was heard to say that before long 'organizers of big London choral concerts, instead of sending to Leeds or Sheffield for a choir, will just send word to the Waterloo Road'.

By this time Holst's classes were also beginning to produce student composers, whose works from now on figured in the College concerts every year. In 1912, for instance, a particularly deep impression was made by *St. Patrick's Prayer,* a work for choir and orchestra by Charles Burke, a student nearer seventy than sixty years of age. It was repeated more than once, and subsequently published. Two other features of the College musical life also became established about this time: the music students' teas—with performances—and the visits at reduced rates (or on the free tickets often provided by Vaughan Williams) to symphony and other concerts in the West End. On a night when a piece by Holst was to be heard, his Morley class was suspended, and his students adjourned in force to the Queen's Hall to hear the *Hymns from the Rig Veda* or the *Beni Mora* suite.

By 1912 it was apparent that, thanks to Holst and the constant assistance of Vaughan Williams, Morley was beginning to enjoy an unprecedented musical reputation for a College that was not primarily musical. It is therefore

167

distressing to find Holst in that year worried because the College could or would not find him enough money to hire the number of parts he required during the session, or to pay the occasional professional needed to balance the orchestra for a special performance. The College income was of course small, and there were no special grants for this sort of thing; but the earliest days, when without the greatest economy the place could not have carried on, had established a tradition of tight-fistedness, and in that the Council for long allowed the College to be imprisoned. By 1913 matters had reached the point where Holst, the least mercenary of men, was threatening to resign unless his salary were increased. Even he, it seemed, had to eat—if only (his sole sustenance on one day's march) currant buns. Conscious of the jewel in their midst, the Council accordingly decided 'to try to raise sufficient money by an appeal to increase Mr. Holst's salary to at least £1 per night'. Two months later he got his rise.[1]

From these mundane matters it is pleasant to turn back to the work in the music department, and to leave Holst in 1914 at a typical moment in the music students' tea. A special piece has been composed for the occasion, in tribute to the most recent developments in music—a *Futuristic Tone-Poem in H* for two voices and orchestra. A future violin teacher, Mr. James Brown, introduces the work. He explains that it is intended to express the 'somethingness of something', and that the instruments include a Contrabass Macaroon and a Tubular Pneumatic Buzza-

[1] Other tutors were at this time (1913) paid amounts varying from about 15*s*. to 7*s*. 6*d*. a night. Holst's £1 seems not unhandsome when one considers that forty-five years later distinguished composers at Morley may receive little more than twice this for an evening's tuition.

168

phone. Among the special technical features will be the use of the 17th inversion of the Metropolitan and District 6th. The two main sections, strings and wind, will play in different times, varying from simple times like 7 or 9 beats in a bar to more complex times such as $\frac{9.666}{16}$ or $\frac{x-y}{4nth}$. The work then begins, and lasts a full 12½ minutes. In view of the differing times maintained by the brass and the strings, Holst conducts it throughout with two batons.

* * *

The growth of interest in literature, the arrival of Holst, and the enthusiasm for economics engendered by the W.E.A. and the unsettled industrial situation, all helped to attract more students to the College. In 1904–5 the membership was under the 700 mark to which it had fallen after the turn of the century. The next session it began to rise, and by 1913–14 it was up to 1,125, where it had been in the mid-nineties before the mechanics began to depart to the polytechnics. These 1,125 students, however, were now much more evenly divided in sex. In 1895 the men had outnumbered the women by four to one; now, in 1913–14, as the inevitable result of the loss of the technical classes, the old male numerical superiority had gone, and at 569 men and 556 women the numbers were almost equal.

Many of these new women students were attracted by the commercial classes, which by 1914 accounted for more 'student-hours' than any other group, with modern languages second. Twenty years before, the scientific classes had held the lead: now they were almost bottom of the list. So great a change was, of course, reflected in the

169

occupation of the students. In 1889–90, in the College's first session, the student roll had included 199 clerks and 87 'engineers'. Now, in 1913–14, there were 392 clerks and only 12 'engineers'. But if the balance of the sexes and of the students' occupations was changing, one factor still remained fairly constant. Despite the introduction of the motor bus and the electric tram during the early 1900s, Londoners were not yet accustomed to travelling great distances as a matter of routine, and the population of the College continued to be drawn largely from the local boroughs. In a census of 908 students taken in 1913–14, the biggest number (163) came from Southwark, and very considerable numbers from Kennington, North Lambeth, Camberwell, Clapham and Walworth. There was, however, a growing element—152—from north of the Thames, and a few brave souls (mostly students of long standing who had moved farther afield) were already finding it worth while to travel to the College from the recesses of rural Surrey and Hertfordshire. But broadly speaking, it was still a College for inner South London—for that land of two million inhabitants almost unknown to superior persons over the river, who were sometimes heard to remark that it contained no big hotel and no good tailor.

In the last years before 1914 there were a number of changes among the staff and Council—changes which marked the end of one era and the opening of another. In 1910 Roden Buxton, elected to Parliament for mid-Devon, resigned his honorary Principalship and ceased to be actively concerned with the College. For a while there were efforts to replace him, and in particular to persuade a young voluntary teacher and member of

Council, Otto Niemeyer, to take on the post. Niemeyer, already fully equipped with those talents which in later days were to carry him to a directorship of the Bank of England, kindly agreed to supervise the College finances (while his sister lent a hand with the Library); but he was much too busy to accept this greater responsibility, and accordingly declined. Soon afterwards, since the College under the guidance of the Vice-Principal continued to forge ahead, it was decided to leave the quest for a Principal until some obviously eligible candidate came in view. Mary Sheepshanks therefore continued, as Vice-Principal, to direct the affairs of the College—as she had in fact been doing for many years.

In 1913, however, Mary Sheepshanks herself departed on a year's leave of absence that developed into final resignation. An ardent suffragist, she had been asked to lecture on the Continent, and in the course of this tour she was invited to edit *Jus Suffragii,* an international journal devoted to the women's movement. Her place was taken, at first temporarily and then permanently, by Miss Clare Brennand, who had studied at Newnham and at the Royal College of Music. Under the direction of this quiet, charming and able woman the College was to continue to prosper for the next twelve years.

Meanwhile there had also been important changes on the Council. The old generation was now giving way to the new, and soon the 'two young men at the end of the table' (as an older member of Council once termed Chettle and Niemeyer) would be shaping matters more after their own pattern. Between 1909 and 1914 Lady Frederick Cavendish, John Keane, Mrs. Crum, R. F. Bowers, and G. W. Johnson, all workers since the earliest days, ceased their active connection with the College; though fortunately another of the old guard—Frederick Black, now Sir Frederick and Director of Contracts at the Admiralty—proved willing to occupy one of the vacant Vice-presidencies. Of the new appointments to the Council perhaps the most important were those of Fabian Ware, voluntary teacher and friend and chief of Chettle's, and that doughty champion of the W.E.A., R. H. Tawney.

The vacant chair in the Council that Tawney occupied was that of a fighter no less gallant and devoted than himself. In 1912, after a brief illness, Emma Cons had died at the age of seventy-four. She had attended Council meetings and been in and out of the College up to four or five weeks from her death. 'Dominating but not domineering' (in the phrase of William Rivers), she had been content to guide and counsel, and had not sought to control: so much so that the new generation was scarcely aware that in losing her they had lost the effective founder of the College. With her passing and with the retirement of Mary Sheepshanks we may mark the end of an era within the College, just as surely as the outbreak of war soon afterwards was to mark the end of an era for the outside world.

There has been little space in this history to record any of the more personal characteristics of Emma Cons, or to mention her work outside the College and the Vic. Lilian Baylis, in her memoir, drew a loving and unforgettable picture of this short, cheerful, round-faced woman. 'I see her striding up the hill at Hever,' she wrote, 'singing in her deep contralto voice: I see her, still, in her delicate little lace bonnet, facing and quelling a gang of roughs in the gallery of the Old Vic. . . . I see her tucking

3*a* Samuel Morley among the Students

Terra cotta by George Tinworth above entrance to Morley College

3*b* A Group of Students at Hever

Included are the hostess Ethel Everest (with dog), Emma Cons, W. Drywood (on left), Percy Eyre (behind Emma Cons), and 'Skrep' (with beard) See page viii

4a Sir Frederick W. Black, K.C.B.

4b Lt.-Col. H. F. Chettle, C.M.G., O.B.E.

up her skirts and climbing on to the roof of one of the tenant's houses, to show a recalcitrant workman how slates and gutters should be fixed. . . . I see her beautiful face lighting up with sympathy for others.' This intensely practical woman, who 'always carried a knife and a piece of string in her pocket, even when she was wearing evening dress', and who managed with the greatest success large groups of dwellings not only in Lambeth but in Drury Lane and Marylebone, was yet also the artist and the creator. Of her creations, only a few have been mentioned in this volume—the coffee taverns, the Old Vic, Morley College, Surrey Lodge (as fine a group of tenement buildings and cottages as any erected in the 19th century, and even today in their damaged state still possessing a great deal more character than the modern block confronting them). But even these activities did not exhaust her good works. She served on Royal Commissions, was co-opted as the first woman alderman on the L.C.C. (and as a woman found herself debarred from speaking or voting), helped to raise the money to establish Vauxhall Park, helped to found and run the first women's horticultural college at Swanley. She was Vice-President of an important woman's suffrage society, a member of the executive of the Women's Liberal Federation. She was concerned with a dozen or more hostels and homes, clinics and crèches. When she took time off to travel it was to Canada to visit her emigrated tenants, or to Armenia to report on the Turkish atrocities. And on the way back from Armenia she called in at Crete to help the refugees, found many of them out of work, and promptly set up a silk factory with capital which she raised in England.

It is difficult to imagine a fuller or more useful life than that of this wonderful woman whose name is still so little known today, whose obituary in *The Times* numbered only a few lines devoted largely to the L.C.C. episode, who never appeared in *Who's Who,* who was not thought worthy of inclusion in the *Dictionary of National Biography,* and who has never been made the subject of any full-length biographical study. In simple truth, she was one of the greatest women of the 19th century. But if this has never been recognized, either then or now, at least there were many at the time who knew her worth and mourned her passing. 'We received hundreds of letters of sympathy,' wrote Lilian Baylis. 'I remember very distinctly that I took in, at the same time, Lord Stamfordham's telegram expressing the regret of the King and Queen, and a similar message sent by a scavenger in Lambeth.' In that conjunction Emma Cons, who strove so hard to bridge the gulf between the classes, would surely have been delighted.

174

IX

Last Years at the Vic

IN the early months of 1914 the Royal Victoria Hall stood outwardly much as it had done for the previous twenty-five years. At the far end of the building, on the Waterloo Road, an arched doorway still gave entrance to a Morley College running 'above, behind and below the stage'. In the tympanum above this door a terra-cotta group of working men, modelled by that master craftsman Tinworth of Doulton's, still surrounded a terra-cotta Samuel Morley growing grimier year by year. At the other end of the building, facing on to the New Cut, the balcony doors of the Vic still offered admission to all who could put down a few pence. Dimly lit, dilapidated and dirty, the whole edifice gave few outward signs of the pulsating life within.

Outside in the New Cut, too, things seemed much as before. The Saturday night 'saturnalias' of the mid-19th

175

century had long since become only a memory, and in general folk were much soberer, more respectable and better off than in the 1880s. Jostling along in the lurid light of the naphtha flares, dazed by the ceaseless shouting of the stall-holders and refreshed from time to time by snacks of hot sausages, baked potatoes, fried fish and chips, pigs' trotters and jellied eels, they were a crowd intent not on debauchery but on bargain-hunting. All the same, there was no lack of drunks and brawlers, or of shrieking women and whimpering children, when midnight came and the pubs poured forth their contents.

But if Saturday night in the Cut seemed much as at any time in the past ten years, inside the theatre things were on the brink of profound change. Free after the death of her aunt to develop those aspects of her work which she considered most important, Lilian Baylis had already struck out along her own lines. In February, 1914, she dropped the Saturday night variety performances, with their New Cut audience intent on the consumption of oranges and saveloys, and began to repeat on Saturdays the opera which had been performed the previous Thursday. Round about the same time, after a spell of showing films on Mondays, she revolted against the ever-increasing quantities of cinematic rubbish, and began to consider how to establish legitimate drama.

Armed with a full theatrical licence from the L.C.C., in the spring of 1914 Lilian Baylis next persuaded her governors to sponsor a Shakespeare season by a visiting company. This was no great success. The plays had to be staged on the opera nights, and few of the regular patrons welcomed the change. Nevertheless from this moment

176

the Vic became dedicated to the production of Shakespeare. By the autumn, though financial troubles pressed harder than ever, the theatre had its own Shakespearean company. In Estelle Stead, Matheson Lang, Ben Greet and others it found a degree of talent and devotion sufficient to triumph over every obstacle. From this point there was to be no turning back. Lilian Baylis went ahead, to give Great Britain its first permanent home of Shakespeare and its nearest approach to a national theatre.

Many years afterwards this remarkable woman was to express what the theatre meant to her: 'The Theatre isn't an excuse for wonderful evening gowns and jewels; it isn't a fad of long hair and sandals or the perquisite of 'varsity men and women; good drama isn't only for the students of training colleges and boys and girls swotting for the Oxford and Cambridge Locals; it is a crying need of working men and women who need to see beyond the four walls of their offices, workshops and homes into a world of awe and wonder. . . . Furthermore, all art is a bond between rich and poor; it allows of no class distinctions: more than that, it is a bond between nation and nation. I think it was Dr. Dearmer who said: "Art is a spiritual necessity. Civilization cannot exist in its absence, for without it civilization is but organized savagery." The theatre is perhaps the most important and accessible and the most easily understood branch of art for the man and woman in the street.'

Within ten years of Lilian Baylis's first venture in Shakespeare, the dynamic of that inspiring creed was to bring the Old Vic and Morley College to a parting of the ways.

* * *

177

The effects on the College of the outbreak of war were immediately apparent in the new session's enrolment. For some years numbers had been steadily rising; but instead of the 569 men who had enrolled during 1913–14, in September, 1914, only 435 men presented themselves. With the progressive mobilization of the nation's manpower, this decline continued; in 1915–16 there were 343 male students, in 1917–18 only 215.

Nevertheless, to the surprise and pleasure of the College authorities, the falling-off in total enrolment was very slight. The men might be otherwise engaged but the women came along in gratifying numbers to take their place. Thanks to this the enrolment for 1914–15, at 1,111, was only a dozen or so less than for the last year of peace, and the next year saw a similar state of affairs. In 1916–17 the total enrolment fell to 1,045, and in 1917–18 to 973; all told, the student population declined during the war by little more than one-eighth—a surprising achievement. In one respect, however, these years set up a new and lasting pattern. As already mentioned, the proportion of women to men had been increasing even before the war. In 1914–15 the women students for the first time outnumbered the men; and from that year to this they have continued to do so.

At its first meeting after the outbreak of war the College Council had to consider, among other things, a request from the L.C.C. to debar all enemy aliens from the College. The request did not find favour. Percy Vaughan, barrister, lecturer in economics and teachers' representative on the Council, was deputed to write a special message on the subject for the College Magazine. It was printed at the front of the first war-time number, and

178

offered a welcome contrast to the behaviour of the London mobs then busy smashing up German-owned food shops:

> OUR FRIEND THE ENEMY
>
> Now that we are at war with Germany and Austria there is a tendency in some quarters to indulge in animosity against Germans and Austrians resident here.
>
> Such sentiments are unbecoming to a humane and civilized nation and no member of Morley College will lower the reputation of his country by giving them play. That we are at war with Germany and Austria is the misfortune, not the fault, of the Germans and Austrians amongst us. That we love our country and wish for her success is counted a virtue among ourselves. Germans and Austrians feel the same about their countries as we do about ours, and what is a virtue among us is not a vice among them. Our German and Austrian guests are entitled to courtesy, consideration and protection from insult in time of war as much as in time of peace. . . .
>
> . . . The debt of civilization to German science, philosophy and music is enormous. It is unaltered by the war. All that can be altered by an inconsiderate treatment of aliens is the reputation of the English for justice and humanity. It is our duty to increase that reputation, not diminish it.

The protest did not avail, and in November the L.C.C., whose annual grant had long since become vital to the College, finally insisted that all enemy aliens be expelled.

This episode was not the only one which shows the

179

College to have taken long views amid the hurly-burly of the conflict. In 1916, for instance, the College sponsored a conference on the economic problems likely to ensue after the war. In the same year, and in the same spirit, it listened with approval to a message from Graham Wallas at the annual prize-giving—a message which asked the students not to think of themselves as merely carrying on during an emergency, but to consider whether on the contrary their function as students had not received new force from the sudden crumbling of age-long barriers, and from the opportunities that might be grasped of shaping matters anew towards a better life for all.

But if in some ways immune to the worst attacks of war-fever, the College, like every other institution, nevertheless fulfilled its duty to the country. How many of the 569 men who were students in 1913–14 actually served could not be ascertained even at the time, but over 200 are known to have done so. Among members of Council, Fabian Ware, H. F. Chettle, R. H. Tawney and Percy Vaughan were quickly in the conflict. Ware survived to become a general and, assisted by Chettle, to do magnificent work for the Imperial War Graves Commission. Tawney was soon gravely wounded. Vaughan, the writer of the 'Our Friend the Enemy' message in the Magazine of September, 1914, was badly wounded in 1915 and killed two years later. Among those who paid tribute to him afterwards was Arnold Bennett, who in the course of a memorable appreciation wrote: 'I never discussed the subject of war with Percy Vaughan, but what he thought of the moral bases of the present war is plain from his action, and what he thought of the institution of war I can guess. Thousands and hundreds of thousands of English-

180

men have freely left the securities of a profession and the amenities of home and the consolations of philosophy and art for the battlefield, as he did. It has been proved that the world is thickly populated with heroes and martyrs. But I am quite certain that no hero and no martyr had a more biting, a more sardonic, a more passionate sense of the gigantic and incredible sheer idiocy of war than Percy Vaughan had. And I am quite sure that none combined with that sentiment a more winning, practical, human loving-kindness than his.'

Among those of the tutors and students whose names were recorded in the ever-lengthening list headed 'In Memoriam', mention may perhaps be made of three, each of whom in some way typified in their service and death the fate of many more. There was Lance-Corporal Sydney Bressey, of the harmony class, who won the Military Medal, and who wrote in the trenches a setting of 'Music when soft voices die', which he sent back to Holst, and which was many times performed at the College. There was young Private G. Skelsey, of the commercial classes, who had a safe job at the Ministry of Munitions, but who felt it his duty to enlist on reaching the age of nineteen—and was killed after one week in France. And there was Sergeant Cecil Coles, ex-member of the orchestra and latterly a tutor under Holst and a gifted composer, who died of wounds received in the course of a volunteer expedition to bring in wounded. To 'Cecil Coles and the others,' Holst later dedicated his noble setting of Whitman's 'Ode to Death'. In the College Magazine at the time Holst wrote: 'Cecil Coles was writing a suite for small orchestra in the trenches. Luckily he sent me the first movement before the rest was destroyed, together with most of his papers, by a shell. We hope to produce it and thus pay our last tribute to our old friend in the manner that would have pleased him most.'

There were other ways besides military service in which the College and its members strove, in the language of the time, 'to do their bit'. A V.A.D. was built up round the nursing classes of Percy Vaughan's wife, Dr. Marion Vaughan. A War Savings Association, formed under Dr. Winifred Cullis in 1916, had a member on duty every evening during term to receive contributions. Invitations to all the main College functions were sent to soldiers from the dominions and the colonies, and special classes and recreational activities were run in the afternoons for convalescents. All this might have been expected from the College. More unusual, and arising from its position near Waterloo Station and the Union Jack Club, was its use as a dormitory for soldiers on leave. This began in April, 1915, when the College offered the lecture hall and another room to the Union Jack Club free of charge for this purpose during week-ends. By the end of 1916 soldiers were sleeping in these rooms every night of the week, at considerable disturbance to College activities, and the Union Jack Club was pressing for further accommodation. As this could have been made available only by seriously curtailing classes, the College felt unable to meet this request. It was promptly confronted by an order from the War Office commandeering the whole building. The last round, however, went against the over-zealous manager of the club. J. D. Gilbert, one of the L.C.C. members of the Council and an M.P., secured an interview with the War Minister, Lord Derby, and persuaded him to withdraw the requisition.

182

Among the other difficulties experienced during the war were the impact of food scarcities and rationing, so that before long it was possible to hold only two 'major teas' during the session. The need for economy, too, told on the College. In 1916–17 the L.C.C. reduced its grant to £400, which was £100 less than the College had been receiving ten years earlier. At the same time the College was faced with additional charges for dark blinds, air-raid insurance and the rest. These were certainly necessary, for from 1916 onwards the enemy made several attempts to hit Waterloo Station. In September, 1917, a major raid occurred on the opening night of term, and thereafter attendance at classes fell sharply on moonlit nights. When raids took place after that the normal practice was for the classes to adjourn to the gymnasium in the basement, which was also a public air-raid shelter. Many times the music classes entertained their fellow-shelterers by giving selections from their repertoire. In circumstances where a rendering of 'Tipperary' or 'Pack up your Troubles' would perhaps have been more conventional, Holst took his choir through a Mass by William Byrd.

Among the College organizations, the first war casualties were the outdoor clubs which depended on the support of the younger men. The Football, Cricket and Tennis Clubs quickly suspended activities 'for duration', and by 1917 the Cycling and Swimming Clubs were compelled to follow suit. Only the Rambling Club managed to keep going throughout the whole four years. The annual Clubs' Dinner, too, ceased, the German Club diplomatically retired into cold storage, and by way of compensation the College could show only a newly formed Esperanto Club.

183

The war also had its inevitable effect on class work. German classes were kept together under Henrietta Baatsch, but numbers became small and the Morley student in general preferred to learn French. By 1916 the electricity classes and the men's gymnastics could no longer be run owing to shortage of men, and about the same time the choir began to experience difficulty for the same reason. The only new class of note to be formed during the four years was one in practical economics given by a panel of lecturers who included Dr. Leslie Burgin, later a Minister of Transport, and Miss Catherine Webb, a prominent member of the co-operative movement who had taken Tawney's place on the Council.

Amid what for the College was educationally and socially a period of recession, the French, Commercial and Musical departments remained remarkable for their vigour. By 1915 303 students were taking commercial subjects, 177 French and 171 music, these between them accounting for more than half of the total enrolment. Commercial subjects (of which typewriting was for long taken by a devoted elderly law clerk and voluntary teacher, W. Drywood) were not, however, the type of work which the founders of the College had intended to encourage; they were provided rather as a facility for students already studying other subjects, and in 1916 the Council took pains to point out that no one taking only a commercial class could be regarded as a 'satisfactory' student from the College point of view. During 1917–18 these classes obtained much poorer results than usual in their Royal Society of Arts examinations—a decline ascribed to the frequent interruptions from air raids.

Shortage of tenors and basses may have upset the

184

balance of the College choir, but it made little difference to the general enthusiasm of the music classes. Rejected by the army for short-sightedness and a neuritic right arm, Holst continued to inspire the work at the College without a break until July, 1918, when he departed on a year's leave to organize music for the troops in Salonika. Into the details of all his activity during these four momentous years it is impossible to go, but one feature of it was the way he drew together his Morleyites and his Paulinas, groups otherwise very different, in common enterprises. Miss Gray, the headmistress of St. Paul's, regularly invited Morley College groups to perform at the school: Vally Lasker, Jane Joseph, Claire Mackail and others from St. Paul's became pillars of the work at Morley. And together the Morleyites and the Paulinas provided the forces for the great Whitsun festivals that began at Thaxted in 1916 and continued there and elsewhere for many years to come.

Of the quality of the College concerts during this time, and indeed throughout the whole of the Holst period, there is ample evidence from the College Magazine. The source may sound partial, but it had become Holst's habit to invite distinguished outside musicians to appraise his student's work, and the criticisms were frank as well as friendly. Edwin Evans, Clifford Bax, Hugh Allen, Herbert Howells and many others of comparable stature made the journey to the Waterloo Road for this purpose. Perhaps what impressed them all more than anything was the spirit of the performances. Typical of the comments on this point were those of A.C.B.—initials which conceal a great musician whom everyone now knows as Sir Adrian Boult—who in March, 1917, wrote after a performance of the *Rig Veda* hymns: 'I must confess, as an outsider who has never been to Morley College before, to have been greatly impressed with the really splendid atmosphere which pervades all the musical doings in the College. All the students go in for the music so obviously because they really love it, and guided and stimulated by Mr. von Holst the whole place seems to throb with the best of all that is implied in the word "amateur", that word which professionals are apt to use with a sneer, but the spirit of which they would do better to study more closely, and which, as seen at Morley, cannot fail to inspire and freshen all those with whom it comes in contact.'

Among the many musical ventures of these war-time years, space can be found to record only two. One was a joke. *English Opera as She is Wrote* gave full play to Holst's riotous sense of humour. It was first performed in February, 1918, and was advertised as a 'work in six acts and five languages (including tonic sol-fa)—with a vast orchestra, five hidden choirs of mermaids and a chorus of Italian brigands disguised as fir trees and food inspectors. The scenery and lighting will be beyond words, even those of an N.C.O.' Further announcements warned the College that the first act would be in the manner of English ballad opera, the second would take on Italian characteristics, and the third (in which the heroine would be reincarnated as Scriemhild) would be deeply Teutonic and philosophical ('The relation of Time to Eternity is obvious,' wrote the composer, 'for I have disregarded the former and the whole drama suggests the latter'). The fourth act would be a subtle conception 'a la Depussy', and the fifth a ballet in the manner of Horridinsky-Kautakoff. The sixth and final act, 'before which the

186

mind reels and staggers' would portray the Opera of the Future. All this was as good as it sounded in advance. Lilian Twiselton and others gave a superb performance, and the Council demanded a repetition of the piece for the annual prize-giving. Parts of it were also performed more informally to shelterers in the tubes.

The other musical venture of which something more must be said was the Whitsun festival at Thaxted, where the Holsts had a cottage and had found a fellow-spirit in the vicar, Conrad Noel. The first occasion, in 1916, was an unforgetable experience for all those who took part. 'Mr. von Holst's choir and orchestra, consisting of Morleyites and Paulinas, arrived on Friday and Saturday, their carriages bursting with double basses, flutes, violins and clarinets, while strains of symphonies and concertos drifted from the windows.' Joined by the Thaxted singers, they then took part in an almost uninterrupted round of Purcell, Bach, Vittoria, Palestrina and Lasso, diversified by country dances and unrehearsed performances of folk-songs and Elizabethan madrigals. 'It was a feast—an orgy,' wrote Holst afterwards to W. G. Whittaker. 'Four whole days of perpetual singing and playing, either properly arranged in the church or impromptu in various houses or still more impromptu in ploughed fields during thunderstorms, or in the train going home. . . . Take Bach's *Missa Brevis*, for instance. The Morleyites had practised it since January. On June 3rd they did it *twice through* at their concert. On June 10th they rehearsed it and other things for three hours in Thaxted church. On Whitsunday we did it during the service in the morning, and again in the evening, and again on Monday morning. And then some enthusiasts

187

went through it again on Tuesday morning. . . . In the intervals between the services people drifted into church and sang motets or played violin and 'cello. And others caught bad colds through going long walks in the pouring rain singing madrigals and folk-songs and rounds the whole time.

'The effect on us all was indescribable. We weren't merely excited—we were quite normal, only rather more alive than usual. . . . I realize now why the Bible insists on heaven being a place (I should call it a condition) where people sing and *go on singing*. We kept it up at Thaxted about fourteen hours a day. The reason why we didn't do more is that we were not capable mentally or physically of realizing heaven any further. Still, as far as it went, it was heaven. Just as the average amateur's way of using music as a sedative or a stimulant is purgatory, and the professional's way of using music as a topic of conversation or as a means of getting money is hell. . . . Music, being identical with heaven, isn't a thing of momentary thrills, or even hourly ones. It's a condition of eternity.'

It was little wonder, with such a tutor as this, that many Morleyites of 1914–18 should have felt that there were bigger and more important things even than the war; or that young Fabian Reeves of the orchestra, who met a pilot's death with the R.N.A.S., should have thought to leave his two flutes to the College 'for the use of students unable to afford an instrument'. And it was little wonder that another student, after the Thaxted festival of 1918, could write: 'At a time like the present let us by all means cling to our music—cling if need be like the proverbial drowning man to a straw. For it is not, as some would tell us, a luxury to be sacrificed at

188

5*a* 61, Westminster Bridge Road, 1924

5*b* 61, Westminster Bridge Road, 16th October, 1940

6

Mural Decoration by Eric Ravilious
Including the Kensington Apartment-House

the bidding of "Dora"; rather is it to be cherished as an ever-present witness for sweetness and sanity in a world deliberately giving itself over to madness and passion—the abiding voice of that power which makes all things new, raised in eternal protest against the Realism which has turned Europe into a slaughterhouse.'

* * *

During the war years there died two elderly ladies whose connection with the College dated right back to the days of the foundation. In 1916 Ethel Everest died at that home at Hever to which she had invited so many generations of Morley students; in her will she left the house and farm to the National Trust in memory of Emma Cons, whose ashes had been buried there in her beloved daffodil wood. But the Trust felt unable to take over the property; nor was expression given to the deceased's hope that a room would be set aside in the house for the use of visitors from Morley College. The following year there died Constance Martineau, a formidable character sometimes nicknamed 'martinet', but one who had never weakened in her affection for the College, and who now crowned her many gifts with a legacy of £1,000. So passed away the last of that little group of intimates who had helped Emma Cons to bring the College into being, and of whom William Rivers now wrote: 'What a potential of all goodness that is humanly possible was stored in and intelligently released by them!'

The inevitable time-barrier between the old and the young, the stalwarts of the past and the stalwarts of the present and future, was now fast establishing itself, and soon there would be few connected with the College who remembered its earliest years. Meanwhile the war, which had offered a far more violent threat to continuity, had at last drawn to its close, and from the spring of 1919 the men were returning from the Forces. With appetites for study sharpened rather than blunted by their experiences, they hastened to rejoin the College, so that 1919 saw classes continuing far into the summer.

The men came back: which was far from providing a reason why the newly joined women should stay away. The 1918–19 session, with 1,216 enrolments including those of 307 men, saw the College fuller than in 1913–14. But it was nothing to what was to come. As the releases from the army continued and talk of reconstruction filled the air, the sap once more rose in the tree of education. A new Education Act, the work of H. A. L. Fisher, promised a higher school-leaving age and a great expansion of continuation work. For adult education, A. L. Smith, Mansbridge, Tawney and others produced that seminal '1919 Report' which 'has served two generations as a store of information and ideas.'[1] In conformity with the spirit of all this, the College population increased sharply. In 1919–20 enrolment reached 1,613, of whom 614 were men; the following session it climbed to 1,797 (673 men), and there attained its post-war peak. By this time hundreds of would-be students were being turned away, the class-rooms were packed almost beyond capacity, the lecture-hall and Common Room could no longer accommodate all those who crowded to the social functions, and in a desperate effort to gain a few more cubic feet the College took to hiring, at half a crown a night, the sitting-room of Church the caretaker.

In such conditions it was not long before the clubs

[1] R. D. Waller in *A Design for Democracy* (Parrish, 1956).

were on their feet again. By 1920 tennis, football, cycling and the rest were in full swing, and the ranks of the clubs which met inside the College were swelled by a newly formed Psychological Society. A year later the scientific branches of the social activity, more or less in abeyance during the war, took on a new lease of life. On the inspiration of William Rivers they were detached from their association with the ramblers, who now became the Rambling Club *tout court*, and linked up with the long-established Lambeth Field Club. For many years after this the Lambeth Field Club and Morley College Scientific Society, as the joint organization was called, did admirable work in many spheres including those of microscopy, photography and wireless.

Of the other clubs, none showed more activity than the revived Literary and Debating Society. The star of this was now William Margrie, who was later to become an alderman of his native borough and the self-styled 'Sage of Camberwell'. A wit and an eccentric with a genius for self-advertisement, allied to an uncommon measure of common sense, he was soon by way of being a local Bernard Shaw. 'In some classes,' he wrote in the College Magazine, 'the majority of the students remain dumb. That is because they are afraid of exposing their ignorance. Such a fear is impossible in the Debating Society, because we are all equally ignorant.' Possibly encouraged by this invitation, the students rejoined the society in large numbers, and soon Margrie was staging a series of notable meetings. Some of these took the form of mock trials or royal commissions, with Chettle, Niemeyer and others of the Council participating. Lloyd George, for instance, was tried on various charges,

191

including that of failing to provide homes for heroes. Later the society considered the question of Home Rule for Animals, and the still more important subject of a New Capital for the Commonwealth. After various places had put forward their titles, South London urged its claims with the statement that it contained Morley College. This argument was regarded as decisive and by unanimous vote the meeting transferred the hub of empire across the river.

Among other social activities the terminal soirées quickly regained their pre-war quality. At one of them Edmund Fellowes, for instance, sang Elizabethan songs to his own accompaniment on the lute—an instrument which at that date few people in Morley College, or indeed in England, had ever heard. Of all the pre-war social functions only one, in fact, could not be successfully revived—the annual Clubs' Dinner. An annual College outing and an annual Christmas Party organized by the Advisory (formerly Consultative) Committee under the energetic chairmanship of A. S. Collingridge was felt to provide adequate compensation.

The class-work in these early post-war years displayed all the same vigour as the social activity. Hard-pressed as it was for accommodation, the College willingly agreed to the transfer of the cookery classes to the Borough Polytechnic, but apart from this it was a question of adding new subjects rather than dropping old. The period also saw the arrival of several highly gifted new tutors. In 1918–19 Miss N. Noble took over the women's gymnasium on the retirement of Miss Daphne Milman. That same year W. B. Honey, a student who was later to become a famous authority on ceramics, began lec-

192

turing on art. The following year Bertrand Russell (who later married Frederick Black's daughter Dora, for some time Honorary Secretary to the Council) undertook a class in psychology. The students found him at times difficult to follow but nevertheless immensely stimulating. Indeed the subject became so popular that a second psychology class had to be started. Half-way through his course Russell broke his collar-bone, but he was evidently as resilient in middle life as in old age, and missed only one lecture. That same session Hugh Dalton began a three-year tutorial in economics, a class remembered not only for the ability of the tutor but also for his geniality and readiness to accompany his students on country walks. Of this class the annual report recorded that 'the lengthy discussions could not be concluded in the allotted time, so that lecturer and students usually adjourned to the refreshment room for an extra hour.'

The following year, 1920–1, Dr. Lionel Tayler was lecturing on occupational problems, Dr. Markham Lee on modern Russian music and S. P. B. Mais on English literature. Two years later Miss St. Clare Byrne began a notable series on historical subjects and by 1923–4 students could listen to H. J. Laski offering an unconventional analysis of 'Modern Social Problems'.

On the musical side the work remained as exciting as ever. During 1919, while Holst was in Salonika (and sending back to Morley for part-songs for the troops), his place at the College was taken by Dr. (later Sir) Richard Terry.[1] Immensely popular with all, and later

[1] The success of Holst's efforts in Salonika may be judged from the following description of a concert written to a College friend in February, 1919: 'Never, never have I seen such an audience. They sat on seats, on

(*continued overleaf*)

193

one of the teachers' representatives on the Council, Terry had nevertheless one weakness. He was so great a lover of conversation, and so gifted a raconteur, that often the evening's practice was over before much strictly musical work had been done. On one occasion, at the final rehearsal before a concert, he consequently found the programme so little ready for performance that he burst into tears and left the platform. Whereupon Vally Lasker picked up the baton and took the students through several hours of the most strenuous practice, with the result that all went well—under Terry—at the concert the following day.

By the beginning of the 1919–20 session Holst was back at the College, though it was Terry who conducted that autumn an admirable performance of Gluck's *Orpheus*, with Lilian Twiselton and Dulcie Nutting in the main roles. The first 'music students' social' after Holst's return took place in February, 1920, and was full of the usual good things, with Steuart Wilson singing 'Onaway, Awake' in an impromptu performance of *Hiawatha*, and Myra Hess discovered among the audience and prevailed upon to play. On this sort of level the musical activity continued. The 1920–1 session, for instance, was notable not only for the choir and orchestra making a clean sweep of the prizes at the newly founded

the ground, on petrol tins, on instrument cases (the double bass one held five men and a dog); they sat among the orchestra, behind the choir and in the green rooms; all round the theatre people were standing from four to six deep, besides the crowd outside. Moreover so many people had to be refused that we were forced to repeat the concert. So that about 3,000 people here are at least aware (*a*) that soldiers are prepared to take music seriously, and (*b*) that there is such a thing as British music. In fact they come and tell me so, which is gratifying and even comic after my efforts to say so to them previously.'

194

South London Music Festival, but also for the presentation, in conjunction with the girls of St. Paul's, of a pageant based on Purcell's music to *Dioclesian.* This was the invention of Holst, who extracted the forgotten music from its original dramatic setting, pieced it together to a mimed story specially written by Jane Joseph, and provided what the *Daily Telegraph* called 'a glorious experience'. The following year there were other excellent concerts, after one of which the visiting critic, Vaughan Williams, was moved to write: 'There is a great danger of the Morley concerts becoming a fashionable institution. How terrible it would be if it became "the thing" for people to form "Morley parties" and to bring down the wild hordes of Mayfair to invade our quiet groves. The danger is a real one, and why? Because there is to be found in these Morley concerts something to be found nowhere else in London—intense enthusiasm controlled and directed by a master mind. When these two factors are in conjunction, achievement seems to have no limits. To me, there are no concerts like the Morley concerts. . . . Morley students are indeed lucky to have Mr. Holst as their musical director; but Mr. Holst is lucky to have the Morley students to direct.'

So Morley music continued, with its hold on the College growing stronger every year. In January, 1923, a special concert to commemorate the tercentenary of the deaths of Byrd and Weelkes found so many students unable to gain admission that it had to be repeated the following week. But at the very height of interest and enthusiasm, Holst and the College met with a cruel blow. In February, 1923, Holst was conducting at Reading University when he stepped backwards from the rostrum

195

and suffered a serious fall. Away from Morley for the rest of the session—P. J. Collis and Vaughan Williams helped to fill the gap—he returned in September only to find his health still gravely impaired by the after-effects of concussion. Medical advice insisted on reduced commitments, and since the Morley work came at the end of the day it was Morley that had to go. Early in 1924 he retired from the musical directorship and thenceforward the College knew him only as a visitor and a friend. His place was taken by Dr. Arnold Goldsbrough, then the organist of St. Martin-in-the-Fields, who within a few months completed a project very near to Holst's heart. At the King George's Hall in June the Morley Choir and Orchestra gave a concert devoted entirely to the works of Vaughan Williams—the first to be given in London. 'With great good humour,' reported the College Magazine, 'Dr. Vaughan Williams honoured the concert with his presence and did his best to disguise any surprise he may have felt at the liberties taken with his music.'

Of other changes during these first post-war years we may note the resignation in 1919 of one ex-student College secretary, A. H. Green, and his replacement by another—Fred Snelling, who had been a pillar of the College social life since the nineties. There was also the retirement from the Council in 1922, and death soon afterwards, of James Clough, one of the original students, who had endeared himself to all by more than thirty years of quiet, devoted service. His place was taken by another of the older generation, William Rivers, who had already served on the Council as a student member at the beginning of the century.

The session of 1919–20 also saw two developments of

196

interest in the daytime use of the building. An Infants' Welfare Centre was started on the initiative of the College authorities; and in response to a request from the L.C.C. accommodation was provided for one of the new Day Continuation Schools. The latter started in a great hurry, as the axe of economy threatened, and Sir Robert Blair at the L.C.C. feared that if the school were not opened at once the whole project would be put back for ten years. The extremely co-operative attitude of the College in this matter doubtless registered favourably at County Hall. At any rate, after the fees charged to the students had been brought into line with corresponding fees in L.C.C. institutes, the L.C.C. went so far as to state that Morley College was being run at a cost below that of lesser aided institutes, and to recommend and subsidize increased expenditure, including higher salaries for the staff. This novel and welcome development might well be counted the most significant of all the changes in the years from 1918 to 1924, but for an even more basic matter which had been gravely concerning the College since 1919, and which now in 1924 was at last brought to a happy conclusion.

* * *

In the years that followed Lilian Baylis's initial Shakespearian season, nothing less was established at the Vic than a permanent home for the great masterpieces of drama. Between 1914 and 1917 Ben Greet produced thirty-eight plays, of which twenty-seven were by Shakespeare. At a time when almost every other management in London was trying to tempt its war-weary audiences with entertainments like *Chu Chin Chow* or *A Piece of Fluff*, Lilian Baylis offered nothing but the highest and best.

197

Her courage was rewarded not only by fuller houses, but also by the enthusiastic support of many of the leaders of the English stage. Ellen Terry, Madge Kendal, Lena Ashwell, Constance Collier, Sir Frank Benson, Sir Herbert Tree—all appeared before the opera audiences to commend the Shakespeare productions. Among the resident company, Sybil and Russell Thorndike quickly won the hearts of the patrons and found, like many others, that the relationship between players and audience at the Vic was closer and warmer than at any other theatre. Perhaps this was not surprising, considering the audience were often called on to provide 'supers' for the next production. For this form of co-operation Morley College students frequently volunteered, to be rewarded by the economical Lilian with a cup of coffee and a slice of cake.

Amid all this the penny popular lectures still took place on Tuesday, though the Friday temperance meetings went by the board. Opera, too, continued on Thursdays and Saturdays to attract full and appreciative houses—even if attendance fell off for Wagner (whose works other managements withdrew). By the end of the war the scene at the Vic was thus one of intense enthusiasm and activity, with notable theatrical achievements already behind and the possibility of great developments ahead. Money, of course, was tight, but then it always had been. In any case, financial difficulties had a habit of yielding to Lilian Baylis's three standard remedies—hard work, economy and prayer.

Into this scene of purposeful and progressive activity there arrived in 1921 what came to be called the L.C.C.'s 'bombshell'. This was a warning that the dramatic licence would not be renewed unless major structural alterations

198

were undertaken in the interests both of safety and of dressing accommodation. The L.C.C. licensing authorities, it appeared, did not approve of class-rooms 'running above, below and behind the stage'. There was only one way of conforming to the L.C.C.'s new requirements. Morley College must go.

In point of fact the bombshell, though explosive enough, was scarcely a surprise, nor to one party at least was it entirely unwelcome. The L.C.C. had been complaining for some years; and if more space could be gained for dressing-rooms at the Morley College end of the building it would certainly be a godsend from the point of view of the theatre. At all events there was no doubt that the actors at the Vic were, to say the least, cramped. Constance Willis has recorded how there were only 'two small dressing-rooms on the side of the stage, four people in each making a crush; . . . principals dressed in the office and choristers who were not able to get in the small dressing-rooms dressed behind a curtain, the wardrobe door, the lavatory door, anywhere they could, and made up wherever there was a ray of light'. All the remaining dressing-space of the theatre had gone to form Morley College. Though now rendered acute by the L.C.C.'s demand and by the rapid expansion of dramatic activity under Lilian Baylis, the problem had for long existed in a less pressing form. It was some years before the war that Mary Sheepshanks had gazed with bewilderment at the Vic dressing-rooms and asked Bob, the stage carpenter, how on earth the performers managed. 'Well, ma'am,' he had replied, 'some of the ladies dresses and undresses in the wings—and us chaps don't look.'

199

It was in March, 1921, that the Governors of the Vic formally approached the College Council about the new development. To enable the Vic to comply with the L.C.C. requirements, they asked that the College should vacate its part of the building. To the College such a suggestion was, of course, highly unwelcome; for while the existing accommodation was inadequate for the ever-increasing numbers of students, the Council had always hoped to remedy this by extending the College over the site of the public house next door. Indeed plans for this purpose had been drawn up before the war, and a few hundred pounds collected for the purpose. To sever all the old associations and depart, even if satisfactory terms for the divorce could be arranged, was not a step which the College could readily contemplate. Nevertheless its Council at once agreed to co-operate. Under the guidance of Chettle it formulated a principle from which it never budged during all the complicated negotiations which followed. It would help the Vic 'in every way consistent with its trusts'. Translated into practical terms, this meant that the College would give up its existing accommodation, legally secured though it was by Order in Council, if the Vic would provide equivalent accommodation elsewhere.

Within two months the College found alternative premises which it was prepared to accept. The Licensed Victuallers' Schools in Upper Kennington Lane were up for sale and the College agreed to move there if the Vic would buy the buildings and meet the bill for repairs. At once a difficulty appeared. The cost of the building, at £20,000, was far more than the Vic had in hand or could readily raise. To help bridge the gap, the Vic

Governors were prepared to mortgage the theatre's foundation endowment of £650 per annum from the City Parochial Foundation; and they considered that the College should do likewise with its £350 per annum. This suggestion was put to some representatives of the College Council at a joint meeting with the Vic Governors; and Sir Wilmot Herringham, the Vic chairman, was in little doubt of its unfavourable reception. 'I do not know how far Chettle can control his Council,' he wrote afterwards to the Clerk of the City Parochial Foundation, 'but there were some uncommon sticky members of it sitting near me. I should not be surprised if they jibbed.' Jib they duly did; for they could hardly forgo the College's only assured income to help another institution, however closely related. Clearly, therefore, only large additional funds could solve the problem. In November, 1921, the Vic, under the names of H. H. Asquith and many other distinguished persons, accordingly appealed to the public to subscribe £20,000 towards the estimated total of £30,000 needed for the twin purposes of improving the Vic and rehousing the College.

This appeal, despite the names of the eminent people and some enthusiastic work within the College, where class collections yielded a few shillings every night, for some time made only slow headway. After six months little more than £5,000 had been subscribed and the chance of acquiring the Licensed Victuallers' Schools had disappeared. Salvation, however, was at hand. In June, 1922, J. L. Garvin of the *Observer*, who had throughout given strong support, announced a princely gift. The donor proved to be Mr. (later Sir) George Dance, the distinguished theatrical manager. The cheque he wrote was for

£30,000—the whole estimated cost of the entire double project.

This seemed to settle any financial difficulties, and the question now became one of suitable premises. A long search, in the course of which Clare Brennand examined not merely scholastic buildings but also mission halls, shops, factories and a motor works, eventually convinced all concerned that the only available place in the neighbourhood which was at all practicable was the Yorkshire Society's disused school in the Westminster Bridge Road. 'Terribly dirty and dilapidated,' ran Chettle's report after seeing the building. Nevertheless to the Yorkshire Society's School the College in October agreed to move, always on condition that the Vic acquired the premises and paid for suitable alterations to make the accommodation equivalent to what was being given up.

At this stage finance once more reared its ugly head. When to the price of the building was added the estimated cost of the renovation and extension considered necessary by the College, the total sum came to £27,000. This would have left the Vic insufficient for its own reconstruction. A distinct acrimony now crept into the proceedings. The Governors of the theatre tried to take their stand upon a superficially reasonable but from the College point of view entirely unacceptable principle—that the College should be compensated only on an agreed value of the premises it was vacating. As these premises were worth very little to anyone except the College or the Vic, this would have produced only a sum which would have been quite useless for obtaining fresh accommodation. Failing to budge the College Council—or the Minister of Education, to whom Sir Wilmot

Herringham also wrote—on this line, the Vic Governors then tried to show that the alterations demanded by the College were excessive. In this they had the support of the L.C.C. official valuer, who at first thought that an adequate conversion could be made for £10,000 and then suggested £14,500. To this the College Council, firmly led by Chettle, retorted that the Vic Governors had never had an architect on the job, and refused to abate any part of its claim. But the Vic would not budge either; and its final offer of £21,000, to include the purchase price of the building, came £6,000 short of the College's claim. At this margin of disagreement the two parties stuck.

In this unhappy wrangle the Vic was naturally able to command much more sympathy than the College. Many influential persons were excited by the new Shakespearian ventures, and few knew of the no less valuable work which went on at the other end of the building. The College, it was said, must be dazzled by the size of Mr. Dance's cheque; and this view became the official one at County Hall after the L.C.C. valuer's report. Chettle and the College Council, however, were the last people to fight for an unjust cause; it must have been singularly galling to them to be informed, as the L.C.C. Education Officer (Sir Robert Blair) informed them in November, 1922, that unless they came to an agreement with the Vic within five weeks the Higher Education Committee would recommend the cessation of the L.C.C.'s annual grant to the College. This communication, perhaps one of the most remarkable ever to be made by an education authority to an educational institution which was striving to fulfil its trust and which had not departed in any way from approved educational policy, served its purpose. The bludgeon had come down, and further argument was useless. The Vic duly paid up its £21,000; and the College, still convinced that the disputed alterations were essential, set out to find the balance of the money.

On top of this problem came another. In March, 1923, the builders were just about to begin when the College and the Vic alike learned with horror of a bill promoted by the London Electric Railway. Two new tube lines were to pass under the site of the Yorkshire Society's School. This in itself might not have mattered; but the Company required the use of the playground for the sinking of two extraction shafts. On this site the College was intending to build a hall, for it had had one in the Vic and the new building possessed none. As the work of extracting soil was to proceed day and night for two years, educational activities in the building might well become impossible. To clinch matters, the Company proposed to arm itself with powers of compulsory purchase.

This new threat rapidly dispersed any remaining coolness between the Vic and its offspring; for if the College could not take possession of its new premises the work at the Vic would have to stop. In firm alliance, Reginald Rowe for the theatre and Chettle for the College fought a stout campaign, rejecting the Company's grossly inadequate offers of compensation and instead lodging a petition against the bill. Advised by the L.C.C.s' Parliamentary Secretary to make a speedy settlement with the Company as the bill was bound to go through, they nevertheless stuck to their guns. Great was their joy when in July, 1923, after five months of acute anxiety and complete standstill on the building operations, the bill quite

204

unexpectedly failed at the committee stage in the Lords.

By this time the College had already surrendered its largest rooms to the Vic, though the work on its own new accommodation had not yet begun. Odd rooms had therefore to be hired in schools and vicarages. In September a contract was at last signed with the builders, who undertook to complete their task within nine months. With the Vic's contribution and the proceeds of money-raising efforts by the students and staff, the College was finally left with some £5,000 to find if it was to have all the desired alterations.

To the hope that this remaining sum might come from the public purse, the Board of Education soon administered a rude shock. In February, 1924, it approved the plans for the alterations on the express condition that no public money was involved. As a reward to the College for nearly forty years' pioneer work in adult education, this was scarcely generous. Two months later, under pressure, the Board relented to the extent of stating that it would raise no objection if the L.C.C. cared to make a grant.

Meanwhile the City Parochial Foundation, which had already made a substantial contribution to the Vic appeal, was coming to the rescue. In April it agreed if necessary to lend the College the desired £5,000; and in July it went one better by offering to give £2,500 if the L.C.C. would do likewise. In September the L.C.C. agreed, and the problem of finance was solved. It remained only for classes to be moved into the rooms as they became ready, and for preparations to be made for an official opening.

The building operations were still uncompleted but the

main work was done and the new concert hall ready when on the evening of December 10th, 1924, the Prince of Wales came to perform the ceremony. Thick fog shrouded the streets, and the Prince, who had travelled by train from the country, arrived twenty minutes late. In the new hall—thenceforth to be known as the Prince of Wales Hall—appropriate speeches were made by Sir Frederick Black, Chettle and Clare Brennand, and by Fred Snelling and A. S. Collingridge for the past and present students. The Prince in his address spoke of the unique character of the College: 'In the first place, every other educational establishment which I recollect owes its origin to the determination of the older generation to drum knowledge forcibly into the more or less unwilling heads of the young. Morley College, on the other hand, originated solely from the determination of grown men and women already busy with their own jobs in life to win that knowledge for themselves. That determination, and the fruits it has borne, give your college as unique and as proud a charter as any possessed by the oldest university in the land. Secondly, this is the only college I know which is the offspring of a theatre. I do not know whether I ought to say that the Old Vic was the father or the mother of Morley College. Perhaps the Old Vic was the mother and the L.C.C. the father. Anyway, between them they have been wonderful parents, and the child, which is what we are concerned with here tonight, is a very fine and healthy specimen. I don't see why it should ever die.'

When he had declared the buildings open and been thanked, the Prince left the hall. The audience stayed to listen to a concert given by the music classes under Arnold

206

Goldsbrough, in which works by Holst, Vaughan Williams, Edmund Rubbra (a former student) and Wilfred Palmer (a present student) occupied a prominent place. Meanwhile the Prince, escorted by Chettle, was touring the building. 'He was extraordinarily jerky,' recorded Chettle in his diary, 'but most easy to get on with. He talked just as one man to another. There was only one hitch. Owing to the lateness of the hour I telescoped the tour and forgot the people in the basement. . . . I was told to keep the Prince on my right hand, but this proved impossible—he was all over the place. He was a terrific success.'

When it was all over, and the excitement had died down, and everyone (or almost everyone) agreed that the College had been successfully transplanted to a much better site and building, his colleagues on the Council made Chettle a little present of a silver cigarette-box. The inscription, composed by Niemeyer, ran: 'H. F. Chettle, Consilium Morliense. Aede Refecta, 1924.'

'The Home having been Rebuilt'. It was certainly an achievement, carried out against every kind of difficulty. And no one could foresee that sixteen years later the new home would dissolve, in a matter of seconds, into a monstrous pile of rubble and dust.

207

X

61, Westminster Bridge Road

THE building which the Prince of Wales opened in December, 1924, was an architectural hotch-potch. Its core was an elegant 18th-century town house, erected on ground leased in 1783 from an old-established institution near by—the Magdalene Hospital for the Reception of Penitent Prostitutes. After serving for forty years as a private residence, this house had been taken over in 1834 by the Yorkshire Society as a school for boys of Yorkshire birth or descent. The school had flourished, with the result that in 1885 the Society had clapped on to the 18th-century structure two flanking portions not unlike Nonconformist chapels. It had also added an extra storey with a steep pitched roof and protruding dormer windows. Thus enlarged, the compilation had served its purpose until the growing provision of education by the state had rendered the school unnecessary. In 1917 it was accord-

208

ingly closed and the building was taken over by the War Office, which established there the Britannia Club for Soldiers and Sailors. Five years later it stood dilapidated and empty when the Vic Appeal Trustees bought it for Morley College.

The main addition now made was a new block joined to the back of the building and containing not only the Prince of Wales Hall but also a gymnasium and a refreshment-room beneath. Besides this various other features such as a laboratory were added, together with an array of doors and passages the only purpose of which was to give independent access to the hall. All told, the building provided a good deal more cubic space but not much more useful floor area than the old accommodation in the Vic. Critically considered, it was a rambling structure far from ideal for its function; and as it was closely hemmed in at one side by shabby little warehouses and cottages there was little room for the free play of light and air. Externally, too, the general effect was not improved by the huge legend in concrete, MORLEY COLLEGE FOR WORKING MEN AND WOMEN, which was now affixed at roof-level across the breadth of the façade—and which, being too high to be read from the pavement, was soon duplicated by notice-boards below. Nevertheless, everyone was extremely proud of the new home; for the full horror of the Victorian abutments was concealed from the street by pleasant trees, the stage in the Prince of Wales Hall was a notable new amenity, and inside the 18th-century core were many excellent rooms. The most notable of these was the combined reception hall and Common Room which had an elegant fanlight over the front door and two near-Adam mantelpieces.

209

In this Common Room, in accordance with the old tradition of the College, the Secretary (but no longer the Principal) still maintained a desk. There were other efforts too, to preserve links with the past. They were the more needed because the Vic, in the throes of reconstruction and full of fresh plans for the future, now dropped both the Tuesday public lectures and the old half-price concession to Morley students. Like everyone else, Morleyites could still see a show at the Vic for as little as fivepence, but their days of special privileges and associations were ended. Moreover, Lilian Baylis, though she remained a good friend of the College, had nothing like Emma Cons's 'parent's fondness' for the place; and her more brusque manner alienated more than one old student who had been devoted to her aunt. William Rivers, for instance, retained a lasting impression of her entering the College, seeing him doing nothing, and ordering him to clean her bicycle; nor could he forget overhearing a row with Charles Corri in which she threatened to put Corri 'back into the gutter where she found him'. Not surprisingly then, when circumstances forced the theatre and the College apart, the break was complete. The two institutions continued to preserve a warm feeling for each other and Lilian Baylis came on occasion to talk at the College, just as groups of College students for their part remained (and remain) among the staunchest patrons of the Vic. But relationships of this kind now became purely unofficial. Of formal links between the College and the theatre there henceforth survived only one—the right of the Vic Governors to nominate two members of the College Council.

The completeness of the severance between parent and

offspring perturbed some students, who missed in the new home the atmosphere of the old and the feeling of being constantly on the fringe of exciting events. To preserve some of the old memories the College Council decided to name several rooms after those who had helped to create the College and its traditions and who were now no longer alive. Sir Frederick Black, Vice-President and doyen of those who still survived from the early days, suggested the list. Soon there was the Emma Cons Common Room, the Caroline Martineau Laboratory, the Constance Martineau Library, the Ethel Everest Gymnasium, the James Clough Council Room, the Florence Acton Refreshment Room. In due course enlarged photographs of most of these former pillars of the College adorned the Common Room. One other souvenir, too, of the Vic days was retained (in addition to the ancient furniture, kept solely for lack of money to buy better). The terra-cotta group representing Samuel Morley amid working-men which had surmounted the entrance to the College was brought across and re-erected within the new building.

If some of the old faithfuls among the students felt lost and strange in the new home, this certainly did not apply to the majority, who were extremely content to be in more impressive and commodious premises. Moreover, newcomers were soon knocking at the gates. In 1923–4, the last session in Waterloo Road, there were 1,520 students; in 1924–5, the first session in Westminster Bridge Road, 1,681. The next year the total was only five short of 2,000, and in 1926–7 it rose to 2,171. Within three years of moving the College thus increased its numbers by more than a third.

To see how far the student body had changed since the

foundation, it is perhaps worth while to glance further at the 1,520 students who enrolled during 1923–4, the last year in the Royal Victoria Hall. A full two-thirds of them were women, as against a mere handful in 1889–90. Almost a half had had secondary education—a dramatic change from thirty-five years earlier, when it seems that no students at all had been to anything more than an elementary school. (The change was not at root due to that malady so frequently diagnosed by historians of adult education, 'capture of a working class institution by the middle classes', but to the fact that much more free secondary education had become available from 1902.) As for occupation, a fifth of the men in 1923–4 and rather more than a quarter of the women were in manual, craft, or workshop jobs; all the rest were in commercial, administrative, professional or clerical work, mostly in offices. In 1889, though it is not possible to state an exact comparison, the 'clerks' had outnumbered the 'engineers' by little more than two to one. The polytechnics, it was clear, had since 1889 proved a bigger attraction for the 'mechanics' and therefore for the males.

Two other differences between the student body at the two dates also stand out. In 1889–90 almost half of the students were under twenty; in 1923–4 the under-twenties numbered less than a fifth. The average age of the student population was steadily rising—a reflection of the later age at which most people now left school, and of the widespread provision of recreational and commercial classes elsewhere in London. The second difference was equally plain. Though there is no reliable record of which subjects were taken by most students in 1889–90, technical classes came top of the list. By 1913–14, as already recorded, commercial classes were at the top, modern languages second and science near the bottom. By 1923–4 modern languages were a very easy first, attracting almost twice as many students as any other set of subjects; and music was second with a short lead over the commercial group. Clearly the curriculum of the institution was moving in a certain direction. And this was the direction, remarkably enough, pointed out by the founders—'the advanced study of subjects of knowledge not directly connected with or applied to any handicraft, trade or business'.

Two further points may also be noted, one of contrast and one of similarity. By 1923–4 there remained only two 'voluntary' teachers in the College—those taking Greek and Latin. In view of the small number of students involved, these classes could not attract a grant, and so still depended on unpaid tuition. Thirty-five years before, unpaid tutors had been the backbone of the staff. The other point shows that whatever else had changed since 1889, Morley in 1924 was still a College for South London. Small numbers of students indeed came to it from all over the Home Counties; but when it moved out from the Victoria Hall, of its 1,520 students no less than 1,200 still lived in the South London boroughs. Within that 1,200, more than half were local folk from Lambeth and Southwark. The College was still mainly serving the neighbourhood which Emma Cons had set out nearly half a century earlier to reclaim from the forces of ignorance and strong drink.

* * *

The continued increase in numbers after 1924 makes it plain that the uprooting of the College brought no

213

set-back in the work. In fact the very first session in the new building saw several interesting developments. Dr. Elizabeth Sloan Chesser, for example, began a series of lectures on health subjects and revived the afternoon class on Infant Care. At the same time book-keeping was dropped from the curriculum as a first step towards the complete elimination of commercial subjects, historical geography and classical dancing were added, and folk-dancing was promoted from an activity confined to Saturday nights to the normal dignity of an official class. A new string orchestra was started, and the following session arrangements were made for another distinguished musician, Herbert Howells, to join the music staff. The concerts and all the other customary activities were continued with success. As for the clubs, their enthusiasm may perhaps be seen from the example of the Ramblers, who not only arranged several walks of thirty miles but also dined together in the Forest of Hainault on Christmas Day.

All, then, went well in the new home; but before long there came the inevitable disappearance of still more links with the past. Lady Frederick Cavendish, one of the original Council of the College and a supporter to the last, died in 1925. In the same year Miss G. V. Young, the Librarian, retired after many years' devoted service, and was succeeded by Felix Webster, a student since 1906 and a true 'Morley character' with a burning love for books and the theatre. A few months later, at the end of the 1924–5 session, the Council learned with great regret but perhaps without surprise that Clare Brennand wished to resign. The strain of the war years followed by the many crises connected with the move from the Vic had been intense, and her health was no longer equal to the burden

214

of continuous evening work. She consented to stay during the following term, and then left at the end of 1925. On her departure the student Chairman of the Advisory Committee well expressed the general feeling when he wrote:

'During the last twelve years she has directed the educational and social activities of the College with conspicuous ability and success, and her self-sacrificing devotion to the best interests of the students has engendered in all who have come into touch with her, deep feelings of respect and affection. In this period the numbers have doubled, the standards have been raised, and the usefulness of the College developed. Under her guidance we have passed through a time of national stress and crisis, and have also had our own crisis in the removal from our old building in the Waterloo Road to the new and splendid College which we now enjoy and which, largely owing to her efforts, we have been able to enter practically free of debt. Her scholarship, her personality, her loyalty to the aims for which Morley stands have been essential factors in the progress of our work. . . .'

It was indeed much that the College owed to the departing Vice-Principal. And it was typical of her that both her speech at the royal opening in 1924 and her farewell speech at her last prize distribution ignored any achievements of which the credit might have redounded to herself, and instead concentrated on two College needs for the future—a week-end camping site and a sports ground.

Faced with the task of finding a new director for the College, the Council first hesitated and then came down

215

unanimously in favour of a bold choice. Once more it was to a woman that they offered the post. Overcoming—in the Vice-Chairman's words—'their fear of her tender years and golden curls', they appointed Mrs. Barbara Wootton, who at twenty-eight already had behind her some years of experience as a tutor in economics at Girton and as research officer to the Trade Union Congress and Labour Party. She took up her new duties in January, 1926; and in response to a suggestion from the L.C.C., the College Council accorded to her the full title of Principal which it had somewhat thoughtlessly withheld from Clare Brennand. In so doing it at last recognized that it was not going to find a suitable active unpaid Principal—a post vacant since 1910, and scarcely canvassed for at least a dozen years.

Barbara Wootton had barely begun work when the College Secretary, A. G. Disney, who had succeeded Frederick Snelling only four terms earlier, fell ill with pneumonia and died. The blow to even the ablest of new Principals must have been severe. Fortunately the new Secretary, when he was appointed in April, 1926, took up his duties as to the manner born. George Cottrell had previously been assistant secretary to the Huddersfield Technical College. Within a few months at Morley he had earned himself a remarkable tribute in the annual report: 'From the first day that he crossed the threshold of the College, Mr. Cottrell identified himself with the work in a manner rarely equalled, so that few could have guessed that he had not been associated with the College for many years. The Council feel that they have every reason to congratulate themselves upon the appointment.' Thirty-two years have passed since those words

216

were written; George Cottrell is still Secretary of Morley College; and successive Councils are still congratulating themselves on the fact.

The new Principal soon showed all her expected energy and freshness of approach. In the class-work, Kingsley Martin began a series of lectures on 'English Ideas of the Nineteenth Century', May Wallas on 'French Life, Literature and History', and the Principal herself on 'Problems of the Wage Earner'. The time given to shorthand and typewriting was reduced by about a half, and plans were made to eliminate commercial subjects entirely the following season—for clearly there would be no difficulty in filling classes of a more cultural nature. In the process of dropping the commercial subjects a reluctant good-bye had to be said to W. Drywood, who unpaid and paid had taught typewriting for more than twenty years; and at the same time the College also said farewell to another teacher of twenty years' standing, Leonard Howard of the elocution classes.

Side by side with these changes went interesting new ventures outside the classes. In response to a suggestion by the Council that the College should carry on the 'penny' popular lectures recently dropped by the Vic, Mrs. Wootton persuaded three eminent men—R. H. Tawney, Sir Josiah Stamp and Lord Thompson—to deliver lectures which were open free of charge to the general public. This proved to be the beginning of a notable enlargement of the College activities. Another innovation arose from the Principal's own recommendation. College examinations were discontinued as having outlived their usefulness; and to compensate for the loss of the annual prizegiving and presentation of certificates,

217

an Open Week was instituted, with special performances on the final Saturday night. The money previously used to buy prizes was awarded instead in the form of small bursaries for foreign travel and attendance at summer schools. At the same time the 'democratic' element in the College organization was encouraged by the complete transfer of the Magazine into student hands, so that it became entirely an organ of student opinion instead of partly an official bulletin. Thenceforth this resilient journal, better in format than ever before and pulsating with renewed vigour, for some years pursued a lively career under an exceptionally able student editor, D. J. Moxley.

There were other developments too which, as so often at the College, simply arose spontaneously from the body of students and ex-students. A Folk Dance Club was formed, straightway won the Harmsworth Trophy at the Hampstead Festival, and within eighteen months had some 200 members. To this day it remains one of the strongest and most active of all the Morley clubs. Also in 1926, an old students' group—the Old Morleyite Association—was founded to provide a focus for all those, whether past or present students, who had put in five years or more at the College. With Frederick Snelling as its secretary it was sure of a good start, and it was soon notable for the enterprise of its outings and the friendly atmosphere and warmth of its gatherings. It also did—and does—much to keep alive in Morley the recollection of the founders and of the old ties with the Vic.

All these were pleasant things, but one task the new Principal must have viewed with a certain distaste. A debt of nearly £3,000 remained from the building operations, and it was among her duties to explore ways and means of clearing it off. In a very short time she was completely successful. Two strokes did the trick. One had strings attached: the L.C.C. agreed to pay the College an extra £700 a year for three years in return for permission to run a day continuation school in the new building. The other came as a gift from the blue—in this case the true blue. Hearing of the situation from Mrs. Wootton at a reception, Lady Astor retired for a few moments and returned to press into the hands of the astonished Principal a cheque in favour of Morley College for £750.

The new Principal's first year, then, was certainly not devoid of incident and success. Already she had a distinctive policy—the development of university extra-mural classes and further links with the W.E.A.; and this policy was fully acceptable to the Council. It was accordingly with something of a shock that that body heard, only eighteen months after Mrs. Wootton had come to Morley, that she desired to move to another post.

The post—the Directorship of Studies for Tutorial Classes in the University of London—was certainly one for which Mrs. Wootton had unique qualifications of aptitude, experience and sympathy. The Council understood her decision, accepted her resignation 'with the greatest regret', and acknowledged 'that the wider opportunities of the new appointment made it impossible to question the wisdom of her decision'. They also placed on record their feeling 'that in the short term of her Principalship she raised the standing and increased the importance of the College, developed its educational and social work, and improved its administration'.

The Principal's resignation was accepted on July 4th,

219

1927, at an 'emergency' meeting called after the end of the session. A small selection committee, including Chettle and Niemeyer, was at once set up. By August 8th this committee had advertised the post, weeded out the applications of more than 130 highly qualified people, interviewed several of the candidates, presented a short list of two to the full Council, and heard that body make a unanimous choice. It was a remarkable piece of work, especially as it produced Eva Hubback.

220

XI

Eva Hubback and the Thirties

LIKE her predecessor, the new Principal had lost her husband in the First World War after a brief married life. Left with three young children, she had continued to keep together a true family home and at the same time engage in a full-time profession. After a short period as a tutor in economics at Newham she had taken a post in the National Union of Women's Suffrage Societies, and had become both parliamentary and general secretary to that body's successor, the National Union of Societies for Equal Citizenship. It was with nearly ten years' experience not only of administration but of British public affairs at their heart and centre, in the lobbies and corridors of Westminster, that in 1927 Eva Hubback came to Morley.

Born in 1886 of a wealthy Anglo-Jewish family, Eva had inflicted two painful shocks upon her devoted parents. The first was when she insisted on going up to a university. In this case opposition finally dispersed when she took a First Class in Part II of the Economics Tripos—a feat achieved in her year by one other woman and no man. The second was when she married a Gentile, F. W. Hubback, a fellow-spirit at Cambridge and later a university lecturer. She was long since forgiven for both breaches of the parental wishes and in the Spielman family circle, together with their relatives and associates the Bentwiches, the Raphaels, the Samuels, the Josephs, the Franklins, the Waley Cohens and others, she enjoyed the friendship and support of the highly intelligent and public-spirited group at the head of Anglo-Jewry. From her Cambridge days, too, she had another wide circle of friends, many of them, like herself, early members of the Fabian Society—Shena Potter (later Lady Simon), Amber Reeves (later Mrs. Blanco White), the Walter Laytons, the Cornfords, the Oliviers, Hugh Dalton, Maynard Keynes, J. C. Squire and others. And from her work for the National Union of Societies for Equal Citizenship she was on friendly terms with all the prominent women of the country (and notably with Eleanor Rathbone and Mary Stocks) and on at least conversational terms with half the public men. So extensive an array of influential and progressive acquaintances was no small help in the tasks which lay ahead.

A multitude of useful friends, however, was not Eva Hubback's main recommendation for the Principalship of Morley College. That, of course, lay in her achievements and her personality. In her work for the National Union she had been one of the main instruments in securing a host of long overdue reforms. Thanks in great part to her activity, by 1927 women were eligible to be

222

permanent officials of the civil service, to become magistrates, to serve on juries, to divorce their husbands for adultery, to enjoy equal right of guardianship over children—none of which things could they do in 1919, when she began active work for the Union. And a year after she came to Morley the Franchise Act of 1928 gave the vote to every woman over twenty-one, and so set the final seal of success on the whole women's suffrage movement. Meantime, too, she had kept up her interest in economics and her skill as a tutor by taking extra-mural classes for Oxford and London universities, and by acting as a visiting teacher at Streatham Hill High School. These were her achievements. The force and attraction of her personality—expressed perhaps most strongly in brown eyes that suddenly awoke to flash amusement or indignation—were obvious enough. Careless of dress and in many ways unsophisticated, she was serious-minded, intensely active, maternal, sympathetic and direct. Possibly her two most important characteristics were a remarkable capacity for going straight to the heart of a matter, and, in the words of Mary Stocks, 'a singular talent for combining pertinacious attack with friendly and reasonable co-operation'.

Eva Hubback had not been in charge at Morley for more than a term when she was confronted by an occurrence calculated to put any educational establishment on its toes—a full-dress inspection by the Board of Education. It was the first that the College had experienced, though reports by individual inspectors had been common enough. In the event, both the College and the inspectorate acquitted themselves with distinction. The former showed up well enough to make a deep impression upon the latter, and the senior inspector's report was a

223

document of remarkable grasp which contained in its introductory paragraphs the best survey of the College history till then written.

The report also offered an admirable summing up of the policy of the College and some of its distinguishing characteristics. 'Three notable institutions,' it stated, 'the Working Men's College, Toynbee Hall and Morley College, have specially fostered adult education in London during the last half century and prepared the way for further developments in the shape of voluntary classes such as those of the Workers' Educational Association on the one hand and of the London County Council's Literary Institutes on the other. With the latter Morley College has much in common, but owing to the circumstances of its growth, by reason of its continuous tradition, its close association with such movements as University Extension and the Workers' Educational Association, and the large-minded policy of its Governing Body, the College has enjoyed certain advantages which it is difficult for publicly managed institutions to acquire. The voluntary element and the association of an independent body of governors with students and old members cannot easily be reproduced. The sense of proprietorship brings an additional sentiment into play. The freedom to experiment and to establish relations with the Universities and other bodies has had a stimulating influence. It is highly creditable to those who have been responsible for its policy that the life of the College has been one of continuous growth, not only in numbers but also in the character of its interests. It has known how to co-operate cordially with outside educational movements without being absorbed by them. It is to be hoped that the close relations with

224

the public authority entered into in recent years will still permit the exercise of the initiative and vigour which have characterized the College in the past. The distinguishing feature of the College on the purely educational side is that during a long course of years it has sought to discover the cultural interests of every section and to provide whatever was demanded. Subjects of every conceivable kind have been offered, from the days when physical and natural science had the glamour of novelty to those in which psychology promised to reveal the secrets of every aspect of life.'

Many favourable references were also made to particular departments of the College. Of the work in English Language and Literature, for instance, the report noted that 'only one or two institutions in London, and only one outside London, provide anything comparable for the student who is not a specialist or seeking a university course'. Of music it wrote: 'Taken altogether the work of the College in music is on a scale quite unique in the whole field of adult education in England.' And many were the tributes to individuals, and not least to Eva Hubback. 'It is seldom,' ran the report, 'that a new Principal can have so quickly inspired the confidence of all who come in contact with her. It is too early to pass judgment upon her work, but everything points to the probability that the College has secured the services of one who, whilst preserving the tradition of the College, will bring new energy and the influence of great ideas to extend its sphere of usefulness and to raise its already high academic standards.'[1]

[1] This very favourable verdict on the College and its directors was confirmed by an L.C.C. inspection two years later, in 1930. The L.C.C. *(continued overleaf)*

The ordeal of the inspection over, the Principal was able to devote her attention to future plans. It at once became clear to the College that a new and immensely fertile influence was at work. This extended not only to the classes but also to the appearance of the College, which soon began to take on a much brighter tone. The change was perhaps typified by the outer cover of the annual prospectus, which ceased to be a dismal concatenation of miscellaneous print on 'grey paper with blunt type' and became instead something at once simple, tasteful and colourful. And very soon she was able to report to the College Council a major development which was to revolutionize the look of the gloomy refreshment-room in the basement, and to add immensely to the appearance of the Prince of Wales Hall.

In the mid-twenties the youthful Rex Whistler had been employed, at the expense of Sir Joseph Duveen, to decorate the refreshment-room at the Tate. He had executed his commission in a spirit of gaiety completely new to British mural painting—an art which had long languished in disfavour. Impressed by the result, Sir Joseph had offered to finance a further scheme of decorations in some other public building to be recommended by Charles Aitken, the Director of the Tate. Aitken recommended Morley College, and Sir Joseph was as good as his word. Rex Whistler had been a student at the Slade, and by way

report referred to the College as 'a centre of learning and social activity which is not only permanently attractive, but is full of inspiration and helpfulness', and concluded: 'There can be no manner of doubt that the College, as at present conducted, is succeeding to a remarkable degree in fostering intellectual and aesthetic interests in a great number of the working population of this part of London. We believe it to be producing a change of outlook as to the manner in which the leisure hours of workers may profitably be spent.'

226

of spreading the benefits of Duveen's patronage Aitken therefore turned to the Royal College of Art. William Rothenstein, then the head of that institution, at once interested himself keenly in the project, and a small committee was formed which included among others himself, Aitken, H. L. Wellington, Mrs. Hubback and R. C. Davison, a member of the College Council. Six senior students and young ex-students of the Royal College were then invited to submit designs, and three of them—Edward Bawden, Eric Ravilious and Cyril Mahoney—were finally selected for the work. They were to be given their materials, and paid by time as working craftsmen—£1 for a full day's painting, ten shillings for half a day.

The result was a revelation. Bawden and Ravilious worked together on the refreshment-room, Mahoney on the hall. Mahoney's decorations, painted on site on canvas fixed to the apsidal wall at the back of the stage, represented the pleasures of life in work and play. Large figures in the foreground, planned somewhat in a 15th-century Florentine manner, represented Dancing, Plastic Art, Music, Philosophy and other pursuits; while above these, groups of country dancers, sportsmen and apple harvesters added animation to the scene. It was an impressive and finely executed work, perhaps a little on the formal side, which Rothenstein had no hesitation in later describing as 'the finest in this country since Ford Madox Brown decorated the Manchester Town Hall', and which drew from Hilaire Belloc the statement that in any other country people would have come from near and far to see it.

* * *

227

The work of Bawden and Ravilious, as befitted the room they were called upon to enliven, was in a very different vein. Here all was gaiety, wit, sharpness, freshness of invention. Taking as their theme London life, they soon found this too overwhelming; so they abandoned it, but not before Ravilious had produced a remarkable *jeu d'esprit* in his 'Kensington apartment-house'. Displayed in section like a doll's house with the front open, this was a clever and amusing piece of work which bore no relation to the rest of the decorations—for the artists moved on to an entirely different theme, the old English drama. This new subject was specially appropriate by reason of the College's connection with the Vic, and as the two young artists had both been soaking themselves in the 'Mermaid' dramatists, it set their imagination afire. Painted directly on the plaster, the resulting decorations were a remarkable combination of illustration and free fancy. The basic conception was to depict scenes from the plays on fantastic stages linked by an architectural framework and set in a landscape populated by allegorical and other figures. Ravilious showed Pomona and the Seasons, together with a series of two-tiered theatres the stages of which were occupied by Mephistopheles and Faust, a vision of the Seven Deadly Sins (with Helen of Troy near by) and scenes from Peele and Ben Jonson. Bawden for his part painted scenes from the Brome Miracle Play *Abraham and Isaac* in a church setting, together with the main wall, which he devoted entirely to Shakespeare. Episodes from *Lear*, *As You Like It, Romeo and Juliet,* and *The Tempest* were all featured, together with such linking figures as Flora, the Sad Muses (with straight hair in the intellectual manner) and the Three

Graces (a plump Semitic trio unclad save for hats and necklaces). Shakespeare himself appeared as a lean and dandified figure arm in arm with a slightly boozed Ben Jonson, and about to be crowned with a chaplet of leaves by an anxious Britannia leaning precariously from a balcony above. In all, the young artists spent about eighteen months of their free time decorating the room; and the whole work, including Mahoney's in the hall, cost Duveen some £1,200.

The impact of these delightful paintings was immediate and considerable, not only on the College but on the outside world. The art critics at once hailed the formal beauty of Mahoney's work and still more the liveliness and wit of that of Bawden and Ravilious. The *Scotsman,* for instance, spoke of 'the most amusing series of figures from classical mythology and other sources that perhaps has ever been assembled . . . there is no question that a more highly spiced and daintily dished entertainment has seldom been offered upon any walls, far less those of a College for working men and women'. In the same vein, the *Daily Chronicle* referred to 'the most entrancing piece of modern wall decoration that one has seen', and *The Times* to 'the constant entertainment to the eye and mind'. No less impressed was the *New Statesman.* 'The Morley College for Working Men and Women, in the Westminster Bridge Road,' wrote its critic, 'was built during the more unfortunate period of Victorian architecture. Half warehouse and half chapel, its unattractive façade has acquired no patina through succeeding decades. A grim edifice in a grim neighbourhood, it typifies the pains rather than the pleasures of learning. Yet the invention of three young artists, supported by the munificence of

229

Sir Joseph Duveen, has brought within its doors something of the splendour of the Muses and the delight of fairyland.'

The critics did even more. They saw in the Morley decorations, following on those of the Tate, and one or two earlier schemes, a true renaissance in British mural painting—and such indeed it proved to be. All this was very gratifying to the College, which received much publicity in the process and which shrewdly added to the effect by inducing Stanley Baldwin, then leader of the Opposition, to perform in February, 1930, an opening ceremony. It proved to be the sort of occasion which called forth Baldwin's best. In introducing him, Graham Wallas recalled that someone had once said of Morley College that nothing useful was studied there. Baldwin seized on this and developed it. 'I thank God,' he said, 'that such a place still exists.' This, with much more in his most reflective vein on the value of the arts, helped to attract further attention to the decorations and the College, and even caused left-wing students to wonder whether Baldwin might not, after all, have something in him. The following month the summit of publicity was reached when Queen Mary suddenly communicated her wish to inspect the decorations and arrived the next day. She saw more than the paintings, and retained a gracious interest in the College for the rest of her life.

* * *

The murals brought Morley College more into the news, and more into contact with the outside world, than anything since the musical activities of Gustav Holst. But they were by no means alone in attracting at this time considerable attention to the College. In 1928, during her second session as Principal, Eva Hubback began the custom of an annual College Dinner with well-known guests—whose speeches were duly reported at length in the press. On the first occasion, Lord Eustace Percy, Ellen Wilkinson and G. S. Ammon (later Lord Ammon—an early student of the College) were the chief guests; the following year Ramsay MacDonald and William Rothenstein occupied the seats of honour; and thereafter until 1938 a succession of distinguished men and women—Gilbert Murray, Lady Astor, Sir Herbert Samuel, J. C. Squire, George Lansbury, Eleanor Rathbone, Herbert Morrison, A. P. Herbert, Ben Greet and many others—graced the occasion with their speeches. In this way the function acted not only as an integrating factor within the College, drawing together some two or three hundred students from many different classes and clubs, but also as a valuable link with the worlds of politics, scholarship and the arts. And it was notable that influential persons introduced to the College in this way tended to preserve their goodwill for it long after the evening's festivities were over.

The dinners, however, took place no more than once a year. Much more important in bringing men and women of distinction into the College, in gaining their lasting friendship, and in giving the College—and the outside world—the opportunity of hearing authoritative discussions of the questions of the day, were the remarkable public lectures which Eva Hubback was soon organizing. As already mentioned, Barbara Wootton had made a tentative beginning in response to the Council's desire that the College should take on this task in succession to the Vic. Eva Hubback quickly brought the whole project to full fruition. Her first big venture, in 1928–9, began brilliantly. Admission was free—the lecturers gave their services—and no less than 800 persons crowded into the Prince of Wales Hall to hear Sir Oliver Lodge talk on 'The Moon'. Thereafter Ellen Wilkinson, Graham Wallas, Sir Michael Sadler, Viscount Cecil and others of comparable eminence occupied the rostrum at fortnightly intervals throughout the two winter terms. As the sessions proceeded, however, attendance varied sharply and in general declined. Drawing the conclusion that this was because the lectures were on unrelated topics, Eva Hubback decided thenceforth to present only connected courses built up round some central theme.

The following session she was ambitious enough to embark on two separate courses, each running at fortnightly intervals throughout two terms. Half a crown paid for either set of a dozen lectures, for the speakers were still unremunerated. For this sum the public and the College could hear Graham Wallas, Wickham Steed, G. P. Gooch, R. W. Seton-Watson, Lord Lothian, Sir Arnold Wilson, R. G. Casey, Lord Lytton and Walter Layton lecture on different aspects of 'The World After the War', or Ramsay Muir, J. J. Mallon, E. D. Simon (later Lord Simon of Wythenshawe) Eleanor Rathbone, Stella Churchill, F. W. Pethick-Lawrence and others discuss 'Social, Industrial and Political Problems'. But once again attendance, excellent in the first term, fell off in the second. This was not merely the normal seasonal decline in adult education; it was because each course was too extended. From 1930–1 onwards Eva Hubback accordingly relied on compact courses, related to the same theme, and given within the compass of a single term.

That autumn saw a series on 'England Today and Tomorrow' with Holst talking on music, Vita Sackville-West on literature, Robertson Scott on the Countryside, and Walter Elliot on the Empire; while the following term ten distinguished scientists lectured to such effect on 'Science Today and Tomorrow' that their talks were later collected and successfully published, with further gratifying results to the reputation of the College.

By 1931, then, the public lectures were an established attraction, and a mounting number of eminent men and women were becoming acquainted with the College. In the classes, too, tutors were beginning work who were known, or would later be known, on a much wider stage. Charles Hill, the later 'Radio Doctor' and Cabinet Minister, and W. E. Williams, later the creator of the Army Bureau of Current Affairs and director of the Arts Council, began lecturing in 1927; C. E. M. Joad and Arnold Foster (who succeeded Arnold Goldsbrough as Director of Music) in 1928; Susan Isaacs and Amber Blanco White in 1929. New subjects, too, appeared in the curriculum—horticulture (with David White), child psychology, the history of London, folk-lore, wireless, contemporary art, 'Studies in Heredity'.

All this, together with the establishment of an annual Open Day and continual development on the social side—and most notably the long overdue acquisition of a Sports Ground (at Eltham) in 1928—made the demand for admission to the College heavier than ever. From 2,051 in 1927–8, the enrolment mounted within three years to 2,822—with an increasing proportion of students taking more than one course. It was entirely typical of the Principal that she saw the implications of this rise as soon as it set in. In January, 1929, less than eighteen months after she had taken office, and less than five years since the move to more commodious premises, the College requested the L.C.C. to finance a substantial addition to the building.

The scheme as it evolved was to buy up and demolish the decrepit cottages and warehouses of Nos. 63–67 Westminster Bridge Road, and on the site thus cleared to build a block of eight class-rooms, a small hall and a library. This would be built in L shape with the shorter arm of the L running at right angles into the existing building, so that the whole College would then occupy three sides of a rectangle, with an open courtyard between. The L.C.C. were favourably impressed, and after negotiation with the Ministry a grant of £10,500 was eventually approved—sufficient to pay for the class-rooms but not the hall and library. To reach this stage took some two years. Meanwhile a limited and friendly competition between two architects, Charles Cowles Voysey and Edward Maufe, had ended in favour of the latter, who had produced a scheme of exceptional clarity and distinction. The whole project was estimated to cost £15,000 and the College undertook to raise the difference between that sum and the L.C.C. grant.

Responses to the College Appeal Fund were coming in, if at a much slower pace than the Council desired, when in the summer of 1931 the full impact of the world economic crisis hit Britain. The May Report, the continued drain on the gold reserves, the resignation of the second Labour Ministry, the formation of the National Government under Ramsay MacDonald, the 10 per cent cuts and the suspension nevertheless of the gold standard—this

234

unforgettable series of events spelt disaster to the Morley building project. By a government ruling, all capital grants were refused for buildings and detailed plans of which had not been completely approved by September 4th. On that date the Morley plans were still going through the official mill. With dismay the College heard that its cherished scheme (on which work would have begun within a few weeks) was to be postponed *sine die*.

Faced with continued high numbers despite the bad times, Eva Hubback found a temporary solution in the use of rooms in an L.C.C. school at West Square, some five minutes' walk away. Meanwhile the College began to do what it could to help in the dreadful problems of mass unemployment. On the suggestion of R. S. (later Lord) Hudson, then Parliamentary Secretary to the Ministry of Labour and a recently co-opted member of the College Council, Eva Hubback undertook to organize classes for the unemployed in the afternoons. Hudson guaranteed £50 to cover administrative costs and the fee of a gym instructor; all other tuition was to be unpaid—and was readily found from Dorothy Robson, José Ugidos and many others of the College tutors. In addition that faithful stalwart William Rivers gave up three afternoons a week to help with the general supervision. The classes began in April, 1932, with a choice of no less than fourteen subjects. Admission of course was free, and for some weeks there was a regular daily attendance of about 140—nearly all men. With the better weather in June this figure declined, but the experiment was successful enough to warrant further classes the following session—especially as the Pilgrim Trust were willing to give a grant of £300. Already however, it was apparent that any educational

235

benefits were greatly restricted by the rapid turnover of students, and that the choice of subjects was needlessly generous. In fact only six subjects in this first session attracted consistently workable groups—psychology, economics, wireless, foreign languages, public speaking and gymnastics—and of these only the last three were really popular.

The following session not merely did these classes for the unemployed continue, but the experiment began to form the core of a wider movement. On the suggestion of the British Institute of Adult Education, the College in November, 1932, convened a conference of all those in the neighbourhood interested in providing occupational or educational centres for the unemployed. Out of this was born the South London Unemployment Committee. This in turn later merged into a yet wider organization promoted jointly by Eva Hubback and Alan Collingridge, who was soon to become a member of the College Council—the London Council for Voluntary Occupation during Unemployment. It was formed on the suggestion of the Charity Organisation Society with the object of co-ordinating the work of all the various voluntary centres, and for the first months of its existence it functioned from Morley College. Meanwhile on the class side the big new success was the creation of an orchestra, some forty strong, of unemployed professional musicians. Their tutor and conductor was the twenty-seven-year-old Michael Tippett, who thus began his first regular connection with the College.

For the next (the third) session of the unemployed classes the L.C.C. now agreed to pay tutors if certain minimum numbers of students were enrolled. Among the

236

groups eligible was the orchestra, which became the South London (Morley College) Orchestra of unemployed musicians, and which began to enter upon a positively busy career of public concerts. Engagements were obtained to play in L.C.C. schools and in churches, settlements, hospitals and parks (for which purpose a separate Military Band was soon formed). On occasion distinguished soloists—Harriet Cohen, Myra Hess, Phyllis Sellick and others—generously gave their services to cooperate with the group, and under Tippett's direction the whole venture resulted in something that was good not only socially but musically. So much was this the case that when employment began to revive to the point where the classes were no longer necessary, the South London Orchestra and the Military Band obstinately continued. The other classes faded away in 1935 and ceased entirely in 1936, but the South London Orchestra was still going strong in 1939. This was not because unemployment among professional musicians remained higher than in other occupations; it was because Tippett had got together a good band of players and by his personality and unusual choice of programmes inspired them with the enthusiasm to remain together.

* * *

Meantime the normal evening work of the College went on unchecked save by the limits of accommodation. The public lectures continued to bring men and women of distinction into the College. 'Biographies' (with Lord Zetland, Philip Guedalla and others), 'The Art of the Cinema' (one course by Francis Birrell and John Grierson and another by Alistair Cooke), 'Shakespeare' (with Dover Wilson, Ernest Milton and others), 'Political

Thought in the World Today' (with Laski on Democracy, A. L. Rowse on Socialism, John Strachey on Communism and Sir Charles Petrie on Fascism), 'Twentieth Century London' (with Geoffrey Crowther, Lewis Silkin, H. M. Tomlinson and Herbert Morrison), 'The Arts Today' (with Walter de la Mare, Edward Maufe, Herbert Read and Eric Gill)—the lists between 1931 and 1939, liberally dotted at intervals with that prime favourite of the Principal's 'The Contemporary World', is far too long to give in more than fractional form.

In the classes, too, many outstanding new tutors appeared during these years. Myfanwy Evans (later Mrs. Piper), Michael Stewart, Gordon Jacob, Frank Darval, Nicholas Pevsner, Norman Fisher—all undertook courses between 1931 and 1938. At the same time old friends known in other capacities also began to lecture. In 1933 R. F. Cosser, a student of many years' standing, commenced a class on the 'Wild Life of the Countryside' which he is still taking in 1958 with no less success; and within the next three years Mary Sheepshanks returned to lecture on 'International Problems', and Barbara Wootton on 'Trends in World Economics'. Perhaps most remarkable of all, J. J. Denton, who had been a student before the formal foundation of the College and who had taken classes since 1895, began in 1933 to lecture on television, and to gather around him as keen a group of experimenters as he had earlier attracted in 1899–1900 to investigate wireless telegraphy.

Under Arnold Foster the music department also continued to do admirable work. A fine musician and a born organizer with a flair for working with amateurs, Foster had played the horn in the College orchestra for some

238

years, and so was well acquainted with the Holst traditions. When he succeeded Goldsbrough as Director in 1928 he was fully convinced of the value of tackling unfamiliar and unjustly neglected works. At his first concert there was Schubert's overture *Fierrebras,* the next year Purcell's *King Arthur,* and in 1930 the first London performance of Vaughan Williams's *Hundredth Psalm.* The following session he began to associate the choir and orchestra with the League of Arts, and together with the dancing classes to assist in the summer performances in Hyde Park. Between then and 1939 he followed this up with—among many other works—the first performances in England of two choral pieces by Moussorgsky, translated by a former student of the College, the first public performance (for the League of Arts in Hyde Park) of Holst's ballet *The Golden Goose,* and a rendering of Dvorak's rarely heard *Te Deum* of which the *Daily Telegraph* wrote that 'the splendidly assured performance would have done credit to far more ambitious organizations'.

Other works to be presented included the first extracts to be sung in English (again specially translated) from Rimsky-Korsakov's opera *Sadko,* a revival of Purcell's *Dioclesian,* and the second performance in London—the first was given by the B.B.C. only four days earlier—of Vaughan Williams's *Five Tudor Portraits.* This enterprising policy, combined with the high standard maintained by the choir and orchestra, helped to keep Morley College music before the general public. At the same time by carrying on the 'music teas' and the Whitsuntide festivals begun by Holst, Foster saw to it that Morley music continued to have a social as well as an educational and aesthetic value.

239

In other aspects of the College social life the 1930s also saw continued liveliness and activity. The Principal and most members of the Council now played a much less prominent part in this than they had done in earlier days: the initiative stemmed almost entirely from the students, who were greatly aided in their projects by the College Secretary. The clubs—there were twenty-five of them by 1939—maintained their vigorous individual life; two dramatic groups—the Dramatic Society and a more 'high-brow' affair, the Morley Players—disputed the stage of the Prince of Wales Hall; and every week-end the newly acquired Sports Ground echoed, according to season, with the thud of boot on leather, the clash of hockey sticks, the sharp ping of gut on tennis balls (together with the not infrequent sound of wood) and the shrill appeals of lady cricketers.

Talented and energetic student direction, too, continued to be applied to the College Magazine. In 1931, under the editorship of Roy Townend, it suddenly acquired considerable elegance of format, and from then until 1936 it remained a journal of surprising distinction. Thereafter, under more 'popular' editorship, it fully maintained its liveliness, but fell sadly off in appearance and intellectual content, its distinctive flavour being an amalgam of crude 'anti-capitalism' and pacifism. This deliberate introduction of politics on a somewhat hysterical note was an innovation. It arose, of course, from mass unemployment and the alarming nature of the international situation, and possibly it reflected the opinions of the more vocal among the politically-minded students. It could, however, only be a dividing force in a College which had thriven on the watchword of 'unity and good

240

fellowship', and which by its foundation scheme was designed to be unsectarian in both politics and religion.

Whether at any particular moment it worked well or less well, student control of the Magazine was one of the 'democratic' features about the College which helped to give it exceptional vitality. A democratic element in the College organization had been present from the first in the form both of the Consultative (later Advisory) Committee of students and teachers, and of the practice of co-opting two unpaid teachers and two student or ex-student members to the College Council. By the active desire of students and College authorities alike, this element had been progressively strengthened as far as the students were concerned; but at the same time the virtual disappearance of unpaid tutors caused the teachers' representation to lapse both on the Advisory Committee and on the Council. In 1928 the latest of several revisions of this democratic machinery produced a scheme by which the Advisory Committee (directly elected by students of at least one year's standing) was confined to student members and given somewhat increased powers. Among these it was allowed to choose two of its own members to serve on the College Council (instead, as had been the practice since 1908, of suggesting four or five names from which the Council selected two). Ten years later a further development took place when Eva Hubback formed the Class Secretaries' Association. In this the class secretaries met to discuss class matters with the Principal and to choose some of their number to serve on the Students' Advisory—now rechristened Students' Executive-Committee. The other members of the Students' Executive Committee thenceforth included a proportion

241

of club secretaries, the editor of the Magazine, and one or two other key figures in the student organization—a form of 'functional' representation which for some years replaced direct election by the student body. The detail of all these changes is not important. What matters is the evidence they afford of a constant desire to find the most appropriate and efficient ways of associating the students in the active running of the College.

The period in which all these advances took place was not of course without its losses on the personal side. The years 1931 and 1932, for instance, saw the deaths of three of the College's oldest and most valiant supporters—Sir Frederick Black, Frederick Snelling and Graham Wallas. All had been with the College, in spirit if not always in presence, from the earliest days; and each in his different way had left on it a lasting impression. Black had been the ideal voluntary teacher who had become successively member of Council, Chairman and Vice-President. Radiating good humour and ever ready to provide hospitality, he had done more than any other person to establish a friendly social atmosphere within the College, and to bridge the gap between the different social worlds of the founders and the early students. Snelling, a more aggressive but no less devoted man, had been the ideal student who in turn had become Council member, College Secretary and founder of the Old Morleyite Association. In him, as in William Rivers and others of his contemporaries, were reflected on the student side the ideals put forth by Black and the Cons-Martineau-Everest circle and the traditions they so successfully established. Wallas, first an outstanding tutor, became the ideal President, eager to play a truly active part in both the adminis-

242

tration and the social life of the College, and able in his public addresses to formulate a philosophy of adult education and a view of the College of the most deeply considered and inspiring nature. And different as were their personalities, with geniality pervasive in the first, determination in the second and intellectuality in the third, all three men had presented to Morley an equally shining example of the spirit of service—the spirit, in fact, on which the College was built.[1]

There were other personalities too, that the College was soon to miss: Frederick Church, a devoted and highly efficient caretaker for more than thirty years; Sergeant Oliver, an impressive doorkeeper during the same period; Henri Bosc, an outstanding teacher of French who met with a fatal accident in a railway tunnel. And, casting a shadow over the music department, with which he kept in touch to the last, came in 1934 the premature death of Gustav Holst.

* * *

Such losses were in the natural order of things. Meanwhile the College showed persistent vigour and gathered fresh strength from its newcomers, among whom Margaret Cowles, assistant secretary and the Principal's right-hand woman from 1931 onwards, was soon prominent. Then in 1935 came the news for which it had long waited. With the national economy slowly climbing from the troughs of the depression, County Hall and the Board of Education were now agreed that the building project cancelled in 1931 might proceed. In due course—after an interval to avoid conflicting with the King

[1] Wallas was succeeded as President by R. H. Tawney, who in turn was followed in 1937 by Sir Arthur (later Lord) Salter.

George V Jubilee Fund (!)—the Council appealed to the public for the £6,000 needed for the small hall and library which the L.C.C. were unwilling to sponsor. Once again the City Parochial Foundation stood the College in good stead, and support came from—among others—the Pilgrim Trust and Miss S. C. Courtauld. Queen Mary generously headed the list of contributions, and the students for their part undertook to raise at least £1,000. Moreover some of the music students and friends of the music department conceived the brilliant idea of equipping the small hall as a music-room in memory of Gustav Holst, and for this purpose a separate committee under Vaughan Williams got to work.

Under the eagle eye of Edward Maufe the building operations went on as planned, and in March, 1937, Queen Mary came again, this time to open the extension. Later the same day the Holst Committee, which had raised £1,157—sufficient not merely to adapt the hall especially for music but also to build two small practice-rooms and supply three pianos—held its own celebrations in what was henceforth known as the Holst Room. Vaughan Williams and J. W. Mackail spoke of Holst and Morley music, Imogen Holst conducted the choir in some of her father's songs, and Harriet Cohen played on the new Steinway selected by Myra Hess.

The new wing had all the qualities expected from the plans. 'An endeavour,' wrote the architect, 'has been made to create a building really simple in upkeep, yet one that also has charm.' In this he triumphantly succeeded. The clean lines of the block of eight class-rooms made an instant appeal, as did the dignity and warmth of the library. The Holst Room, in fan shape, was equally or still

244

more attractive. Outside, above its double windows, keystones representing the planets and carved by Edmund Burton paid tribute to one of Holst's best-known works. Inside great thought had been given to the decoration. 'As this room will be used principally for chamber music,' wrote Maufe, 'the scheme leads away in colour from violins and 'cellos; the floor being in Jarrah wood; the resonator at the back of the platform and the rest of the woodwork in pear wood; the walls are a very pale Italian pink and the ceiling a summer night blue, and on this again a suggestion of planets.' Moreover the whole extension had another virtue: it opened up the College to the air and sun. Before, the College was hemmed in by dilapidated warehouses; now the buildings surrounded a quiet court open to the south. In fact the only slight imperfection in the whole operation was financial: the appeal brought in £1,500 less than was needed. This difficulty, however, was overcome by a notable gesture on the part of the students, who suggested that the inevitable loan should be serviced and repaid over twenty years by means of a shilling increase in their annual registration fee.

With a handsome addition to its accommodation, the College confidently expected, and got, a record enrolment for the 1937–8 session. The following session might have been better still; but with Hitler working up for war with Czechoslovakia, 'enrolment week' was naturally overshadowed. After Munich, however, normal interests quickly revived, and in the end the 1938–9 total of enrolments was only 33 short of that of the previous year.

These last two years of peace saw no slackening in the College's manifold activities. The public lectures attracted a regular attendance of over 400 persons; new tutors of

245

the quality of Karl Polanyi, Dorothy Pickles and J. Ormerod Greenwood joined the lecturing staff; Eva Hubback launched an ambitious scheme for a large social science department for professional as well as voluntary workers. Through the kindness of Mrs. Trevelyan, a cottage at Coldharbour became available for the use of the students at week-ends. A new pavilion diminished the ardours of dressing and undressing at the Sports Ground. In the College a fresh set of murals, done 'for love' by the young artist Anthony Greene, embellished the link between the old and the new buildings with representations of College activities in a vein of witty fantasy entirely in key with the earlier decorations of Bawden and Ravilious. They were unveiled in January, 1939, by the Duke of Kent, whose signature was the last to be inscribed in the College 'distinguished visitors' book' before that disappeared, with much else, in October, 1940.[1]

By the summer of 1939 Morley was in many ways different from the College that earlier generations of students had known. The building was much more commodious, gay and beautiful. The curriculum, always wide, had grown still wider, and Eva Hubback was rapidly expanding it in the direction not only of the social studies but also of the arts. The biggest group of students—fully twice as large as any other—was still that enrolled for foreign languages, as it has been for the past twenty years; but the next largest was now country and other dancing, a development that would have horrified Caroline Martineau. Of the 3,300-odd students, over a thousand now came from districts outside London; the growing reputation of the College and the greatly improved facili-

[1] It turned up again in 1950.

246

ties for public transport were together making it no longer a local but a metropolitan institution. Nevertheless 1,600 students still came from the South London boroughs and of these nearly 500 still lived in Lambeth and Southwark. More pervasive in its influence, the educational background of the students was changing; by 1939 two-thirds had enjoyed secondary education, and more than a tenth had been to a university or training college. As for occupation, all but a few hundred were in office, clerical or professional jobs. In sum the College had become less homogeneous in local, social and educational background, and more of a cross-section of the intelligent middle and working class of London and the Home Counties. This presented certain dangers in the way of dilution and even conflict of interest. But the intellectual vigour of the place was unimpaired, and its social life, under the direction of the students, more vigorous, if less united, than ever before. Above all, amid the excitement of expanding numbers and interests, its staff and its hard core of regular students held firmly to the traditions of service and self-help established by the founders. These qualities, so evident in 1889, were no less evident fifty years later. This was as well, for they would all be needed in the days that lay ahead.

247

XII

Ruin—and Recovery

SEPTEMBER, 1939, was the Jubilee of the official foundation of Morley College. In celebration a programme of more than 150 classes had been advertised, together with an attractive series of public lectures under the title 'Living London'. The new social science department had been enlarged, and the fresh projects included a Theatre School under the direction of Rupert Doone, who had recently been doing distinguished work as producer for the Group Theatre. An enrolment heavier than ever was confidently expected. Instead the beginning of the month found the College officers helping to evacuate mothers and children from London.

On the outbreak of war, government orders precluded the College from opening until it possessed officially approved shelters. The whole place had also to be fitted with black-out curtains—no mean task in the warren of

248

rooms and corridors which constituted the older part of the building. As soon as the College officers had fulfilled their roles in the initial L.C.C. plans for evacuation, they accordingly set about these tasks. As no money was available for the purpose from public funds, the expenses were met by a supplementary charge of a shilling a head to each student. Sufficient black-out material was conjured from some untapped source and made up by the College staff; and since sand-bags were also 'in short supply' flour sacks (twice as large and correspondingly heavy when filled) were used instead. Sand too was unobtainable, but there was earth to be had from Hyde Park, and some twenty tons of this were transported by the L.C.C. to the College. There George Cottrell, James White the groundsman and Albert Exten, a student, aided by one or two others, spent a strenuous week in filling the bags and piling them up in front of the gym and refreshment-room windows under the Prince of Wales Hall. Thus protected, this part of the basement became a reasonably good shelter. Meanwhile Eva Hubback had reorganized the programme of classes to meet the new situation and the inevitable loss of many tutors. When all these things were done, she announced her intention of restarting classes on October 16th. No official objections having been received by that date, the College duly reopened—only four weeks late on the date arranged in peace-time.

Almost the major inconvenience of war in the West at that moment was the black-out. Against the severity of this the College Council quickly protested, alleging its 'very serious effect on social and cultural life and its depressing effect on the morale of the population'.

249

Nevertheless plenty of people still seemed eager to find their way to Morley College. By the end of November, on a programme of 87 classes instead of the 150 planned, 1,400 students had been enrolled; and by the close of the session this figure had risen to 1,785—more than half the recent peace-time totals. Among the classes originally planned, the gravest casualty was the entire social science department: so many social workers were involved in war-time tasks outside London, or in the evening hours, that the whole scheme had to be abandoned. On the other hand the newly projected Theatre School, with a talented teaching staff and a gleaming list of 'advisers' including Denis Johnston, John Piper and Michael Tippett, got off to an excellent start, despite the fact that its students had to enrol for two years and undertake to attend three evenings a week. Correspondingly it was found that a course of public lectures in the spring term on 'The War and the Peace' was but indifferently supported, while a course the following term on 'The Arts Today' arranged by Alan Collingridge, proved extremely popular. Music, too, continued to flourish. The Holst Room saw a series of chamber concerts organized by the Incorporated Society of Musicians, and enterprising concerts also came from Foster and the College Orchestra and from Tippett and the South London Orchestra.

So the first war-time session drew on, with its strange lack of interference from the enemy, and Open Day on April 6th, 1940, was as lively, as interesting, and—despite the lesser number of students—as well attended as ever. Thereafter things happened. The German *Blitzkreig* was unleashed in the West: Norway was overwhelmed, France fell. In that memorable 'invasion summer', when names of railway stations disappeared overnight and men on church towers scanned the skies for the flutter of parachutes, the College staff found themselves preparing for the new session with an increasing sense of unreality. Saturday, 7th September, came, and with it the intensive night bombing of London. Enrolment week opened as planned the following Monday, but two nights of it were enough. On September 11th the L.C.C. decreed that all evening classes should cease until further notice.

A fortnight passed, with the bombing continuing night after night, and it became plain that evening classes were 'out' for some time to come. Like other heads of evening colleges, Eva Hubback thereupon began to devise a still further reduced programme, in which all classes would be held during the daytime at the week-ends. These week-end classes were advertised to start on Saturday, October 19th, 1940, and students were enrolled for them at the College on the previous Saturday and Sunday.

Meanwhile the districts round the College, being so near to important target areas and that excellent aid to night navigation the Thames, were inevitably suffering. Among the many 'incidents' three blocks of Council flats in Kennington—Lidford House, York House and Colwyn House—had been hit or damaged on the night of October 1–2. The familes had to be housed elsewhere, and as the College had been designated an emergency rest and feeding centre it at once offered to receive them. This was possible because classes had temporarily ceased. During October 2nd the families accordingly moved in and occupied the main block of the College, where they were cared for by workers from the Lady Margaret Hall Settlement in the Kennington Road. A few days later they

251

were joined by a fresh contingent from Mountain House, Vauxhall, which had been made uninhabitable by a time bomb. All told, some 250 men, women and children of the district were now being housed in the College and supplied with three meals a day. At night about a third of them went across the road to Lambeth North Underground station; the remainder slept in the gymnasium and refreshment-room.

On Tuesday evening, October 15th, the alert sounded as usual. Most of the families gathered in the two protected rooms, but many others continued to chat and play elsewhere in the block. At 7.45 p.m., an hour or so after the College officers had left the building, a 1,000 kilogram high explosive bomb seared through the roof of the Prince of Wales Hall, on the King Edward Walk side, and exploded on the floor. From end to end it shattered the entire block, which collapsed like a pack of cards. Chunks of masonry and concrete, hurled high into the air, obliterated many of the houses opposite. When the wardens from the nearest post rushed out to investigate, all they could at first see, though it was full moonlight, was an immense cloud of thick dust.

Within a few moments rescue work began. With the help of information from Dovey, the College schoolkeeper, the rescuers were able to reach most of the trapped families fairly soon; but it was twenty days before the last two bodies were recovered. In all, it was found that 195 people had been on the premises. Fortunately the flour sacks had helped to sustain the floor of the hall over the gym and refreshment-room and the 84 persons who came out unhurt were nearly all in those two rooms. Of the remainder, 54 were injured and 57 were killed outright or died in hospital. The dead included the assistant schoolkeeper, Rosser, and three of his family—the only casualties connected with the College.

As far as material damage was concerned, the entire block to which the College had moved in 1924 had completely gone. With it had gone the Prince of Wales Hall, all the splendid murals, all the souvenirs of the days at the Vic, and every single documentary record except the Council minutes. Three-quarters of the College accommodation, and all its working papers, had disappeared at one stroke. From total destruction only one part of the College had in fact escaped—the extension opened in 1937. Though heavily blasted, this proved to be repairable; and a few day's work by a volunteer party armed with picks, shovels and sledge-hammers established a path to it through the wilderness of debris.

Amid all this it was entirely typical of Eva Hubback that she made no fuss about the loss of the building but deplored only the loss of life. Morley, she declared, would get a much better building when peace returned. Typically, too, she at once concerned herself with certain imperfections which had been revealed in the organization of the rescue services, so that the lessons could be applied in future incidents. It was also entirely characteristic of her that two days later, dashing off on some other urgent task, she should instruct the Secretary to find premises where the College could still begin the new session at the week-end as planned.

That Thursday the Secretary and the Assistant Secretary accordingly presented themselves at County Hall, where a skeleton staff in the Education Officer's department at first suggested that the College should accept the

253

inevitable and close down for the 'duration'. This suggestion falling on unreceptive soil, it was followed by an offer to lend an L.C.C. school if the College could find one with vacant accommodation. The two College officials set out on a search of the neighbourhood, and later that day tracked down some unused rooms in a school in Johanna Street, a side turning off Baylis Road. Some sheets of paper found in the street yielded the addresses of some of the students who had registered the previous week-end. Two days later, on the Saturday, the new session scheduled to begin that day in Morley College opened in Johanna Street School. The number of classes was 21 and the total enrolment 164 students.

* * *

In the weeks that followed, great efforts were made to get into touch with other regular students. By the middle of December attendance at Johanna Street had almost doubled. Meanwhile the surviving part of the College was being patched up. Very soon invitations were going forth to a special 'Christmas week-end' to celebrate the reopening of the 1937 extension. It proved to be an interesting and indeed inspiring occasion. On Saturday afternoon, December 21st, 1940, there was tea in the Holst Room with an entertainment by the Theatre School and the orchestra; the next morning, an extremely profitable discussion in the Holst Room on the future Morley and its needs—educational, social and architectural; and on the Sunday afternoon, a carol service in Christ Church near by with the College orchestra and choir.

So the fabric of Morley life was slowly stitched together again; but while the classes continued to be held at week-ends attendance remained small. In compensation and typical of Eva Hubback's promptness to respond to some new social need, the College began in March, 1941, to organize special evening classes for the Southern Railway staff in two of the large shelters underneath Waterloo Station. In various corners, tuition was given to small groups in music, drama, 'keep-fit', boxing, dressmaking and other subjects, and George Cottrell ran a lending library of 'Penguins'. With the summer term and the longer daylight, it was then possible to resume evening classes at the College. Attendance at once improved, and was so constant that the classes, instead of ceasing in June as normally, were continued into the middle of August. The session ended up with a total enrolment of 495—the lowest since the foundation of the College, but not discouraging in the circumstances.

The systematic bombing of London ceased in the spring of 1941, by which time the surviving part of the College had suffered further damage from blast and the Holst Room had seen its grimmest moment, when it became the mortuary for corpses from a neighbouring lodging-house. From May, 1941, until the 'Little Blitz' of early 1944 and the V weapon attacks of June, 1944–March, 1945, the capital enjoyed comparative quiet. During this prolonged lull the College was able to offer increasingly comprehensive programmes and despite deficiencies of accommodation to attract more and more students. From 495 the enrolment rose in 1941–2 to 1,270; the next year it was 1,800; and the last two years of the war both saw an enrolment of over 2,000. To accommodate this number, there were the eight repaired classrooms of the 1937 extension and the Holst Room. The offices having been destroyed, the College administration

255

was carried on from various corners of the Library, which also served as the student Common Room.

On the social side, the College life of these years was inevitably restricted. Many of the clubs, as in 1914–18, had to suspend activities, and only the Ramblers and the Folk Dancers managed to keep together really strong groups. The Magazine, too, ceased publication; and in the absence of much social life to organize except some extremely well-attended Christmas parties, the Students' Executive Committee also ceased to function. Nor did the emergency canteen in a corridor, though highly welcome after no canteen at all, encourage bouts of student discussion such as had taken place over the tables of the refreshment-room.

But if social activity was at a low ebb, there was no lack of vitality in the classes of these war-time years. Most of the old subjects found their way back into the programme; and new ones, such as Russian and recorder-playing, were successfully introduced. At one time Joad found himself with a class of 70 for a course in philosophy. The public lectures, too, continued to arouse a good deal of interest. Some of those on topics connected with the main problems of the day—such as a course of five by Sir Bernard Pares on Russia—still drew excellent audiences; but in general attendances at lectures on social and political affairs now became small compared with those at lectures on the arts. Numerically speaking, much the most successful of all the war-time public lecture courses was one on the Ballet, with Ninette de Valois, Kurt Jooss and other speakers. Many of those who came along for this had to be turned away. Another course, on the Opera, with Vaughan Williams, John Christie and others was little less popular; and a course on the Theatre, with the speakers including C. B. Cochran and Tyrone Guthrie, again saw the Holst Room packed to overflowing. Another great success was 'Writers on Writers'. By contrast an attractively devised series on local government drew an audience of barely twenty-five.

This increasing concern for the arts among intelligent men and women of modest means was seen perhaps most clearly in the realm of music. A decade and a half of missionary work by the B.B.C. had had its effect, and by 1939 the level of musical taste and appreciation among the general public was steadily rising. With the outbreak of war and the later bombing, this valuable gain was inevitably jeopardized. Certain artists, however, and foremost among them Myra Hess, with her lunch-time concerts at the National Gallery, remained determined to sustain music-lovers in the capital, bombs or no bombs. In this matter of providing the London public with good music amid the exigencies of war the Morley College music department under Michael Tippett bore an honourable and by no means insubstantial share.

Already in the first winter of the war Tippett had given two unusual concerts at the College with his South London orchestra. The first introduced one of his loveliest works, the Concerto for Double String Orchestra; the second had Solomon as a guest artist. The devastation of the College in October, 1940, then appeared likely to end all such public performances: for without the Prince of Wales Hall the larger College groups had no room in which to perform. At the same time Arnold Foster moved from London, and the groups themselves practically disappeared. Before the war the College orchestra had

257

numbered about sixty and the choir about seventy. When Tippett, appointed Director of Music in Foster's place, took his first classes at Johanna Street at the end of October, 1940, the orchestra had fallen to nine students and the choir to eight.

During the war-time sessions which followed, Tippett was never able to rebuild more than a very small College orchestra, and the South London orchestra dispersed entirely. But by the beginning of the 1941–2 session he had built up the choir to an effective unit of some thirty voices, and by 1944–5 it was again at a strength of over seventy. During the same time he was able to attract to the College teaching staff such admirable musicians as Walter Bergmann, who introduced recorder-playing to the College in 1942, and Matyas Sieber, who in 1944 began to teach composition and also took over the music appreciation class (earlier given for some years by W. R. Anderson). Several talented young musicians, including Maria Lidka, Norbert Brainin, Antony Hopkins and Peter Pears also became associated with the individual tuition. The bomb thus caused only the briefest interruption to the musical activity of the College. Within a few months, the orchestra apart, Tippett had restored it to the standards which Holst had introduced and Goldsbrough and Foster maintained.

Moreover he was soon making a significant and unusual contribution to the public music of war-time London. Among the monthly concerts he planned for the Holst Room, the College choir gave a whole programme of Monteverdi directed by Peter Pears; and other complete concerts or half-concerts were devoted to the works of Dowland, Purcell, Telemann and Orlando Gibbons, as

258

well as to pieces for the recorder. Further notable occasions included the first performance of Tippett's solo cantata *Boyhood's End*, given by Peter Pears and Benjamin Britten, and the first concert performance in England of Stravinsky's *Dumbarton Oaks,* played by an instrumental ensemble under Walter Goehr. Still more unusual, in October, 1944, Tippett presented anthems by Purcell and Gibbons in which the counter-tenor parts were, for the first time in many generations, sung in the original pitch—by Alfred Deller. From this occasion dated the revival of the counter-tenor voice and the increasing fame of that great singer.

Outside the College, the College choir performed with success under Tippett's direction at—among other places—the National Gallery, Friends' House, and the Wigmore Hall. Possibly its most memorable appearance was at the Adelphi Theatre in March, 1944, when it joined forces with the London Civil Defences Choir and the London Philharmonia Orchestra in the first performance, under Walter Goehr, of Tippett's remarkable oratorio, *A Child of our Time*. Among the soloists on that occasion was not only Peter Pears but also Joan Cross, who many years later was to start an Opera Group for the College.

All this received its due measure of appreciation from the music critics, who were delighted to come across acceptable performances of great but unfamiliar music. In November, 1941, for instance, *The Times* gave a very favourable review of a performance of Purcell's *Ode for St. Cecilia's Day* and then in a subsequent article went on to plead for other institutions to follow suit and so revive a knowledge of Purcell's great odes, at that time 'practically unknown'. In May, 1943, after a concert of works

259

by Purcell and Holst, the *New Statesman* was equally complimentary, praising Tippett for having turned 'his little choir into one of the best ensembles in the country', and congratulating him on his enterprise. 'Morley College,' the critic concluded, 'does not yet cater for the Stoll Theatre public, but, if all goes well, the post-war years should find that public enjoying works and performances which have been brought to light and trained by that far-sighted institution.'

All this was as nothing, however, compared with the blaze of publicity which greeted Tippett's oratorio. With its passionate sympathy for the persecuted, its unusual text (written by Tippett himself) and its controversial use of Negro spirituals as chorales, it aroused the strongest reactions. These were doubtless sharpened by the fact that Tippett himself, a conscientious objector, had recently spent three months in Wormwood Scrubs for refusing to accept direction to agricultural labour. The performance itself came in for a good deal of criticism, but few were unimpressed by the power and beauty of the work. From this moment Tippett was a leading figure in English music, and the College music drew fresh strength from the reputation of its Director.

To these developments Eva Hubback was both sympathetic and helpful. Music, however, though it was something which she much enjoyed, was very far from being her main interest. Not surprisingly, therefore, she was herself more directly concerned in satisfying other war-time needs. Her flair for promoting informal discussion of social and economic problems, her position as co-founder (with Lord Simon of Wythenshawe) and secretary of the Association for Education in Citizenship, and

260

her close contacts with government offices, brought her into the heart of many new war-time developments. In 1944, for instance, she helped the War Office to evolve techniques of discussion for the groups which the Army Bureau of Current Affairs (under W. E. Williams, an outstanding former lecturer) was then fostering. In the course of this assistance she organized week-end courses for army discussion group leaders at the College and wrote a pamphlet—*How to Run a Discussion Group*—which was published by the Association for Education in Citizenship and purchased wholesale by the Army.

Such a development was only typical of many. In 1942, after her appointment as one of the regional advisers to the Ministry of Health on child welfare, Eva Hubback established (as her predecessor had done in the First World War) a Nursery Course for the benefit of mothers and nursery workers. At the same time a group of experts gave a course on 'The Social Services Today and Tomorrow', and special lectures on the history and future of the Social Services were provided in the afternoon for rest centre welfare advisers. During the same session fifteen lectures on the Beveridge report were also arranged for care committee workers, a course on public speaking was organized for selected members of the A.T.S., and week-end study courses were arranged for youth leaders on such themes as 'Education for Citizenship', 'Music and Drama', and 'The Psychology and Moral Training of the Adolescent'. By this time it seemed that any organization which had an educational problem on its hands automatically applied to Eva Hubback. In 1943, for instance, she was asked by the Ministry of Labour and the Institute of Personnel Management to run

261

courses on personnel management: by the National Association of Local Government Officers to run courses on local government: and by the L.C.C. to arrange weekly talks on London for members of the Allied and Dominions forces on leave. All these requests were met, and the course on personnel management proved so popular and successful that the College was soon asked to organize another, on parallel lines, to be held in the Cripplegate Institute for the benefit of workers in North and East London. The next year, 1944, the Air Ministry requested, and got, a three-day course in parenthood for members of the W.A.A.F. Finally, the 1944–5 session opened with a whole group of public lectures designed to educate the general public in matters then much under discussion—a lecture by Beveridge on his proposals, a short series on 'New Ideas in Education' by Professor Lauwerys, and a somewhat longer series by Dr. David Mace on 'Marriage and the Modern World'.

For a College which in October, 1940, had seen three-quarters of its accommodation disappear overnight and its student roll shrink to one-twentieth of the peace-time total, this was no bad war-time record. By 1945 large numbers of students were again coming forward, and within the diminished premises the spirit of the College survived intact. Under Eva Hubback's leadership, the College had not been content merely to carry on, though that in itself was no small feat. It had also responded actively and imaginatively to the special needs of the time.

* * *

As in 1919, the return of peace brought a quickening in the world of adult education. For the first post-war

262

session the College advertised sixty-four classes. They attracted more than 2,500 students, with the result that the depleted accommodation was at once filled to overflowing. Many groups had to meet in other buildings: in a school on the other side of Westminster Bridge Road, in a school in Walnut Tree Walk off the Kennington Road, and before long in a school, named with unconscious irony the Paragon, a full half-mile south of the Elephant and Castle. All of these provided useful classroom space, but little else. They were extremely unpopular with those students who were accustomed to the College, partly because they lacked essential facilities—at the Paragon Greek Dancing failed to survive the absence of any means of washing the feet—but still more because the students there missed the cheerful atmosphere of the College and felt cut off from its social life. By November, 1945, the College Council therefore began to consider ways and means of providing temporary accommodation on the College bombed site.

The story of what ensued in this direction in the next three years is a dismal one, and not least because the College authorities themselves contributed substantially to the muddle. Since government controls made the permanent reconstruction of the lost buildings obviously impossible for some time to come, Eva Hubback suggested as a measure of temporary relief that some huts should be erected on the bombed site. This proposal being approved by the College Council, an architect was engaged, and a scheme worked out not only for hutted class-rooms but also for a large hut to serve as common room, canteen, and hall. These huts were to be placed on top of the surviving class-room block, and on the site of the old gymnasium and refreshment-room. The whole project, it was estimated, would cost no more than £5,000.

The plans were then put to the L.C.C., whose officers some five months later declined to pass them unless provision was also made for more lavatories. To increase the sanitary accommodation, however, involved not only spending much more money but also extending the works to the front of the bombed site on the Westminster Bridge Road, where the main drains lay. Confronted with this requirement, the College went one better: since a permanent or semi-permanent block must now appear at the front of the site, the College Council asked its architect to develop the scheme still further to include a Principal's room, an office, and a staff room. By February, 1947, the architect had done this and in addition provided for a temporary theatre with dressing-rooms. The buildings as planned, though still mainly of a temporary nature, were now to be on two floors and would cover the entire site. The estimated cost, originally £5,000, had risen to more than £50,000. With some misgivings the College Council nevertheless approved the scheme, and re-submitted it to the L.C.C.

Throughout the rest of 1947 and the early months of 1948 the architect strove to steer the scheme through the network of authorities at County Hall. In the course of his negotiations he encountered objections which decided him to produce a new scheme altogether, in which all the rebuilding would be of a permanent nature. His reaction was no doubt natural and logical: but unfortunately he omitted to consult the College authorities beforehand. By mid-1948 the latter thus found themselves

264

confronted with a scheme which was no longer temporary but which at the same time exploited only about half the potentialities of the site. Dismayed and perplexed, the College Council thereupon decided that if it was to be a question of a permanent building, they would ask a more established architect, Mr. Charles Cowles Voysey, to take over the prime responsibility, and to work as far as possible with the existing architect on the basis of the plans already prepared.

Not surprisingly, this highly unrealistic proposition could not be translated into practical terms to the satisfaction of all concerned. In September, 1948, Eva Hubback accordingly found herself recommending to the Council a bold but belated step—to scrap the whole project as it had developed, and to begin afresh on a permanent scheme with Cowles Voysey as sole architect. This decision was duly taken, with excellent long-term results for the College. Meantime, however, three years' work had gone for nothing; and bills of some £4,500 had been incurred for professional fees. The settlement of these swallowed up the whole of the College's small financial reserve. All told, it seems to have been the one occasion in the College history when a substantial sum of money was wasted.

This false start on the rebuilding problem fortunately made little or nor difference to the continued vigour and vitality of the College. In 1946–7 there was a decline in enrolments compared with the previous year, but the next session saw the numbers leaping up again, and in 1948–9 they reached a post-war peak with 3,030 students. Of these rather more than a third were men—a proportion somewhat greater than in the years immediately

265

before the war. As for the subjects studied, these displayed the trend which had set in with the outbreak of war and was to continue for long to come: the trend, in general, towards the study of the arts. In 1938–9, foreign languages had been easily the most popular group of subjects with 1,268 students; physical training and dancing had come next with 914; and several groups of subjects—English language and literature, social studies, science, and music—had followed a good way behind, each with about 400. By 1948–9, foreign languages, with 621 enrolments, were only just ahead of English language and literature; physical training and dancing had declined by almost two-thirds (as also had science), and were now half-way down the list; music and social studies each attracted about 500 students and were third in popularity. The visual arts, which had attracted 134 students in 1938–9, now attracted nearly twice that number.

Among the many fresh classes started in these post-war years were three or four which represented new departures for the College. Agriculture, begun in 1947, at once aroused a response among townsfolk interested in the land. Eleven years later the class still attracts an excellent enrolment. Modelling in clay, begun in the same year, also at once established itself and under the direction of Hermann and Erna Nonnenmacher now has to be given three nights a week. A third class, in mural painting, made no less impression, and under Angela Latham produced both notable work and a new method of protecting wall paintings from the atmosphere. Unfortunately this class had to be dropped after a year or so as the students had nowhere to paint except on the walls

266

of the corridors, and their activities proved too much of an obstacle to others.

Together with these new classes Eva Hubback also planned a number of courses designed to appeal to special vocational interests. There were daytime courses, for instance, for members of the army and the R.A.F. intending to become teachers or unit instructors. There was a whole series of courses on marriage and the family —presented in conjunction with the Central Council for Health Education. And there was a series, repeated every year, on latest developments in the Social Services—a series in which men and women actively associated with these developments like Helen Bentwich, Winifred Raphael and Harold Shearman came along to talk on some subject which they had made their special concern. All these courses with visiting lecturers were in addition to the normal weekly public lectures, which continued to arouse great interest and which were especially successful when they were about the arts. Particularly memorable in this last category were a course in 1946 on The Film, with Anthony Asquith, Dilys Powell and others, and a course the following year on Shakespeare, in which the lecturers included Robert Speaight, E. M. Tillyard and Harcourt Williams. Even these, however, were outshone in popular appeal by two other courses—on the Novel and on 'Remembering Great Writers'. The first offered the London public the chance of hearing, for five shillings, twelve lectures by novelists of such eminence as Phyllis Bentley, Compton MacKenzie, V. S. Pritchett, L. A. G. Strong, Frank Swinnerton and H. M. Tomlinson. The second provided the chance of hearing, among many other reminiscences, Swinnerton's personal recollections

267

of Arnold Bennett, Ian Hay's of Rudyard Kipling, and Herman Ould's of John Galsworthy.

Much notable work was also done by those classes of the College whose activities include occasional public performance. The Theatre School, after its initial productions during the war, proceeded to a number of memorable presentations including that of Louis MacNeice's translation of *Agamemnon* in 1945 (directed by Rupert Doone), Dibdin's *The Waterman* and A. P. Herbert's *Plain Jane* in 1947 (directed by Winifred Radford), and Marc Connolly's *The Green Pastures* in 1948 (directed by Archie Harradine). In 1949 in collaboration with Roy Muscott Walker it also began the custom, to be continued for some years, of presenting its students and ex-students in a Shakespearian play in the yard of the George Inn, Southwark, on the occasion of Shakespeare's birthday. Distinguished artists such as Robert Medley helped with the décor, and several times the production was revived during the summer holidays and given by invitation of the L.C.C. in the London parks.

Needless to add, the music department under Michael Tippett also continued to make its mark in public. So far as its concerts outside the College were concerned—there was no place for choir and orchestra to perform together inside the building—it had to do this without any financial backing from the College; for the concerts usually lost money, and the Council felt that the College resources were far too small to underwrite any such risk. Fortunately help was to be forthcoming from the Arts Council, which from 1947 onwards made special grants to the organization responsible for these activities—the Morley College Concerts Society. With this aid—usually a matter

268

of one or two hundred pounds a year—Tippett was able to present many programmes of astonishing novelty and interest. It is impossible to detail them all, but a typical concert given within the College, in the Holst Room, was that of January 12th, 1946; Mewton Wood and Ilona Kabos opened by giving Hindemith's 'Sonata for Two Pianos', the College Choir followed with motets by Byrd and Tallis, and the concert ended with two works by Stravinsky, including the first performance in England of his 'Sonata for Two Pianos'. Outside the College, in the Central Hall, Westminster, Walter Goehr took charge of the concerts where the choir was joined with an orchestra—either the College one or on occasion a group of professional players. Again the interesting items presented in this way are too numerous to mention, but prominent among them were the first performances of Tippett's *Symphony* (1947), Frank Martin's *Le Vin Herbé* (1948), and Matyas Seiber's cantata from James Joyce's *Ulysses* (1949). There was also the first concert performance of Stravinsky's ballet music to *Les Noces* (1947), with Peter Stadlen, Eric Harrison, Mewton Wood and Franz Osborn playing the four pianos, and a performance of Vaughan Williams' *Riders to the Sea* with Kathleen Ferrier among the soloists (1948). Greatest of all in the immediate and enduring impression it made, was the first performance in modern times of Monteverdi's great *Vespers* of 1610—a work of which only one portion (the Sonata) was at all known, and which in 1946 the College now presented in Dr. Redlich's new edition complete except for two items. So great was the interest aroused by this piece in musical circles that repeat performances were given both in 1946 and 1947, and the B.B.C.

commissioned a broadcast on the Third Programme. Spurred by this triumph Tippett and Goehr went on to explore further neglected works by Monteverdi, and in 1948 gave with the College Chamber Choir and Orchestra the first London concert performance of the great Italian master's *Coronation of Poppea*.

All this received a generous measure of attention and appreciation from the press. Of the *Vespers*, Desmond Shawe-Taylor in the *New Statesman* wrote that 'A musical event of the first magnitude occurred at the Central Hall last Tuesday. . . . There is a chance that the Vespers may be repeated in the near future; and in that event I implore London concert-goers to absent themselves on no account whatsoever'. What this critic felt was echoed throughout the musical press. The power and beauty of the work as it emerged during the first performance were a revelation even to Tippett himself, who later wrote: 'When the day came . . . there was little to encourage us in the pre-booking figures, and we feared the worst. But as Goehr and I reached the Central Hall we were strangely excited to see a queue of people in the street waiting to pass by the box office. We were to have an audience after all! When the music began I sat high up in a balcony to listen. Bit by bit all sense of the imperfections of the performance went, and like many another in the audience, I submitted to a profound musical experience such as I had never expected to receive. Monteverdi's music became as substantial as that of Beethoven or Bach.'

It could not be expected that every newly presented work would make such an impression, but over and over again the critics expressed their pleasure in these concerts. Of *Les Noces*, for instance, the critic of the *Observer* re-

270

marked: 'What especially delighted and astonished me was the chorus. Before the concert I had misgivings. How could a parcel of amateurs be expected to pick their way, without falling on their noses, through the wilderness of shifting time signatures and clashing keys! But the spills and fiascos did not happen. The Morley College singers went to work with unflurried efficiency, as though the business in hand were a little glee by Macfarren or Stainer.' And perhaps the most comprehensive verdict on the whole of the Concert Society's work was that given by the *Scotsman* after the performance of Seiber's *Ulysses*: 'The Morley College Concerts are famous for the discriminating nature of their programmes, the standard of amateur choral and orchestral performances (backed by solo artists), and the smallness of their audiences. Last night's performance at the Central Hall, Westminster, was in the best traditions.'

On the purely social side of College life, the immediately post-war years saw a rapid revival in club activity, particularly that connected with the Sports Ground, and the formation of several new groups. Prominent among these were the Ballroom Dancing Club, formed in 1946, and ever since a powerful stimulus to the social life of the College, and the Art Club, formed in 1947. The Magazine, in abeyance for most of the war, came to life again in 1945 with a declared programme of eschewing politics and religion, and since then in varied forms and under several able student editors has continued to make a most valuable contribution to the corporate life. To this, direction and force were given by the revival in 1945 of the Students' Executive Committee, with its distinctive function of organizing much of the social life of the College and its

271

prerogative of selecting two of its own members to serve on the College Council.

Of the many other developments which aided the social life of the College during these years mention can be made of only two. In 1948 the students organized a competitive Arts Festival at the end of the summer term; prizes were offered within various groups, and distinguished artists, musicians and writers judged the entries. The whole thing was an outstanding success, but when an effort was made to turn it into an annual event interest waned. The other development was something which, simple as it was, perhaps did more than any other single thing to hold the social life of the College together throughout the following eight years. In 1949 the old pavilion at the Sports Ground, consisting merely of a long timber hut, was dismantled and re-erected in the courtyard at the College. Painted up, equipped with water, furnished, and beautified by pictures and posters, it made an admirable canteen for students who were tired of drinking their mid-evening coffee leaning against the walls of a corridor. Indeed, there was only one drawback to the whole operation: it cost about £700 and as a temporary work did not qualify for a grant from public funds. Contributions from the students, an allocation from the small foundation income, and a bank overdraft, solved this problem.

Among the newcomers to the Council in these years were several whose connections with the College were destined to be close and enduring: Norman Bentwich, Harold Nicolson, David Layton and Lady Walton all joined between 1946 and 1949. Among the losses, perhaps the biggest gap was that left by the death in 1947

272

of Catherine Webb, a devoted member for more than thirty years. Changes in membership of Council, however, were liable to interest the students less than what to some of them appeared to be a change in the name of the College. In 1948, Eva Hubback proposed to the Council that the words 'For Working Men and Women' which seemed from the printing on the College stationery and prospectus to be part of the College title, should be dropped, and that all College documents should thenceforth bear only the heading 'Morley College'. The Council waited for student reaction to be tested, and then accepted the change. This grieved or annoyed a few old hands, who thought that the College was pandering to middle-class snobbery and being false to the intention of the founders. In point of fact, however, what was proposed was rather the removal of an innovation. At the foundation the title of the College was Morley Memorial College, or in shorter form Morley College; but in official propaganda the words 'For Working Men and Women' were always added, usually in parenthesis, by way of explaining that the College was for students who had to work for a living in the daytime. Within a decade or two this purpose was thoroughly well known and understood, and the phrase had become less necessary. It had already disappeared from several official documents and was decreasingly used, though it was blazoned in concrete across the front of the building, when an upsurge of political feeling in the late 1920s brought it back into even greater prominence. Instead of appearing as an explanation, it began to be printed on all documents in a continuous phrase with the name of the College, which accordingly always appeared as 'Morley College for Working Men and Women'. The reason behind this development, which happened long after the number of manual labourers in the College had fallen to insignificant proportions, was probably the desire to link the College in sentiment with the 'workers' and with the labour movement generally. By 1948 Eva Hubback was clear that in the conditions of the time the phrase 'Working Men and Women' was almost meaningless as a definition of any particular part of the community, and that to continue employing it in the title of a College whose members were overwhelmingly middle-class in virtues, vices, outlook and income was becoming simply a form of pretence. The College from 1949 thus reverted, in all its official documents, to its older and more correct style—Morley College.

This change was one of the last of the many to be effected under the Principalship of Eva Hubback. In June, 1949, while she was spending a few days at the first Aldeburgh festival, she was overtaken by an illness from which she was not to recover. For years she had given almost too generously of her time and strength to a multitude of causes and activities. In addition to all her work at Morley she had undertaken lecture tours for the Forces to Malta, the Orkneys and Germany, and for the British Council to Iraq and Persia; a Justice of the Peace from 1939, she had also sat from 1945 onwards as a Labour member of the L.C.C. and been Chairman of the Schools Committee; and after helping to win the battles for the 'children's minimum' (including free milk at school) and for family allowances, she had devoted months of close thought to those problems of population in Britain which she foresaw were destined to bulk large. Her 'Penguin'

274

study on the *Population of Britain*, published in 1947, anteceded by some months the report of the Royal Commission on Population, and was a no less valuable contribution to the study of the subject. With all this she had never flagged in her personal interests and devotion as friend, mother and grandmother. In serving Morley and many other causes so well, she had taken too much from herself to possess the reserves to survive a severe operation. In July, 1949, at the age of sixty-two, her life was suddenly severed and the College lost a Principal recognized on all sides for her largeness of mind, her fertility of thought, her keenness of vision, and her outstanding ability to translate dreams into reality.

275

XIII

Battle for a Building

FACED with the death of the Principal during the summer vacation, the College Council decided that an acting Principal who would not be a candidate for the permanent position should hold office until a more lasting appointment could be made. They accordingly invited Amber Blanco White, Eva Hubback's friend and brilliant contemporary who had been lecturing in psychology and ethics at Morley since 1929, to 'hold the fort' during the ensuing session. This she most successfully did, carrying to fruition a number of projects and initiating others. The present writer also considers that among her many services to the College was the running of a preliminary but highly selective eye over the candidates for the permanent post.

The years from 1950 to the present day it is not for the author of this history to record in any great detail. The

276

task of selection would be too invidious, the conclusions perhaps too partial. Nevertheless, at the risk of offending by gross omissions, he will attempt a few generalizations, and conclude, while his memory of the events is fresh, by setting down something of the struggles to achieve the rebuilding.

So far as numbers of students go, the eight years from September, 1950, have seen first a decline and then a recovery. The Korean crisis and a general increase in fees in 1950–1 caused a drop of nearly 400 enrolments compared with the total of the previous year. The next session, with many students becoming tired of the journey to the Paragon School or the conditions they found there, saw a further falling off to a figure of 2,476. Then the newly rebuilt school at West Square, only five minutes' walk from Morley and used by the College before the war, was obtained in place of the Paragon. Many students still resented attending classes outside the College, but West Square was an altogether more attractive proposition than the Paragon; the fall in numbers ceased and a gradual increase set in. This has continued uninterruptedly from 1952–3, despite adjustments to fees which have nearly trebled the cost of a weekly class. The present session, 1957–8, sees the College with some 3,200 students—the highest figure since 1938–9. It is pleasant to record that the proportion of men, at substantially more than a third, shows a slight increase on the corresponding figure in most of the post-war years and a considerable increase on the figure immediately before the war.

By way of occupation, nineteen out of twenty of the present-day students (to judge from a recent sample

277

count) are now engaged in office, administrative or professional tasks, as opposed to tasks in factories and workshops. There is still, however, a great variety among their jobs. In addition to its large numbers of secretarial workers, civil servants and teachers, the College is proud to number among its students representatives of such diverse callings as those of fitter, film technician, hairdresser, toolmaker, bricklayer, compositor, waitress, policeman, pastry cook, carpenter, nun, and taxi-driver. So far as age is concerned, those under twenty-one are now an almost insignificant proportion. In 1889, it may be remembered, nearly half the students, and in 1923 about a fifth, were under twenty. If one had to hazard a guess, it would be that the average age of Morley students nowadays is certainly nearer thirty than twenty, and possibly nearer thirty-five than thirty. With regard to residence, about 45 per cent live in the administrative county of London south of the Thames, 33 per cent in London north of the Thames, and 22 per cent outside the L.C.C. area altogether.

During the years 1950 to 1958, all the standard subjects of study have continued, and at the same time it has been possible to offer various additions and refinements. Among those which may be regarded as subjects new to the College are archaeology, comparative religion, statistics, microscopy, ornithology, wood-carving (though this was taught in the earliest days), bookbinding, and italic handwriting. More usually there has been some development of an existing study—painting, for instance, is now taught in oils as well as in watercolours, and for some years now it has been possible to run advanced classes (fourth year and beyond) in philo-

278

sophy and other subjects. In all this the general trend has continued very clearly towards the arts. In the music department, for example, in November, 1938, there were 10 classes with 399 students; in November, 1957, there were 23 classes with 651 students. Among the new music classes formed since 1950 alone are an Opera Group, a Wind Ensemble, a Consort of Voices and Instruments, a large Symphony Orchestra of over 100 players, and many additional groups for the study of musical history, appreciation, composition and interpretation. Such a development has of course come about partly because of the special musical tradition of the College; but a similar story could be also told of the classes studying the visual arts, which contained 134 students in 1938 and today contain nearly 300. By contrast, the social studies, foreign languages and the physical activity classes all show a decreased enrolment compared with before the war.

These things have their explanation, or rather explanations. Physical activity has declined at Morley because much more of it is nowadays provided in the men's and women's institutes; also, most men who have served in the Forces have had enough 'P.T.' to last them a lifetime. Classes in foreign languages, too, are nowadays provided on all sides. Some very different reason is required, however, to explain why classes in the arts have boomed, while those in the social studies—and particularly in economics and international relations—have temporarily lost their former wide appeal. This trend, which was pointed out by Eva Hubback in an article in *Headway* as early as 1942, has in fact gone on uninterruptedly since the outbreak of war in 1939, not only in Morley College

279

but throughout the whole world of British adult education; and it represents on the part of the providers not so much a deliberate policy as a response to pressing public demand. The sterner school would dub this demand 'escapist': the student averts his gaze from the perplexities of the economic situation and the horror of the H-bomb to find a blinkered and precarious satisfaction in the study or practice of the arts. But this is far from the whole truth. It is also necessary to point out that sheer exasperation with the economists and the politicians has played its part in causing the trend: much of the point in studying economics seems to be lost when the doctors are in hopeless disagreement, there is no general confidence in their remedies, and in any case it is not they who finally prescribe for the patient. Similarly in international affairs: careful study of the rights and wrongs of issues in dispute between the major powers seems almost irrelevent when the international 'line-up' is as hard and fast as it has been since 1945.

Apart from mere exasperation, there have been other factors, too, at work. The exercise of the arts, it is clear, satisfies a creative need which in our everyday life is decreasingly satisfied by our ordinary occupations. Many of us in other times would have been craftsmen: today the instinct is still there, but the means of satisfying it in daily work is not. Beyond this, too, there is a deeper point. The world is indeed full of horrors, and we must be strong to face it. The contemplation and exercise of the arts, many no doubt unconsciously feel, can help to provide this strength—not by the technical knowledge acquired, but by the opportunity to store the mind with beauty, so that if the darkness falls without, there will

280

never be lacking riches within: riches which not merely develop the personality and fortify the soul against disaster, but also give assurance of what man at his best has been, and may again be. Looked at from this point of view, the trend towards the arts is not so much escapism as its very reverse.

The interest in the arts evidenced by enrolments in the classes has also been seen in attendance at the public lectures. These have continued to provide talks and discussions of extraordinary interest on a wide range of subjects, but those dealing with public affairs have not attracted audiences as large as those dealing with literature. Of several memorable series, 'The Theatre today' (with Christopher Fry, Henry Sherek, Sir Donald Wolfit and others), 'My Favourite Novelist' (with Charles Morgan, Joyce Cary and others), and 'The Craft of Writing' (with Sir Harold Nicolson, L. P. Hartley and R. C. Sheriff) have been among the most outstanding on the literary side; and the largest crowd ever to seek admission to the Holst Room—the queue stretched far down the Westminster Bridge Road—was that which came to hear Dame Edith Sitwell give the opening evening in a series entitled 'Poets Reading'. The closest rival to this was the crowd, largely of College music students, which flocked to hear Vaughan Williams talk on Holst in the series 'Great Men Remembered'. Outside the sphere of the creative arts, extremely popular courses which saw the Holst Room packed to capacity have been 'British Monarchs' (with Sir John Neale, C. V. Wedgwood and others) and 'On the Frontiers of Science' (in which the lecturers included Sir John Cockcroft, Martin Ryle, Sir Heneage Ogilvie and Lord Boyd-Orr).

The success of this last series was particularly encouraging in that since 1950 an effort has also been made to expand the College scientific activities, which had fallen off through the loss of the laboratory. Few problems in education today are more important than that of 'bridging the gap' between the scientific man and the artistic or humanistic man—of making the former more acquainted with the abiding cultural values, the latter less ignorant of the fundamentals of modern scientific knowledge. To this end the College has in the last few years started a number of classes in those peripheral ranges of science such as medicine and natural history which are most likely to appeal to the literary man; and it has also sought to find ways of interesting the latter in broad scientific developments. Courses in the 'History of Science' and in 'Science in the Home' have not been unsuccessful in this respect. With the rebuilding of the College and the acquisition once more of a laboratory, it has now been possible in the most recent months to start an experimental class in microscopy, to organize a Directorate of Science under Raymond Rivers (whose connection with the College through his parents goes almost back to its foundation) and to plan for the near future a revival of College classes in mathematics, chemistry and electronics. There is no danger in all this of trying to do what the polytechnics are equipped to do better: the Morley scientific courses are not for budding professional scientists but for ordinary men and women, who may well find it easier to capture an interest in science in a humanistic than in a technical setting.

In the sphere of public performance, the music and dramatic classes of the College have continued since 1950

282

to play a part of some prominence. The Shakespearian 'birthday' performances at the George, Southwark, and subsequently in the parks gave much pleasure until 1954, when they ceased owing to financial losses. Other notable productions have included Thornton Wilder's *Our Town*, Planché pantomimes, and revivals of the *Agamemnon*, *The Green Pastures*, and *Plain Jane*. A show in Vauxhall Park, *Vauxhall Gardens 1851*, was one of several College con tributions to the Festival year of 1951. As for the concerts, their number has been almost bewildering. Until July, 1951, when he retired into the country to complete his opera *The Midsummer Marriage*, Michael Tippett remained in charge of the music department. In collaboration with the Arts Council he arranged for the Concerts Society to take the Festival Hall—at £250 a night—for three concerts during the initial 1951 Festival season. Under Walter Goehr and with the Philharmonia Orchestra the choir gave again the great Monteverdi *Vespers* ('a performance of the finest quality,' according to Ernest Newman) and *A Child of Our Time*; and other works included the first performances of Stravinsky's cantata *Babel* and of Carl Orff's controversial essay in percussive rhythms and unison singing *Carmina Burana*. The gamble came off. All three concerts were well attended and expenses were covered. The following year the Society took three more dates at the Festival Hall for concerts devoted to the works of Bach, Handel and Monteverdi (*Orfeo*). The Bach concert, with Schwarzkopf, was a glorious affair which lost about £250; the Handel concert, an inglorious affair which went on far too long and lost about £450. In face of these losses the Monteverdi concert could not be given. Six years later the

283

Concerts Society is still—slowly but devotedly—clearing off the debt incurred for these two concerts; and from that season to this it has never arranged for the choir to perform in any place more ambitious than churches and town halls.

Restricted in scale as the concerts have been since 1952, they have not been restricted in scope. Under the direction of Peter Racine Fricker, who became Director of Music in 1952, they have tried to live up to the encomium of Charles Stuart, who in the *Musical Times* in 1951 wrote: 'For six years the Morley College Concerts Society has been giving us more to think, dispute and be grateful about than any other concert-promoting body in London. . . . For musical trail-blazing and general daring, Morley is much more conspicuous in a timorous world than even the Third Programme.' How far Fricker and his fellow music-tutors at the College (who include such well-known composers as Matyas Seiber, John Gardner, Iain Hamilton and Anthony Milner) have been able to sustain the tradition may perhaps be judged from *The Times*, which in 1955 began a review with the pleasing assertion that 'The Sunday night concerts at Morley College invariably provide choice and rare programmes', and a year later wrote: 'The seed which Gustav Holst planted a long time ago at Morley College, and which was subsequently watered by Arnold Foster and Michael Tippett, has grown an astonishing number of plants in these recent years.' To detail all the developments and interesting performances would be tedious; it is sufficient, perhaps, to mention that Saturday night concerts in the Holst Room with College groups have been varied by Sunday night concerts mainly with professional artists,

284

and that the Choir and Symphony Orchestra have normally given at least one concert a term outside the College. Among the more interesting concerts have been those devoted to finding new English songs (which inspired notable contributions from Lennox Berkeley and Howard Ferguson), those celebrating the fiftieth birthdays of Michael Tippett and Matyas Seiber, that in which the College Symphony Orchestra contributed to the great 'Hoffnung Festival' of 1956, and those in which favourite artists with long Morley associations, such as Alfred Deller or Ilse Wolf, have delighted with their art. So far as novelty goes, there have been first performances of works by—among many others—all the Morley College tutor-composers, younger British composers such as R. R. Bennett and Alexander Goehr, and such well-known foreign composers as Stravinsky, Hindemith, Henze, Husa, Liebermann, Frank Martin, Aaron Copland and Roger Sessions. The standard of performance has naturally varied, but in general it has been such as to pass with the professional critics and on occasion—as when the Symphony Orchestra under Lawrence Leonard gave an exhilarating performance of Stravinsky's notoriously difficult *Rite of Spring*—to inspire them to enthusiasm.

As is inevitable in a place like Morley (of which *The Times* once wrote that 'Like Africa, it can usually be relied upon to produce something new'), there have been several fresh developments in the College life since 1950. Among them may be mentioned—though it has not the slightest claim to originality—the Morley Summer School. From 1952 onwards it has been the custom for a group of students—twenty-five has been the smallest number, fifty the largest—to repair into the country in

July with three or four tutors and the Principal to study some subject sufficiently broad to appeal to diverse tastes —'Elizabethan England' for example, or 'The Classical and the Romantic'. The meetings have so far been held, in collaboration with the Wardens, at Urchfont Manor, near Devizes, at Westham House, near Stratford-on-Avon, and at Madingley Hall, Cambridge—in the last case in co-operation with the Cambridge University Board of Extra-Mural Studies. The mornings have been devoted to lectures and discussions, the afternoons to local sightseeing, and the evenings to appropriate recitals, plays and other forms of agreeable illustration. In each case a strenuous week has left the party a trifle tired, but with a warm glow of comradeship and intellectual stimulation which in many cases proves to be a permanent enrichment. Introduced in this way to some of those residential centres the growth of which has been the most striking feature in adult education since the war, many of the students have later returned on their own to sample other courses. So Morley has developed links with a great new movement, and in this new form encourages its students—as it did in the nineties with the Summer Extension Meetings at Oxford and Cambridge—at least to sample the benefits and pleasures of residential education.

Another interesting development, and one which has proved of outstanding value, has been the formation of the society known as 'The Friends of Morley College'. Such societies have become a commonplace wherever a great institution needs support and cash, and very soon after his appointment the present writer suggested to the College Council that Morley could well do with one. Eventually an organization was worked out, and students,

286

ex-students and outside well-wishers were invited to join. The object of the society was proclaimed as 'to make the College a still more useful, vigorous and beautiful place than it already is', and its distinctive role was visualized as giving help in matters for which the College had no claim on public funds. It was also to promote special lectures and social activities, at which outside 'Friends' and students would have the opportunity of meeting together. In the five years since the formation of the society, it has more than justified the hopes that brought it into being. By way of social activity, it has organized 'star' lectures and 'Brains Trusts', and has arranged dances, theatre parties, and visits to many places of interest, both in London and outside. By way of helping to acquire articles which were unobtainable from public funds, it has presented to the College pictures, reproductions, long-playing gramophone records, sports ground equipment, scientific apparatus, furniture and a host of other things: and its contributions, allied to those of the students as a whole, have enabled the College to acquire such desirable but expensive items as an electric pottery kiln and a harpsichord. In 1958 it has some 400 members, and its annual income, all devoted to College purposes, is £250—no great sum these days, but still a very useful amount for the little 'extras' that mean so much.

On the student side, the years since 1950 have seen a gallant attempt to maintain a vigorous social life in premises devoid of many of the necessary facilities. Christmas parties and the like, when run outside the College in a town hall or a swimming bath, are apt to lose much of their attraction; and even the most enthusiastic of Saturday night dancers may tire of the weekly battle for a few

287

inches of floor in the Holst Room. Nevertheless, such obstacles have been overcome; and the Students' Executive Committee, reconstituted since 1953 to include students directly elected as well as representative class and club secretaries, has carried out its tasks not only with undiminished ardour but also with notable success. For the greater part of the time under the able chairmanship of Jack Tidy—one of the outstanding Morley figures like James Clough or William Rivers, who have been in turn student, student representative on the Council, and finally member of Council in their own right—it has organized with great efficiency the Christmas Party, the Morley Ball, the Garden Party, the New Students' Social, and many other occasions, besides welcoming new students during enrolment week. It has also continued, as before, to ventilate student opinion on all matters to the Principal, and to supervise the whole range of club activity. Of the latter, it can be said that it remains as richly diversified as ever—indeed perhaps more so since Scottish Dancing and Bridge have come on to the scene—and that some clubs, such as the Rambling, the Folk-Dancing, the Ballroom Dancing, and the Tennis, are organizations of perennially impressive strength. And all the clubs, whether old or young, big or small, seem to be completely lacking in the 'splinter group' mentality which was sometimes complained of in earlier days; while naturally concerned to further their own pursuits, they are also entirely devoted to the larger interests of the College as a whole. Of their many individual achievements it is impossible to write; but none can have been more meritorious than that of the Tennis Club, which with an annual subscription of only a couple of pounds

288

and never more than eighty members, in the past few years has managed to raise £850 for the construction of three hard courts on the Sports Ground.

Of the various changes in Council and staff it is possible to mention only three or four of the most outstanding. Lord Salter resigned from the office of President in 1953 and was succeeded by Sir Harold Nicolson. In the same year H. F. Chettle, who had been continuously connected with the College since 1907, resigned the Chairmanship of the Council after discharging that duty officially and unofficially for thirty-four years. This shrewd, kindly and utterly sincere Christian gentleman, whose services to the College had been so great over so long a time, retired to spend his declining years in Wiltshire; but to the last he continued to make special journeys to London for the meetings of the Old Morleyites, of whom he was the revered President. He died in 1958, not long after his beloved wife. His successor as Chairman, Lady Walton, is one of the two representatives on the College Council of the local education authority. Her unanimous choice by her colleagues to succeed Chettle is a tribute not only to her own virtues but to the unfailingly cordial relations which the College enjoys with the L.C.C.

Another of the old generation, William Rivers, whose continuous membership as student and later councillor stretched back to 1891, was also lost to the Council in 1953. Only death could sever his connection with the College. He left among the many thousands who were privileged to know him an indelible impression of the constant thirst for knowledge, and the unfailing friendliness and goodness of heart, that in his own creed marked out the genuine Morleyite. Three years later another old

289

friend of the College, Mrs. E. M. Lowe, died shortly after her resignation from the Council, of which she had been a member for thirty years. She had been the first woman chairman of the L.C.C., and her strikingly upright figure seemed the very epitome of her character. No one who sat at Council table with her in her last years, when she was turned eighty and completely blind, will forget her splendid courage and the lightning speed with which her brain still reached decisions.

Fortunately there are some losses which prove not to be losses after all. Felix Webster, who had first joined as a student in 1906, retired in 1954 from the position of Librarian, which he had held for nearly thirty years. It was feared that his friendly chat on matters artistic and political would no longer be heard in the College. But in his middle seventies he promptly became a student once more, and at the time of writing, attends (together with his wife, who for many years helped him in the Library) classes on opera and other subjects which will never cease to interest and delight him. Such is the true Morley breed, and long may it continue.

* * *

After the unfortunate episode of the 'temporary' accommodation, a fresh start was made on plans for permanent rebuilding. With Cowles Voysey as architect, work progressed quickly, and by the spring of 1949 sketch-plans agreeable to the College Council had been produced. The basis of these was a restoration of the College to its pre-war size. The plans were then put to the L.C.C.—it was obligatory to submit them both from the safety and the maintenance-grant angle—and forthwith encountered an objection. Before the war the College

290

had accommodated 3,300 students in the year of maximum enrolment; but in the L.C.C.'s post-war plan for London's further education this number was visualized as rising to 4,000. The L.C.C. accordingly requested an enlargement of the projected building to cater for this increase.

This suggestion was of course very agreeable to the College, and when Eva Hubback died in the summer of 1949 the enlarged scheme was with County Hall for approval. The fact, however, that the College was now to be expanded by the addition of an extra storey both on the existing block and the block to be rebuilt, involving expenditure by the local education authority and the Ministry of Education, meant that the whole work would have to find a place in the country's official educational scheme. The L.C.C., in other words, would give the project a place in one of their annual programmes; and this would then be put to the Ministry of Education for approval. War damage compensation, to be paid on the value of the building destroyed, would cover the greater part of the cost; but an additional grant from public funds, payable in the proportion of 60 per cent from the the Ministry and 40 per cent from the L.C.C., would also be needed.

Shortly after Eva Hubback's death these new plans were returned from County Hall with a number of observations, including an objection on grounds of expense to the provision of a theatre, complete with raked floor, gallery and orchestral pit. This, it was suggested, should be dropped in favour of an all-purpose hall, with movable seats and flat floor, which would also be suitable for activity classes and social functions. The construction

291

would be much cheaper, and the general utility to the College greater. To this suggestion, and others, the College Council agreed; and all points of objection having been met, the plans were then finally approved by the L.C.C. Such was the position when the present writer was appointed Principal in 1950. He has a vivid recollection that when he was offered the position, and accepted, the final words of the Chairman of the Council to him were: 'And it will now be your very pleasant duty to preside over the erection of the new Morley.' He was often to reflect somewhat grimly on these words in the years to follow.

During 1951 the L.C.C., which had intended to allot the approved plans a place in their 1952–3 programme, decided after all not to include the Morley item. This was because the Ministry of Education, which had been working ever since 1945 on the policy (in general fully agreeable to the L.C.C.) that educational building within its province should be devoted solely to the needs of schoolchildren and vocational education, indicated that it was unlikely to approve the proposal.

This decision it was impossible for the College to accept without protest. For eleven years a gallant fight had been waged to maintain the full activities of the place in hopelessly restrictive conditions; but what students and staff would accept during hostilities or their immediate aftermath they would not accept indefinitely. The classes split between three or four different places; no place for the choir, the orchestra, or the Theatre School to perform in; every interview and every telephone call of the Principal and the administrative staff conducted in public in the library; lavatories inadequate to the point of

292

unhealthiness—all this, prolonged for much longer, might inflict irreparable harm on the distinctive character and traditions of the College. Moreover, the College was conscious of its pioneer services to adult education, and felt that it was wrong for a general government policy on fresh educational building, however correct in principle, to be interpreted so strictly as to preclude the restoration of war damage in an existing institution. The case, too, was unique—there was, after all, no queue of bombed adult education centres awaiting repair. The rebuilding of Morley College would establish for the Ministry no embarrassing precedent.

The College accordingly felt fully justified in protesting strongly against the omission. The first step was to persuade the L.C.C. to think again. This was not difficult: relations with County Hall were excellent and the whole scheme had been planned as a joint project with the L.C.C. After the matter had been raised in the Council Chamber the Morley item was therefore inserted after all in County Hall's 1952–3 programme—only to be promptly disallowed by the Ministry. From this point onwards the L.C.C. felt that it could do no more; it could not undertake to put the project forward again before 1956–7, and even then there would be no guarantee of approval by the Ministry. Still unwilling to take 'no' for an answer, the College decided to continue the struggle on its own.

At this stage the Labour Ministry went out of office and the Conservatives took over. The College Council accordingly asked the new Minister of Education to receive a deputation: the Minister refused, but offered an interview with a senior official. The Council decided that a

293

deputation in these circumstances would be inappropriate, and the Principal attended alone—to find the official extremely sympathetic, but so far from hopeful as to inquire whether the students themselves might not tackle the rebuilding. Disappointed in this direction, the College appealed to local M.P.s, who willingly raised the matter in the House. At the same time a number of distinguished friends of the College, representing all shades of political opinion and none and including Elizabeth Bowen, Sir Richard Livingstone, Albert Mansbridge, Gilbert Murray, Earl Russell, J. T. Sheppard, Vaughan Williams and William Walton, protested against the Ministry's decision in a letter to *The Times*. All was in vain. The rest of 1951 and 1952 passed without the slightest progress. Disgruntled students were heard to remark that there was only one thing on which the two main political parties were agreed—not to allow the rebuilding of Morley College.

During 1953 these guerrilla tactics were continued. Acting in her private capacity, the Chairman of the L.C.C. Further Education Sub-Committee, Mrs. Margaret Cole, also made a spirited sally on behalf of the College. She wrote to the Prime Minister, Sir Winston Churchill, putting the matter fully before him. He arranged for her to see the Minister of Education—who merely reaffirmed the decision taken by the Ministry two years earlier.

At the beginning of 1954, when there was still not the faintest sign of movement, the present writer put to the College Council a radical proposal—that the College should scrap the scheme carefully prepared in co-operation with the L.C.C. and abandon all thought of a larger student population than before the war. If the plans could

294

be purged of the small element of expansion, the College would be on unassailable moral grounds in demanding the right to rebuild. Moreover it might be possible in this way to escape from the choked channels of educational building 'programmes', and tackle the war damage by means of a civil building licence obtained through the Ministry of Works. To this new line of policy the Council agreed, subject to the L.C.C.'s having no objection, and to one more effort being made to secure the acceptance of the prepared scheme.

A new assault was therefore opened on a wide front. Since the government was proving unhelpful, the Chairman of the Council and the present writer sought to enlist the sympathies of the leader of the Opposition. He received them courteously, and promised to look into the College's case. Shortly afterwards he wrote to say that he had not understood, when he undertook to make inquiries, that the Prime Minister himself had already been approached without result. This being so, he could do nothing further—an answer which both surprised and disappointed. Meanwhile, however, addresses had also been made to two members of the government. One of the members of Council wrote to the Chancellor of the Exchequer (in whose constituency he lived) and pleaded generally on behalf of the rebuilding; and the present author wrote to the Minister of Works asking if he would help the College to escape from the impasse of educational 'programmes' by granting a civil building licence for strict war-damage restoration alone.

The answer of the Chancellor came first. It followed the Ministry of Education brief, and repeated the customary regrets. The member of Council did not accept these in

295

the conventional way, but wrote back in terms designed to stimulate personal concern in one who was known to care greatly for education. An interval elapsed, and then one magical afternoon the Principal became aware that things were on the move. Within the short space of two or three hours, telephone calls arrived from the Ministry of Works, from the Ministry of Education, and from County Hall. They all revolved round a common theme —the possibility of taking the Morley College project out of the educational building channel, and accomplishing it on strict war-damage restoration by civil licence. It was apparent that all the authorities concerned were in touch, and that things had been happening 'on a high level'. The great governmental machine, for so long prodded in vain, was at last stirring into action.

At no long interval the Minister of Works then rose in the House, in reply to a further parliamentary question, to announce that Morley College could have a building licence as soon as its plans were ready. The architect and the Principal at once settled down before the plans which had been in existence for the past five years. Four sessions of six hours apiece yielded the result. The extra storey to be added to the existing block was sliced off; so was the top storey of the new main block. Rooms were juggled around and re-allocated to different uses. The height of the main hall was reduced, and a second hall broken up into smaller units. By the end of the week new sketch-plans were ready, in which the cubic content of the building, the number of rooms, and their allocation, corresponded almost exactly to what had existed before the war. The construction, of course, would be that of a modern building instead of one which exhibited the work

296

of three different centuries; but no one could now say that the new Morley would be bigger than the old. Restoration (or its equivalent) of war damage, and that alone, was the order of the day.

This basic task completed, and with all apparently now set fair, Cowles Voysey, who had by this time reached an age when he wished to give up his practice, retired from business; and all further work in connection with the project devolved on his successors, Messrs. Brandon-Jones, Ashton & Broadbent. There was soon a gratifying development. The economic situation was fast improving, and general licensing restrictions on private building were abolished. In this new atmosphere County Hall inquiried of the College whether there were not some omitted item of the original plans which could easily be reincorporated. The answer was promptly given by the College that the biggest possible help would be the re-inclusion of the extra storey on top of the existing classroom block. In what turned out to be only a brief and golden moment between crises, the L.C.C. received the Ministry's approval for this additional expenditure. The formula for the rebuilding of the College was now that the work, expected to cost in all about £150,000, would be virtually done from war damage funds, except for the new extra storey. For this a sum of £14,500 was included in the L.C.C.'s 1955–6 building programme and approved by the Ministry.

A rude shock now awaited the architects and the College. Up to the point where tenders for the work were actually in, the War Damage Commission in accordance with its normal practice had declined to agree on any figure for the replacement of the lost building. In

297

October, 1955, the tenders came in, and the lowest was for £150,000, including the new extra storey. A war-damage payment in the neighbourhood of £100,000 had been contemplated in correspondence between the Commission and the architect as far back as six or seven years before; and the College confidently anticipated that with rising costs of replacement this would have grown to the full sum now required. Great was its consternation when the War Damage Commission's 'permissible amount'—based in this case on quantities taken out by the Commission itself from the plans of the old building, for the College itself had no funds to employ quantity surveyors for this task—was announced as only £85,000. More than £50,000 would thus have to be found from other sources—or the building reduced to little more than a half of its pre-war size.

The College had in fact taken too starry-eyed a view of governmental financial methods. When, for instance, parts of the site were cleared and an examination was made of foundations, it was discovered that the earlier parts of the old structure had had virtually none. Clearly the College could not erect a new steel-framed structure—or for that matter a brick one—without foundations: and the public authorities would have been the first to insist that they should be entirely adequate. Certainly no one would now have permitted the exact re-erection of the old building: standards and methods had changed far too much since the 18th and 19th centuries. Yet because the old building had only the slightest of foundations, the Commission would contribute virtually nothing towards the foundations of the new building, with the result that on this item alone the College found itself some £20,000

298

short. Similarly with regard to all the elaborate safety and fire precautions insisted on by the authorities at County Hall—the double doors, continuous hoses, screened staircases and the like. These had not existed in the old building, and though they were now included only by public requirement the Commission would meet none of their cost.

Clearly the College could not solve this problem by reducing the building to half the pre-war size. To do so would have been false to its students and its responsibilities. It had therefore to find some £50,000—and at once, for the expiration date of the tenders had approached and the lowest tender had been provisionally accepted. The College could indeed have tried a public appeal; but it had no wealthy friends and being non-vocational could expect no support from industry. The precedent of the 1937 appeal suggested that at most it might scrape up £5,000. The Council therefore decided, before committing the College to a long and dreary round of begging, to try once more the obvious source—the L.C.C. and the Ministry.

Once again there was no difficulty at County Hall—a fact not unconnected with the quiet persistence and great personal popularity of the College Chairman. The circumstances were fully understood, and the requisite sum approved, subject as always to the approval of the Ministry. It was at the Ministry, where no major building project for non-vocational education had as yet been passed since before the war, that the appeal might fail. Fortunately there was one propitious circumstance. The Minister of Works who had promised the building licence was now Minister of Education. If approached

299

personally, he might remember and perhaps once again interest himself in the matter.

While County Hall put the project up through the usual channels, the College therefore broached the matter less officially. In a surprisingly short time there came another of the memorable afternoons in this story—the afternoon that brought a letter from the Minister stating that there were a number of inadmissible features in the project which worried his officers, but that if representatives of the College would get into touch with a certain official it would be possible to see on what basis the plan might go forward. The last words were as water to the desert traveller—so much so that perhaps the bottle of sherry promptly produced in celebration by the College officials was almost unnecessary. From 1947 sporadically, and from 1951 intensively, the College had been agitating for the rebuilding, and had been meeting with sympathetic but uncompromising refusals. Now here at last were the wonderful, almost incredible, words 'might go forward'.

At the earliest opportunity, in December, 1955, the College representatives duly attended the Ministry. The officer whose duty it was to receive them evidently spoke to brief. In tones friendly but firm, he informed them that he had some rather unpleasant things to say to them, and then a pleasant one. He told them that the Ministry did not in the least like the way the College had handled the affair. In 1954 it had cut adrift from the whole procedure of educational building to manage the project on its own under war-damage compensation. Without any backing from the Ministry it had gone ahead with detailed plans, agreed to pay fees, put the project out to tender, and

300

brought everything to the point where a contract should shortly be signed. And now, having committed itself deeply, here it was back again at the Ministry, cap in hand, asking for £60,000 or more because the war-damage payment was not enough—asking, in other words, to be put into an educational building programme after all, and that forthwith. To this the College representatives listened with surprise; the speaker seemed unaware of the fact that the College had tried for years to get its building by means of the Ministerial procedures, and would doubtless have still been trying, with equal lack of success, had it not started things moving along other lines. However, they said little—as was clearly intended—and waited for the pleasant thing in store. It did not come straight away. The College had also, the speaker continued, included many items in its plans which were beyond the current standards of educational building; acoustic tiles, for example, were incorporated too freely, and there was wooden panelling in the hall. Such luxuries could not now be afforded in any new building under the purview of the Ministry.

The pleasant part was now fully due, and slowly it came. As the College, the officer continued, had got itself so involved, and had landed itself in such a muddle, the Ministry proposed to come to its rescue; it would approve the L.C.C.'s request to include the Morley item in the current 1955–6 programme, on condition that the marginal sum involved beyond the war-damage payment was reduced by some £20,000. The lowest tender figure of £150,000 must come down to £130,000. If this were done to the Ministry's satisfaction, the College could go ahead with its scheme and its financial problem would be solved.

The interview—and the long struggle for rebuilding—was over.

Could £20,000 be sliced off the cost of the building without any sacrifice of accommodation? This was the question which the College immediately posed to its architect, Mr. J. D. Broadbent. The architect got to work, and in a short time produced solutions which were ultimately approved by all concerned. The panelling went from the hall: acoustic tiles were reduced in number: rubber flooring in the class-rooms gave place to linoleum; the lavatory cabinets became shorter and less substantial. Built-in cupboards, the lift and the front railings were all omitted. By these and other economies—not all of them long-term ones—the contract price was duly reduced by £20,000. Against the background of a fresh economic crisis and the threat of new educational building cuts—which fortunately turned out not to relate to the current programme—a contract for approximately £130,000 was then hastily signed with Messrs. Miskin.

The work on the new structure began in May, 1956. Into the problems which arose in the course of construction, the difficulties, technical and administrative, the present writer will not delve. They were by no means few or negligible. They were not lessened by the fact that all the College classes and activities continued as usual throughout the operations, even when an extra storey was being added to the existing block. This made matters easy neither for the builders nor for the students, who experienced much dirt and discomfort. As for the administrative staff, present also in the day, they have had the additional pleasure of concrete-mixers, diesel motors

302

and electric drills. Nevertheless it is some satisfaction to know that in two years only two events have been cancelled because of the rough conditions—a staff dinner and an open day.

In the summer of 1958, when these words are being written, the new building is finished except for some of the fixtures and final decorations. Thanks again to generous help from the L.C.C., the furnishing is also very nearly complete. Among the various features of the building, none will perhaps lend it a more distinctive character than its large hall—to be called the Emma Cons Hall—its refectory, and its Common Room. Each of these rooms is to be embellished with mural paintings, for which a special war-damage payment is available. The three painters commissioned are Edward Bawden again, John Piper, and a younger artist, Martin Froy. If their work provides as much pleasure as was given in the 1940s by the earlier series, they—and the College—can be well content.

Much more could be written about the new building, but enough—perhaps too much—has been said already. The subject would not have been dealt with at such length but for the fact that few evening schools possess premises of their own; and Morley College is too well aware of the advantages of having its own building ever to forgo them lightly.

* * *

The College of 1958 is in many obvious ways different from that of 1889. With the rebuilding, it is much more elegantly housed. With the financial help of the L.C.C., its future is no longer a matter of constant anxiety. Its students, now preponderantly female, are drawn from a much greater variety not only of neighbourhood but also of social and educational background. They are also in general older and better off. Yet beneath all these changes the College remains in fundamentals what it always has been. It is still a place where those who work in the day come to study in the evenings; it is still devoted to the liberal, humanistic side of education, divorced from any aspect of vocational training; and it still aims to carry its students to an advanced level of study. In addition it still rejoices in a wide range of social activities; and its fees, like those of evening classes in general, are still such as all can afford. In essentials it is the same Morley College that was brought to birth in the dressing-rooms of the Vic.

Of all the developments mentioned above there is only one that could seriously threaten its character—the fact that most of its students no longer live in the immediate neighbourhood. This has become inevitable with the increasing fame of the College and the educational, social and financial progress of the most intelligent parts of the local population since 1889—a progress so often registered by a move into some smarter and less grimy district. The way in which such a change could possibly endanger the character of the College is not through any difference it may bring about in the social class of the students, but through the fact that students living far afield usually attend the College only once a week, instead of being constantly about the place. With the rising cost of public transport, many students are already unable to afford to come in for a Saturday dance or a Sunday concert. There is no threat from this to the educational side: but if it weakened the social activities the College could lose some

304

of its old cohesion and individuality—and in the long run this would inevitably lessen the exceptional vitality of its educational work.

Fortunately there appears to be little danger of this at present. Morley in essence still goes on as before, combining constant change and development with a fundamental continuity. This combination struck very forcibly H.M. Inspector who was in charge of the Board of Education inspection of 1927. Throughout his whole report he implied that the aims of the College were permanently valid, and that not only had it enjoyed remarkable success in the past but also that it would go on doing so in the future. For this to come to pass he laid down only three conditions, all of which, he tactfully explained, he expected to be realized. They were that 'the Council and its officers will exercise the same energy and public spirit, and the same practical wisdom in the internal management of the College and in its relations with outside bodies, as they have in former years'; that 'the growing popularity and educational efficiency of the College . . . stimulate the financial support for those extensions which are already beginning to be necessary'; and that the public education authority should 'co-operate on generous lines, whilst leaving a large measure of liberty and initiative to a body which has achieved such conspicuous success in the face of great difficulties'.

To these conditions, as important today as they were thirty years ago, may be added a fourth. The essential Morley also depends on the continued willingness of a considerable number of students and tutors to devote time and trouble to many things beyond the immediate work of their class—not only to the organization of club activities but also to the broadest interests and needs of the College. In an age where the emphasis is on getting rather than giving, on rights rather than duties, this is especially important. What animated the founders of the College above all, as has been pointed out many times in these pages, was the spirit of service. This spirit they fostered within their foundation, and to this spirit the College owes its distinctive qualities. In honouring it, we link hands across the years with a succession of great Morley figures—with Emma Cons, Caroline Martineau, Frederick Black, Graham Wallas, Gustav Holst, William Rivers, H. F. Chettle, Eva Hubback and many others. And in emulating it, we ensure that the College will continue to possess the strength and resilience to play a useful and creative part in a rapidly changing world.

306

Appendix I

Presidents, Chairmen and Principals of Morley College

Presidents

1894–1902	James Stuart
1902–28	E. J. Urwick
1928–33	Graham Wallas
1933–37	R. H. Tawney
1937–53	Sir Arthur (Lord) Salter
1953–	Sir Harold Nicolson

Chairmen of Council

1891–94	J. A. Fleming
1894–98	G. W. Johnson
1898–1903	F. W. Black
1903–28	E. J. Urwick
1928–53	H. F. Chettle (acting from 1919)
1953–	Lady Walton

Principals

1889–91	— Goold
1891–1902	Caroline A. Martineau
1905–10	Charles Roden Buxton
1926–27	Barbara Wootton
1927–49	Eva M. Hubback
1949–50	Amber Blanco-White (acting)
1950–	Denis Richards

Vice-Principals

1891–94	Ella Sieveking
1894–99	Florence Action
1899–1913	Mary Sheepshanks
1913–25	Clare Brennand

307

Appendix II

Sources

1. The following were the main sources used for the writing of this book:

The Annual Reports of the Royal Victoria Hall (1881–90).
The Annual Reports of Morley College (1891–1939).
Minutes of the Morley College Council (1891–1958).
Morley College Magazine (1892–1958).
Correspondence, memoranda, propaganda, etc., preserved at Morley College (1940–58); (everything prior to 1940 destroyed by enemy action).
Files and reports relating to Morley College and the Royal Victoria Hall in the possession of the Charity Commission.
Ditto in the possession of the Ministry of Education.
Ditto in the possession of the London County Council.
Ditto in the possession of the City Parochial Foundation.
Files relating to the Coffee Taverns Association, the Coffee Music Halls Company, etc., in the possession of the Public Record Office.
Files relating to the South London Dwellings Co. in the possession of the Registrar of Public Companies.

308

APPENDIX II

The files of *The Times*, The *Daily Telegraph*, and the *South London Press*; and the press cuttings (1928–58) preserved at Morley College.

Personal recollections, written and otherwise, from past and present students and others connected with the College.

2. The following books, among others, were consulted for special aspects:

Social

Henry Mayhew: *London Labour and the London Poor* (1851, expanded 1861–3).

Octavia Hill: *Homes of the London Poor* (1875) (collection of earlier articles).

Coffee Public House Association: *The Coffee Public House* (1878).

Charles Booth: *Life and Labour of the People in London* (1889 onwards: definitive edition in 1902–3 in 17 vols.).

Beatrice Webb: *My Apprenticeship* (1926).

Sir W. Besant: *London in the Nineteenth Century* (1906).

Alex. Paterson: *Across the Bridges* (1912).

(Survey by Lady Margaret Hall Settlement): *Social Services in North Lambeth and Kennington* (1939).

Topographical

(various): *The Survey of London.* Vols. 23 & 26 (1951 and 1956).

Biographical

(ed. C. E. Maurice): *Life of Octavia Hill* (1913).

E. Moberley Bell: *Octavia Hill* (1942).

William Hill: *Octavia Hill* (1956).

E. Hodder: *Life of Samuel Morley* (1888).

Lilian Baylis: *Memoir of Emma Cons* (1926) (in 'The Old Vic' by L. Baylis and C. Hamilton).

309

Victoria de Bunsen: *Charles Roden Buxton: A Memoir* (1948).
S. & R. Thorndike: *Lilian Baylis* (1938).
Imogen Holst: *Gustav Holst* (1938).
Diana Hopkinson: *Family Inheritance*: A Life of Eva Hubback (1954).

The Old Vic

John Hollingshead: *My Lifetime* (1895).
John Booth: *The Old Vic* (1917).
H. Chance Newton: *The Old Vic* (1923).
Lilian Baylis and Cicely Hamilton: *The Old Vic* (1926).
Edwin Fagg: *The Old Old Vic* (1936).
ed. Harcourt Williams: *Vic–Wells* (1938).
E. J. Dent: *A Theatre for Everybody* (1945).
Harcourt Williams: *Old Vic Saga* (1949).
Robert Speaight: *William Poel and the Elizabethan Revival* (1954).

Educational

Thomas Kelly: *George Birkbeck*: Pioneer of Adult Education (1957).
J. F. C. Harrison: *History of the Working Men's College* (1954).
H. C. Barnard: *A Short History of English Education from 1760 to 1944* (1947).
T. L. Jarman: *Landmarks in the History of Education* (1951).
A. D. C. Peterson: *A Hundred Years of Education* (1952).
E. Eaglesham: *From School Board to Local Authority* (1956).
Mary Stocks: *The Workers' Educational Association: The First Fifty Years* (1953).
ed. R. Forbes Adam: *A Design for Democracy*.
(The '1919' Report of the Adult Education Committee of the British Ministry of Reconstruction, with an introduction by R. D. Waller) (1956).

310

Index

311

INDEX

INDEX

313

INDEX

314

INDEX

315

INDEX

9780415860659